W9-CPX-882

"Pioneer or Perish"

"A community of scholars is bound together by a dynamic idea. They either pioneer or perish. An institution becomes great by daring to dream and then bending every effort to make these dreams come true."
— Robert E. Burns' Inaugural Address, 1947

"Pioneer or Perish"

A History of the University of the Pacific
During the Administration of Dr. Robert E. Burns,
1946–1971

by Kara Pratt Brewer

For Michael,
With best wishes,
Kara Brewer

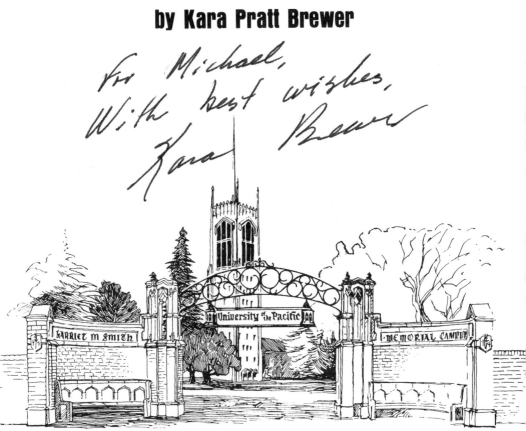

Printed in the United States of America

Pioneer Publishing Company
Fresno, California

Acknowledgements

The author is grateful to the numbers of Dr. Burns' friends and associates she interviewed in the course of writing this book. Their personal insights were essential in gaining a sense of the quality of the man and the institution. A list of these persons who gave so generously of their time and interest is a part of the Bibliography.

Especially significant were the conversations with Grace Burns, Alice Saecker, Catherine Davis, and Harold Jacoby. Gratitude must also be expressed to the Editorial Committee, whose constructive criticism and encouragement were invaluable. And as Dr. Wood has noted in the Prologue, the book would probably never have been written had it not been for Ellen Deering's perseverance, her kindness in sharing her remarkably detailed and accurate memories of the Burns years.

Over 200 individuals and organizations contributed to the memorial fund which supported the research and writing of *Pioneer or Perish*. Friends, faculty, students, even the nurses who had become so fond of him during his brief stay at the Presbyterian Hospital, believed that a history of Dr. Burns' administration would be the most fitting memorial to this man who himself had written a history of Pacific's early years.

Table of Contents

Prologue

As Senior Editor, I must take a few lines to express appreciation to some of the people who were of great help in preparing the manuscript. Dr. Kara Brewer deserves the most commendation for she has researched and written these chapters in a thoroughly professional manner by interviewing, consulting records, reading reports and summarizing all her findings into a fair, honest and readable manuscript. She undoubtedly knows more about the University of the Pacific than anyone, even those who lived and worked for many years on the campus.

To the late Miss Ellen Deering, the registrar of the University for forty-five years, which included the years of Dr. Burns' presidency, must be given the major credit for urging and insisting that this history be written now. She was of inestimable value to Dr. Brewer in the researching for the manuscript by advising, interpreting and consulting with her on many aspects of the history. No one living today has been as intimately and closely involved in the operation of the University as she, and her amazing memory of events, people and details has made her indispensable in preparing the history.

When President Stanley McCaffrey invited me to assume the responsibility for preparing a manuscript on the history of the University during the years of Dr. Burns' presidency and asked that if possible it should be completed within a year, I proposed that it be made a group effort by the faculty and staff of the Pacific Center for Western Studies since we already had a publishing program with our monograph series and the quarterly *The Pacific Historian*. He agreed that he would consider whatever plan we proposed, just so we accomplished the project as quickly as possible. Therefore, preparing the manuscript and publishing the history became a group effort of the faculty of the Pacific Center. Kara Brewer agreed to write the manuscript with the advice and cooperation of our editorial committee.

I would like to express my appreciation for the competent and enthusiastic cooperation of the members of this editorial committee: Dr. James Shebl, Martha Seffer O'Bryon and Dr. Ronald Limbaugh. Each of these members has critically read the rough draft of the chapters of the manuscript. We feel we have had a practical and efficient organization and have completed the manuscript in 1976, the bicentennial of our great nation.

I am honored to write this prologue because I was personally acquainted with the three great men involved in this history—Dr. Tully Knoles, Dr. Rockwell Hunt and Dr. Robert Burns. I have also been involved in Pacific affairs ever since I first arrived on the Stockton campus in September, 1928, to enroll as a freshman student. I have seen the institution and campus grow in those forty-nine years from an enrollment of less than five hundred students to nearly six thousand students and from an alfalfa-covered campus of small, newly planted trees and poorly paved or graveled streets and sidewalks to the beautiful, tree-shaded campus of today.

The main reason for my enrollment at Pacific after graduating from the little Bishop High School in the lovely Owens Valley was that my family had known and greatly admired Dr. Knoles. He had been on leave from the University of Southern California to regain his health by ranching in the healthful climate near Bishop. While in Bishop he taught in the high school and preached in the Methodist Church. However, I never dreamed that I would become closely associated with this great man who was persuaded by the Board of Regents to come to San Jose and to give dynamic leadership to the College of the Pacific. It was just four years after Knoles and the College moved to Stockton that I came to Pacific, to an unfinished campus of alfalfa fields and new buildings.

It was Dr. Knoles more than anyone else who brought the College of the Pacific to the new Stockton campus and developed the pioneering program and atmoshpere that Dr. Burns continued and expanded. It was his dynamic personality, his vision and his superb speaking ability that succeeded in persuading people to help with and become a part of this new venture in higher education in the uncontested interior valley of the San Joaquin. Although he asked for and received the support of leaders in the community and collected an excellent faculty of outstanding and devoted men and women, he still was personally involved in almost every phase of campus activity and development.

xii

Dr. Knoles' keen sense of appreciation of people and their ability brought the energetic and pleasant Robert Burns into his office as his assistant. It also enabled him to attract the great Amos Alonzo Stagg to Pacific after he had retired as a famous football coach at the University of Chicago.

In 1946 Dr. Knoles learned that a former colleague of his, Dr. Rockwell D. Hunt, who had been Dean of the Graduate School of the University of Southern California for thirty-seven years, was retiring but was still active and alert. It is said, "Dr. Knoles sent Robert Burns to Los Angeles to persuade Dr. Hunt to come to Pacific and organize a program of activities around California and Western history." It probably wasn't that simple, but Dr. Hunt agreed to come to Pacific and Dr. Burns was very much involved in it as he loved California history.

Bringing Dr. Hunt to Pacific was a great achievement and he and Dr. Burns worked closely together to organize the California History Foundation. Hunt was to write and publish a history of California, offer seminars and do public speaking as well. Looking forward to the centennial of the College of the Pacific in 1951, Burns encouraged Dr. Hunt to write a centennial history of Pacific. Dr. Hunt was qualified not only as an author but as an alumnus of Pacific. He had graduated from Napa College in 1890 before that college was merged with Pacific in 1896. He had taught in the Pacific Department of History and had written an article in 1901 on the fifty year history of the College of the Pacific. Dr. Burns had written his Master's thesis on the History of Pacific and thus gave the project his personal support and attention. He also strongly supported the work of the California History Foundation which Dr. Hunt was directing. When the well-researched manuscript was completed, Dr. Hunt asked the new president to write the foreword. In this Dr. Burns pointed out some of the characteristics of the College of the Pacific as observed through the study of its history, asserting that "the pioneering which has been the characteristic feature in the past should continue during the next one hundred years. Our next century of service looms larger because we have the past to build upon." Dr. Burns had used this pioneering theme in his inaugural speech.

The *History of the College of the Pacific* was published in 1951 and became an important part of the centennial celebration. Kara

Brewer has used it extensively for obtaining background material in writing this manuscript. Dr. Hunt continued to publish other books on California and his last one, *Boyhood Days on the Sacramento*, was written after he was confined to a rest home and not too long before he died in Stockton at 98 years of age.

The third one of these great men I knew well at Pacific was Robert Burns. I knew him intimately as a student from the time I enrolled at Pacific in 1928. We were interested in many of the same activities. He was on the debate team, in the a cappella choir, the campus chapter of Y.M.C.A. and student politics, and was president of the student body. We were both especially active on what was called the deputation programs. Groups of talented students would visit and provide programs for many of the churches and high school assemblies in Central California and the Mother Lode. During this time I developed a great admiration for his ability to please, influence and entertain his audiences. This was important training for his later career. I found him to be a friendly, happy and optimistic person. He loved to play practical jokes but also could take them. He was a good student but not a "brain" and never attempted to appear as a great intellect either as a student or as president. It was always fun to be with him or take a trip with him.

We were both interested in California and Western history and we were both involved in the organization of the Conference of California Historical Societies. As the executive secretary of the Conference for eighteen years and later, as director of the Pacific Center for Western Historical Studies, I was closely involved with Dr. Burns and benefited by his interest and concern. On one occasion he stated to me that "very soon now I'm retiring as president and I plan on coming over and helping with the work of the California History Foundation." He was never happier than when participating in California history activities, as Western history was his major in his undergraduate studies. He loved the California Spanish missions and supported the annual Mission Tour by Pacific. He found time to serve on the California Parks Commission for several years and told me on one occasion he was going to visit every state historical park personally and as many other of the state parks as possible.

He was a member of the Yerba Buena Chapter of E Clampus

Vitus and was somewhat active in its programs, as he enjoyed the humor and horseplay of the uninhibited Clampers at their gatherings and supported their serious effort to mark and preserve California history.

In his undergraduate days he became interested in the program of the Y.M.C.A. on the campus and became president of the campus chapter. For four years he attended the stimulating "Midwinter Y" Conferences at Asilomar near Monterey. This led to a wider interest and support of the Y.M.C.A. program in Stockton and the "Y" program in general.

His interest in the Masons resulted in his becoming a 33rd Degree Mason and Grand Chaplain of the Masonic Lodge of California.

For five sessions, from 1952 to 1968, he was an elected delegate of the California-Nevada Conference at their worldwide quadrennial General Conference of Methodism.

One of his fine memorials is the Fallon House Theater at the Columbia State Park. Dr. Burns learned that the property was for sale and the chances were great that the building would be destroyed as it was in neglected and weakened condition. He launched a successful campaign to purchase and preserve the building. The property was then deeded to the State Department of Parks and Recreation, with the agreement that the College of the Pacific be granted the right to use the building for a summer theater for its drama students. Under the inspiring direction of DeMarcus Brown, this summer theater was very successful and gained a wide reputation for the quality of the performances. Dr. Burns with his second home in Columbia was very fond of the theater and donated his home as a dormitory for some of the students and faculty.

This list of "extracurricular" activities beyond his area of administrative responsibility could be extended indefinitely but I believe it is long enough to illustrate that Robert Burns had an amazingly wide range of interests. One wonders how he ever found time for the pursuit and participation in all of them. He never lost his zest and interest in them—music, art, drama, athletics, religion, fraternal orders, travel, public speaking, collecting antiques, and people—all were within his range of interest. He was always fun to be with and to talk to even when confined to his bed in the

Cowell Health Center. His final ebbing strength was expended in his efforts to again see the "other side of the world." He was truly a great, kind, happy and successful man. What more could be asked? I'm so glad I could call him friend for some forty years and have the opportunity to help write the story of his achievements.

R. Coke Wood
Senior Editor and
Director Emeritus
Pacific Center for Western Studies

Editorial Committee

Dr. James M. Shebl
Martha Seffer O'Bryon
Dr. Ronald H. Limbaugh

Chapter One

THE ANNUAL meeting of the Board of Trustees of the College of the Pacific was convened at the California Hotel in San Francisco at ten o'clock in the morning on October 22, 1946. Twenty-two of the thirty-six members were in attendance for what was to be one of the most momentous gatherings in its history. Tully Cleon Knoles, who had been President of the College for twenty-seven years, delivered his annual report and then electrified the Trustees with the announcement that he wished to resign. The minutes report dryly what must have served as a shocking blow to these supporters of the college who recognized the significance of the continuous leadership of Dr. Knoles.

Dr. Knoles stated that from time to time he has suggested to the Board because of his age [70 years] and inability to be of value in the financial side of the life of the college, there should be a change in the presidency. Certain developments of the last three or four days have made it seem best to again bring this suggestion to the attention of the Board. Dr. Knoles thinks the trustees should consider relieving him entirely of the responsibility or make some adjustments to throw the burden on someone younger.[1]

The minutes omit any explanation of "the developments of the last three or four days," though everyone was evidently apprised of them.

On a trip to the East Coast, Robert Burns, the Assistant to the President, had contacted foundations to seek financial support for the college. He had also visited the Methodist Board of Education offices in Nashville, Tennessee and had spoken to his friend the Director, Dr. John Gross, who suggested that Burns apply for the position of president at Dakota Wesleyan College. Subsequently, at Dr. Gross's behest, he went to Chicago to talk with Dr. Leland Case, noted editor and supporter of the Methodist school in South Dakota. Dr. Case spent several hours with "the vigorous, dynamic young man,"[2] and then phoned the president of the college's Board

1

Olin D. Jacoby, Board President.

of Trustees to advise that they give strong consideration to Robert Burns' application. An appointment was arranged, and Burns left immediately for South Dakota to visit the school.

The interview was evidently successful; the Board of Trustees offered the position to Robert Burns who, although youthful, had gained valuable experience working with President Knoles for fifteen years at the College of the Pacific. After graduating from the College in 1931, he had worked there as fund raiser, alumni secretary, recruiter, registrar, and assistant to the president. His own life had, in fact, been so caught up in the life of Pacific he hesitated to leave. He told Dr. Case, however, that he hoped someday to be president of his alma mater, and that he believed that some experience in administration at another institution would be beneficial.

Dr. Knoles, however, was very distressed at the thought of losing his able young assistant. He had come to depend heavily on Robert Burns, especially in that area of administration he loathed—money raising. After being told of the new position on Sunday evening, he immediately called Olin D. Jacoby, the President of Pacific's Board of Trustees, described the emergency, and urged that the young man he had trained for the position be immediately appointed President of the College of the Pacific. On the following Tuesday the question of Dr. Knoles' resignation was brought before the Board. Bishop James C. Baker voiced strong support for the nomination;

2

and Mr. Jacoby reported that during meetings of faculty and alumni on the campus the day before, the general consensus was "that the College should not lose the services of Mr. Burns. It was also the opinion that the College should not lose Dr. Knoles." [3]

An accommodation was therefore proposed: that Robert Burns be elected President and Tully Knoles become the Chancellor. The Board agreed and adopted the following statement of intent:

> It is our desire in advancing Dr. Tully C. Knoles to the Chancellorship of the College of the Pacific to retain for the College all of the accumulated understanding, experience and influence which make him unique among college presidents. We are exceedingly anxious to have the full benefit of his counsel, advice and direction in this important period as we come to the objectives of the centennial of the College. We are not in any sense thinking of allowing him to retire from the life of the institution. We want him to take the inside academic administration, continue his work with the relations between the Stockton Junior College and the College of the Pacific. We want him to live on the campus. We want to hear him speak for various gatherings in the state and nation as he has the strength for such activities. Mr. Burns, as President of the Institution, should take over rather complete control of the financial side of the organization, with the Vice-President and Comptroller, and of the business relations of the institution as they have to do with the friends and prospective friends of the College. He will give himself to the understanding of the departments already established in the College and such new phases of their development as the Board of Trustees shall agree upon. Together with Dr. Knoles he will present to the Board of Trustees the general shaping of the College. [4]

Dr. Knoles agreed to become the college's first Chancellor and Robert Burns accepted the presidency, thus becoming, as the headlines announced, "the youngest college president in the West."

The college he was to administer for nearly a quarter of a century, the College of the Pacific, is the oldest chartered institution of higher education on the Pacific Coast. Two years after the discovery of gold in California, a group of Methodist ministers and laymen applied for its charter, which was granted by the California Supreme Court on July 10, 1851. First named California

Robert E. Burns with Chancellor Tully C. Knoles shortly after Burns was named President of the University.

Wesleyan College, the institution was soon to be called the University of the Pacific—a reflection of the ambitious confidence in the future that its founding board of trustees shared. Such audacity was not uncommon in the history of American Methodism. By 1939 the list of Methodist schools included some of the country's strongest colleges and universities. Boston, Northwestern, Syracuse Universities, the University of Southern California, Duke, Emory, and Southern Methodist Universities all owe their beginnings to the Methodist concern for education, as do several smaller universities, seventy-one liberal arts colleges, twenty-eight junior colleges and seven semininaries or schools of theology.

4

The Methodists were not alone, of course, in this educational effort. Most of the colleges founded in this country before the Civil War owe their establishment to groups of churchmen who were concerned about the education of their children. Harvard College was founded by the Puritans only eight years after the Commonwealth. Subsequently Yale, Princeton, William and Mary were instituted by other church bodies, a reflection partly of their desire to be known as "civilized" but more importantly of their determination to promulgate their own variety of denominational orthodoxy among their young people. Later, as the frontier moved westward, a new motivation was added to the desire to protect orthodoxy. Parents and ministers sought to protect students from what they perceived to be the godless materialism and sophistication of the prosperous urban centers on the coast. Williams, Amherst and many other colleges were established so that students could remain safely in rural environments. Indeed, the safeguarding of doctrinal purity and of the ethical character of young people was the predominant motivation in the foundation of hundreds of church related schools during the first hundred years of the nation's history—Catholic as well as Protestant.[5]

Methodists were relatively late on the scene; during the early decades of this country's history the church avoided the temptation to embark on a program to found schools and colleges. That delay was probably providential. Jencks and Riesman, in their analysis of historical trends in American higher education, have contended that the pre-Jacksonian colleges "influenced neither the intellectual nor the social history of their era. Indeed, it could be argued," they continue, "that America overinvested in higher education during the Pre-Jacksonian years."[6] The same authors, however, conclude that "The eclipse of established colonial hierarchies after 1828 created a vacuum which almost every one was eager to fill..."[7] The election of Jackson was a sign to many that upward mobility was indeed more than a dream in nineteenth century America, and the explosion of new colleges between 1830-1860 can be seen as a result of that realization.

Schooling was perceived more and more to be a means toward upward mobility and the Methodists, in spite of dire warnings by conservatives within their ranks of the danger of intellectual pride, embarked on an extraordinary campaign to educate their young people in academies and colleges. They were sensitive to the growing demand for higher learning, and were not willing to sit by while their children were forced to attend institutions which might be dangerous to their faith. The following statement appeared in the *Quarterly Register*, August 1831: "These young men, generally the most promising of our best families, will be educated somewhere. If there be not proper and elevated institutions under our own patronage, they will be sent to others . . . Many of them return with prejudice against the religious opinions and practices of their parents . . . Think of the immense loss in this way and then think of the means to remedy it."[8] Seeing the new program as a mission, Methodist Conferences everywhere set themselves to the task of instituting colleges and universities—with a zeal and vigor that is astonishing. By 1865 Methodists had established two hundred schools in thirty-three of the thirty-four states![9]

Soon after the Civil War, it was apparent to church leaders that an effort must be made to raise the standards of these schools and to regularize the ways churches supported them. In 1868 the Methodist Board of Education was formed "to act as the perpetual custodian of education in the Methodist Episcopal Church."[10] Then in 1892, sensing the need for even more drastic action, the Annual Conference brought into being the Methodist University Senate to tighten supervision. This new body had the power to issue sanctions against institutions which failed to come up to standard. Subsequently many colleges too small to be viable were closed, and others were consolidated with stronger institutions. It was a courageous move and a revolutionary one. The Methodist University Senate was the first accrediting board constituted in the United States.

Among the institutions under its charge were many which had been founded in established centers on the Eastern seaboard. Wesleyan University in Connecticut and Allegheny and Dickinson Colleges had been educating young Methodists since the 1830s. But even more numerous were the colleges which had been established on the Western outposts of settlement. Iowa Wesleyan was the first college in Iowa. Baker University was founded before the admission of Kansas as a state, as were Hamline University, Lawrence College and Denver University before the admission of their home states (Minnesota, Wisconsin and Colorado respectively).

6

This fact is not surprising in the light of Methodism's being peculiarly fitted for work on the frontier:

> On the frontier the ties of tradition, whether religious or cultural, were loose. Yet those who had left their old ways behind them still needed and wanted what was essential in the tradition, stripped of the frills and accretions but renewed in its vigor and presented with power. A church that had been forged in the heat of one man's search for such vigor and power and in his rediscovery of the essence of evangelical Christianity was ideally suited to the demands of the frontier.[11]

At first the circuit riders ministered to the needs of the new settlements; although frequently their formal educational experience had been minimal, they were indeed "voices crying in the wilderness," sometimes the only voices raised for the values of culture and order. Later, after the new settlements were sufficiently established to support their own resident ministers, these leaders began to look for ways to build academies and colleges.

This pattern is apparent on the West Coast where Jason Lee established a school in Oregon in 1842. And it can be seen again in the events which led to the development of California Wesleyan College in California, though in that state the movement was accelerated by the dramatic influx of new settlers occasioned by the discovery of gold. Isaac Owen, William Taylor, Edward Bannister and the other Methodist ministers and laymen who acted as founders of the new institution were following in the footsteps of many of their brethren when they perceived the necessity of an institution that would both educate and inculcate Christian principles of character in young Californians.

In his unique analysis *The Founding of American Colleges and Universities Before the Civil War*,[12] Donald G. Tewksbury writes of the high mortality rate among such institutions. His study indicates that of the approximately 800 colleges that were founded before 1865 only 180 had survived until the time of his study (1929).

> Among the many factors that have been responsible for the death of colleges in this country, the following may be selected for special consideration, viz., financial disaster,

denominational competition, unfavorable location, natural catastrophes, and internal dissensions.[13]

During the early decades of its history, the College of Pacific faced all of these trials. That it was among the survivors Tewksbury cited was owing to positive factors—especially the sheer tenacity and determination of its leaders—which outweighed the very real problems the institution faced.

From its inception, the college was confronted with the danger of "financial disaster." The founders were able to raise only $27,500 to qualify for the charter; in 1851 most Californians were engaged in the search for gold and uninterested, to say the least, in higher education. A subsequent President, William W. Guth, wrote of the obstacles faced by the college which "at first was most handicapped because the conditions in the early days of California were anything but favorable to religion or education." Unlike the eastern pioneers who had founded Harvard College, 49'ers were often motivated by "the wild search for material wealth."[14]

In spite of manifold difficulties the "preparatory department" opened for classes on May 3, 1852. Soon afterward the main college building and the Female Collegiate Institute were erected and on June 9, 1858, the first baccalaureate degrees were conferred, in spite of the uncertain financial status of the college. In April President Gibbons had written "We are teaching this year on half pay, for the sake of trying to get through."[15] In 1861 his successor, Edward Bannister, reported to the Trustees that "The professors are in arrears to the amounts of nearly a half year's salary."[16] Thus a pattern was established; lacking endowment funds to carry it through times of crisis, the University (in 1911 renamed the College of the Pacific) frequently owed its continuance to the generosity of its faculty.

At the meeting of the Board in June, 1862 the question of continuing the college at all was discussed at length. Finally it was resolved "That it is not expedient to suspend the regular College sessions, nor shall the vacant chairs be filled for the present"[17] —scarcely an enthusiastic note of support. In 1864 the Annual Conference once again alluded to the "pecuniary embarrassment of the University which is such as to make it impossible for the Trustees to continue the support of a Faculty of instruction in the institution for the present..."[18] Had it not been for the fact that President

Bannister agreed to assume personal responsibility for the Male Department, Preparatory and Collegiate, and Professor D. Tuthill for the Female Collegiate Institute, the whole enterprise would have foundered. As Burns later analyzed the situation, "the instructors were laboring with only enough compensation to eke out a living. The situation certainly could not last long. It is highly possible that the school might have closed its doors and never reopened them." [19] "Militant Christianity" and "self-sacrifice" are cited as the factors which enabled the college to survive, along with the providential appointment of Greenberry R. Baker as agent and money-raiser. During the first year of his work for the College he raised over $9,000 "which was considered near to the miraculous." [20]

Baker evidently perceived at once that the college in its Santa Clara location was in an untenable situation. He proposed, therefore, that the Trustees buy the Stockton Rancho, between San Jose and Santa Clara. "About twenty of the 435 acres were to be reserved for a campus and the remainder was to be subdivided into blocks and lots and offered for sale at an advance of one hundred percent of the cost."[21] Once again, the Board moved audaciously ahead—supported more by hope than by actual sums in hand. "The purchase was made April 1, 1866, consisting of 435 acres of land, for the sum of $70,000 with interest at one percent per month. The purchase was made almost solely on the strength of faith in the sale of lots to meet the payments, as the amount of cash to pay down at the time of purchase was but $2,000, and $1,000 of that borrowed." [22] The venture was successful, fortunately, and by September of 1870 enough lots had been sold to start the construction of the first building on the new campus.

The move to San Jose injected new hope and optimism in the life of the school, but financial crises continued to plague its existence. Presidents came, often worked bravely against overwhelming odds, then resigned in discouragement. In 1885 President Stratton was faced with a new challenge to the survival of the institution. The other Methodist school in Northern California, Napa Collegiate Institute, announced its intention of "incorporating as a college, and extending the course of study,"[23] and the already meager base of support was divided between the two struggling schools. In 1887 Stratton resigned to become President of Mills College.

His successor, Dr. A. C. Hirst, came to the post with high hopes that in spite of the financial difficulties the University would continue to serve the community. "We do not desire," he said, "to be known through costly buildings and a large endowment but through scholarship." [24] He set out at once to strengthen the academic life of the school, and for a while he succeeded. During the school year 1890-91 enrollment in the "college department" increased to 86 students. But Hirst was unable to settle a student disturbance and suffered an irreparable loss of trust in his administration. In the spring of 1891, four of the most popular faculty members resigned and students left en masse, many of them enrolling in the newly established Stanford University. College enrollment for the following year dropped to 32 students.

Interested observers must have doubted that the school would survive. It had been faced with four of those factors Tewksbury cited as causes of the death of such institutions: "financial disaster, unfavorable location, denominational competition and internal dissension." In a few years it would be troubled by the final factor "natural catastrophe" when two of the main buildings on the campus burned to the ground. Yet somehow, despite repeated changes in leadership (during the years between 1891-1919 seven different men served as president) the College managed to survive.

When Dr. John Seaton resigned in 1919, the Board members gathered once again to choose a new president. They made a far-reaching decision when they chose to ask Tully Cleon Knoles to accept the post. He was to hold it for 27 years before resigning to become the Chancellor in 1946. The Trustees of the University of Southern California, where he had worked as head of the history department and assistant to President George Bovard, were sorry to see him go. Their statement of appreciation of Dr. Knoles' work there is impressive. It reads, in part:

> The high scholarship of Professor Knoles, his vigorous and attractive personality, his genuine gift for teaching, his insight into the problems of young life, the sound judgement with which he has dealt with the issues of the day and his inspiring interpretation and exemplification of the ideas of the Christian faith have made him a tower of strength of the faculty of the University of Southern California and have given him a large

place in the life not only of the city of Los Angeles but all Southern California.[25]

The formal declaration of praise registers unusually strong commendation for the departing faculty member. But the words barely scratch the surface in describing the handsome young man who was to become Pacific's president. Austere in his religious beliefs and the possessor of a wide-ranging yet incisive intellect, Tully Knoles brought to the task a determination to see the college play a respectable role in the academic life of California. He was a proud man and something of an autocrat, but evidently those qualities were informed with such integrity and genuine paternal concern there were few who bridled under his leadership. Paradoxically, his personality was touched with a kind of flamboyance; till the end of his long life he delighted in demonstrating his skill with the lasso, leading parades on horseback, dressed in elegant cowboy garb. This sense of drama informed his teaching, and he was one of the most sought-after public speakers in the state. The sometimes conflicting tendencies in his character led occasionally to bouts of ill health, but they also combined to make him an extraordinarily vital human being.

His colorful personality and broad interests derived from the varied experiences of his childhood. The descendant of two signers of the Declaration of Independence, he was born on January 6, 1876, during the centennial year. His maternal grandmother entertained the children with stories of her experiences during the Mexican and Civil Wars, so the future historian was introduced to historical narrative at an early age. His formal education during those early years in Petersburg, Illinois was frequently interrupted by sickness, but he learned the rudiments of spelling and grammar as an apprentice typesetter for his father's newspaper. The oldest son in the family, he was assigned numerous tasks on the family's small farm and learned while still a boy to assume positions of authority.

After the family moved to California he was admitted to the Chaffee College of Agriculture, which was at that time a Methodist academy. Situated in Ontario, it served as one of the prep schools for that young, burgeoning institution, the University of Southern California. To pay for his tuition, he assumed the care of the grounds of the College. And the man who was one day to help lay out the landscape design of the new College of Pacific campus in Stockton gained his first experience in gardening there at Chaffee, where he "laid out an extensive irrigation system for the gardens." [26]

While he was at Chaffee he attended one of the revival meetings then so popular in the Methodist Church. After hearing Dr. J. W. Phelps deliver a powerful sermon, Tully, along with 23 other young people, accepted the call to the altar where they professed their conversion to Christ. It was a momentous decision for Tully Knoles, because he lived out his commitments to the full; for the rest of his life he was a deeply religious man. Carrying out his decision at this point led him to become Sunday School Superintendent at his parents' Presbyterian Church. He also became very active in the Young Men's Christian Association and there made lifelong friend-ships with two men who would later share with him the distinction and the trials of the presidency of California colleges: Ray Lyman Wilbur of Stanford and George Barrows of the University of California.

Piety and hard academic and physical work were not all that occupied his time, however; he enjoyed the ordinary social life of young people at the time. Although he soon gave up such pleasures, R. R. Stuart reports the surprising (given his subsequent stern eschewing of such "vices") fact that he "learned to smoke cigarettes and he enjoyed the taste of the sweet California wines." [27] He enjoyed sports, played football and participated on the track team as pole-vaulter. His favorite outdoor activity, though, continued to be horseback riding. While still in Illinois he had learned from a traveling cowboy how to use a lariat to rope steers and throughout his life he enjoyed demonstrating his skill at lassoing. During his high school years, in addition to his school work and church work and all that they entailed, he also trained and cared for the horses in his father's stable.

Perhaps his activities on horseback served as a psychological release valve for this young man who made such stern demands on himself. But during subsequent years his skill at trading and training horses had far more practical value; it enabled him to work his way through college. Jotham Bixby, the founder of Long Beach, and wealthy landowner in Southern California, had known the Knoles family for some time. When the young man was struggling through U.S.C., working to support his wife Emily and his growing family,

12

Bixby encouraged his son George to hire Tully Knoles to train some of the horses he had brought back from the Chicago International Livestock Exhibition. Over the period from 1901 to 1912 the student and then professor trained 152 horses for the Bixbys. Later he reflected that: "Frankly, I do not know how I would have lived as a student and a young professor without that added income." [28]

During his senior year at U.S.C. his major professor and mentor, Dr. James H. Hoose, became seriously ill and asked Tully to take over his classes. The students and administration of the University were evidently impressed with his ability, for after his graduation in 1903, Dr. George Bovard, the President, offered him a job on the teaching staff at U.S.C. That was no small order; he was to take over the classes in history, economics, political science and sociology. If he chose not to accept the post, Dr. Bovard told him, he could become the minister of a church in San Fernando with a salary of $800 a year and a parsonage. Tully Knoles had evidently enjoyed his teaching, however, for he decided to stay at the University though the salary there, with no parsonage, was only $600. The knowledge that the "horses would keep me going for a while" [29] helped him make what was to be the watershed decision. Because although Tully Knoles preached throughout his life—at churches and at college chapel services and baccalaureates—from this time on he was to be engaged primarily in all aspects of higher education, first as Professor and then Head of the Department of History at U.S.C., Assistant to the President there and then President of C.O.P. and Chancellor.

Throughout this long career his wife Emily played a tremendously significant role. She not only mothered her own children, she cared for the students of the college, many of whom lived with the Knoles during times of stress. Perhaps her greatest task, though, was to nurse the paradoxical, mercurial man who was her husband during the periods of his depression and ill health. In spite of—or perhaps because of—his strenuous activities, driven by his desire for perfection in them all, Tully Knoles suffered periodic bouts of illness. The most protracted of these occurred between 1912 and 1915 when the breakdown was so severe he had to leave the University. Emily packed up the family and they went to her father's ranch in Owens Valley. For three years her husband virtually lived out of doors, on horseback, of course, and gradually he regained his health. When he returned to the University, friends saw in him a new maturity and strength, and once again he immersed himself wholeheartedly in the life of teaching and administering the Department of History.

Soon after his return, Dr. Bovard also began calling on him for extracurricular activities. All college presidents are called upon for numerous speaking engagements, but frequently lack of time and the pressure of other demands interfere. As the community of Los Angeles was growing by leaps and bounds and the University grew apace, Dr. Bovard referred more and more of these "goodwill," public relations speaking requests to Professor Knoles, who became his assistant and informal vice president of the University. When in 1919 the Board of Trustees of the College of Pacific in San Jose asked Professor Knoles to assume the presidency of that institution he went to Dr. Bovard for counsel. "Take it," the older man said, without hesitation. "Put in a few years up there until you gain the administrative know-how, then come back here and take over my job." [30]

Knoles followed the first part of his advice and accepted the position, but when he learned of President Bovard's retirement in 1921, he wrote to the Board of Trustees and told them he could not leave Pacific (then in the midst of planning to move to Stockton), thus forestalling a motion which had been drawn to nominate him to the presidency of his alma mater. That he refused that offer was indeed significant for the College of Pacific, which benefitted from the continuity of his 27 years as President and 13 years as Chancellor.

He brought to those offices not only the skills and experience he had accumulated during his childhood and 14 years at U.S.C. but also a religious devotion to the task of seeing to it that the college endured. Dr. Rockwell Hunt has written of "the profound significance" of the continuity President Knoles brought to the College's administration. "The administration of no earlier president had continued for more than a single decade—some terms had been far shorter."[31] The job had become, in fact, a kind of jumping off base for men of ambition. Dr. William W. Guth, President of the College from 1909-1913, left to become President of the well-known college for women, Goucher College in Maryland. And Dr. Knoles' immediate predecessor, Dr. John L. Seaton, resigned to become the head of the national office for Methodist higher education in Chicago. Seen in this context, the long tenure of Dr. Knoles as President is clearly a factor of tremendous importance in the life of the institution.

Even more important than his continuance in the office, however, was the quality of leadership he brought to the post. At the very beginning of his administration, he warned the Trustees that he would not be of assistance in money raising. He evidently loathed asking people for money. "But from the time of his acceptance of the Presidency, Dr. Knoles built his life into the active development of the college—indeed his incumbency became his great absorbing life work, occupying twenty-seven intensely busy years."[32] The skills and talents he had accumulated over the years in Illinois and Chaffee and at U.S.C. were all brought to the test during his years as President of the College of Pacific; the wide-ranging scholar, the dramatic speaker, the able administrator, the gifted Christian teacher in this man, all had their parts to play in the turbulent years from 1919 to 1946.

He assumed the office during a critical period; the academic standards of the College had been lowered in the effort to attract more students. The college was poorly endowed, like most schools of its kind, and had resorted to this diminishment of requirements because of the desperate need for tuition income. Other small church-related schools had followed the same path. But Dr. Knoles was determined that Pacific should not founder because of standards which were too low. He immediately insisted, therefore, that admission requirements be strengthened. The Trustees were dismayed; they feared the loss of students. Dr. Knoles persuaded them—as he was to persuade them throughout his presidency—of the critical importance of the move. Almost at once, enrollments began to climb.

The improved academic standards, however, did not solve the major problems faced by the institution. It had been clear to Dr. Knoles from his first visit to the campus that the college was in an impossible situation. Two large important institutions were already in the area: the University of California, supported by the state, and Stanford University, splendidly endowed by the Stanford family. In addition to these great universities numerous smaller schools (six Catholic colleges and the state teachers college at San Jose) were competing for students and endowment. Tully Knoles spent considerable time after his appointment studying the options for the small struggling school he was so determined would survive.

One alternative lay in the possibility of becoming a private junior college. Separation of the upper division university from the lower division had for some time been actively recommended by some of California's leading educators. In 1907 the state legislature had passed "the first law in the nation to permit the board of trustees of any city district, union, joint union or county high school to pre-scribe post graduate courses of study for the graduates of such high school . . . which courses of study shall approximate the studies prescribed in the first two years of university courses." [33] Alexis F. Lange of the University of California and David Starr Jordan of Stanford had also recommended "the amputation of freshman and sophomore classes to prevent university atrophy." [34] By 1917, six-teen California high schools had established junior college pro-grams. In 1919, the Southern Branch of the University of California (later U.C.L.A.) opened as a junior college. The development was too slow, however, to enable either Stanford or U. C. Berkeley to close its lower division. In 1920 Ray Lyman Wilbur, who had be-come President of Stanford in 1916, renewed President Jordan's plea that the University concentrate its resources in the upper division and graduate schools and cease "duplicating work that now or soon will be, handled admirably by forty or fifty insti-tutions in the state." [35] Discussions were then held between Stanford and C.O.P. exploring the possibility of C.O.P. assuming the role of junior college, preparing students for upper division work at Stanford.

At the January meeting of the Board of Trustees Dr. Knoles also presented another possible resolution to the problems faced by the college: that its property be sold and the proceeds be used to build Wesley Foundation Halls at Stanford and U. C. But he saved the option he himself favored till the last and argued once again so forcefully that the Board consented. They agreed "to seek a new location and build a real college from the ground up physically, and on the old cultural beginnings foster the development of a new modern Christian center of living and learning." [36]

The Trustees were understandably reluctant to embark on such a revolutionary path, but as soon as he had their consent Tully Knoles set to work, with his typical driving energy, to find the right location. While in New York for a meeting of the Methodist Board of Higher Education, he made an appointment to see Dr. E. C. Sage of the Rockefeller General Education Board. Between 1902 and 1940 this body dispensed $250,000,000 to schools and colleges throughout the country, and President Knoles sought the support and counsel of its director. Dr. Sage agreed with Pacific's President that the college could not continue to exist if it remained in San Jose, and pointed to a map of the central San Joaquin Valley. "There is the center of the largest area in the U.S. having the largest high school population not served by any college in the vicinity." [37] On his return to the campus, Dr. Knoles verified Dr. Sage's statement. Vice-President John L. Burcham was dispatched to Modesto, Stockton and Sacramento to sound out community leaders who, he hoped, would lend financial and moral support to the new venture.

In the end Stockton was chosen as the site for the new campus, partly because of its central location and partly because of the enthusiastic support for the project voiced by prominent business-men and churchmen in the community. The J. C. Smith Co. offered a forty-acre site for the campus. Urged on by Dr. E. C. Bane, an alumnus of the College and minister of a local Methodist Church, the Chamber of Commerce agreed to sponsor a crusade to raise the $1,250,000 necessary for new buildings, $600,000 of which was to come from Stockton itself. Under the leadership of a local businessman, Thomas F. Baxter, Dr. Bane, and Dr. Burcham, the crusade was launched. On April 24, 1924, the first brick was laid for the new buildings.

Later President Burns was to speak of the move as a "pioneering" effort; indeed the faculty and students on the new campus did face some formidable challenges. When classes opened on September 15, 1924, the buildings had not yet been finished. "There were no doors, few windows, no heating." [38] Members of that first class still recall (humorously, it should be noted) the summer's dust and the winter's mud, for the site on which the new buildings were erected had been a grain field. The proud new brick buildings stuck out like the proverbial sore thumb because there were few trees and no shrubs to soften their outlines. In spite of the physical hardships, students enrolled that first year, 142 more than had attended the

Framework for the Conservatory of Music as the new campus began to develop in Stockton.

college the year before. Tully Knoles' determination to move the institution had immediately proved beneficial.

Thirty-one of the College faculty and eleven of the Conservatory faculty chose to move to Stockton and continue their work with Dr. Knoles. It cannot have been an easy decision for many of them—to leave the culturally stimulating San Francisco Bay Area to come to the relatively isolated agricultural community in the Central Valley. But the President had convinced them of the need for such an institution there; a sense of mission coupled with their loyalty to him urged them to make the move. A group of these "pioneers" purchased a piece of land across the road from the campus on which twenty-two faculty families built their homes. The development of Pacific Manor was subsequently criticized by some townspeople; had the faculty homes been interspersed with Stocktonians' their influence in the local community would undoubtedly have been culturally beneficial. Nevertheless, the advantages to the college were apparent from the beginning. The close relationships between students and faculty that had always been a significant element in its attractiveness were nurtured by the proximity of the campus to faculty homes. Furthermore, that sense of community among the faculty members themselves was strengthened by social and neighborhood ties.

18

Both their sense of mission and their solidarity as a community were soon to be sorely tried—for the college enjoyed scarcely five years in its new home before the calamitous Great Depression shook the economic foundations of the entire nation. Many similar institutions suffered in the 1930s, and the College of the Pacific itself suffered severe diminishment in enrollment (978 students attended the college during its peak year before the outbreak of the depression 1928-29. By 1932-33 that figure had dropped to 707). Students were unable to pay even the minimal ($6.00 per unit) fees for tuition, and retrenchments were obviously necessary if the institution was to survive. Tully Knoles led the way and announced that he would take a forty percent cut in salary during the year 1932-33. Then faculty members, rather than see any of their members dismissed, agreed as a body to accept a similar cut. Even then there were months that the college could not pay its staff. Fortunately, local merchants allowed them to charge groceries, and groups of families were invited to glean the fields of neighboring farms. It was a trying and difficult period. The generosity of the faculty, their devotion to the College and its educational task, were crucially significant in its survival.

Another of the factors which enabled the institution to endure lay in the willingness of its administration to innovate, to adjust to changing conditions. Tully Knoles and the Trustees had already demonstrated that vital flexibility in the decision to move the college to Stockton. In the early 1930s it was apparent that new experiments must be tried, new directions followed, if the college were to remain viable. Both the faculty and the administration were determined, however, that the academic standards which had been achieved after Dr. Knoles' accession to the presidency not be weakened.

The Faculty Coordinating Committee was charged with the task of discovering and exploring ways to save the college. During the ensuing discussions Professor of Speech Dwayne Orton recommended that a separate but allied division be established, a junior college. Such a division, he believed, could appeal to and meet the needs of a broader group of students without diminishing the educational life of the parent body. President Knoles was already familiar with the arguments in favor of such institutions. One of the options considered in 1921 had been the possibility of C.O.P.'s becoming a junior college to prepare students for Stanford University. He had rejected that alternative, but these were different circumstances, and the proposal did not involve the elimination of programs but an addition. Once again he sought counsel from educational leaders in the East; and after receiving encouragement from Robert Lester of the Carnegie Foundation for the Advancement of Teaching, he supported the new plan, and the Trustees agreed.

In 1934 the new division, called the General College of the College of Pacific, opened its doors to 65 students who would otherwise not have been able to meet the admission requirements of the college. The new development came in the knick of time. President Knoles reported to the Trustees that "had it not been for our Junior College offerings our freshman class would have been the smallest in our history on the Stockton Campus."[39] Students were evidently drawn to the new division because its "survey-appreciation courses" would be taught by regular faculty members. Besides, all students enjoyed "the privilege of participating in all college and class activities in accordance with the general regulations of the college."[40]

In spite of this infusion of new students, enrollment was insufficient to maintain the institution, whose facilities were still not being utilized to the full. At the same time the Stockton School Board was considering the establishment of a potentially competitive junior college of its own. Under state law it was required to pay other junior college districts for the tuition of post-high school students, a sum which amounted to $30,000 during 1934-35. Active in local service groups, well known throughout the area because of his public speaking, Tully Knoles had numerous friends in the community. He was also undoubtedly supported by the numerous teachers in Stockton who were graduates of Pacific's School of Education when he suggested some kind of cooperative arrangement between the School Board and the College. The main impediment lay in the Constitution's insistence on separation of church and state, a principle which the Methodist Church had always actively upheld. Informal discussions with state officials revealed, however, that the rental of facilities by a public school system was legal. The urgency of the situation, both for the school district and the College, led to quick action.

20

The Stockton School Board voted on August 23, 1935, to open its own junior college. On October 3 the rental agreement with the College of the Pacific was signed. After receiving final state approval, the public junior college of the Stockton School Board opened on the Pacific campus with 301 freshman students. Sophomores were to be admitted in 1936. No immediate financial gains accrued to the College. According to state law the school district could receive no state support until after its first year of operation, so the rental of the facilities amounted to $5.00, the payment to teachers $2.50 a month. Clearly the College entered the agreement as an investment in the future, gambling that the State Attorney General would affirm the legality of a more permanent and reasonable contract. The first step toward a cooperation that was unique in the history of American higher education had been taken.

The precipitate action, however, had led to considerable confusion. The junior college division of the college continued to exist side by side with the new public junior college. Such duplication over the long run would obviously have been costly and wasteful. Knoles recommended almost immediately, therefore, that the College abandon its own freshman and sophomore years, concentrating instead on the upper division and graduate offerings. Surely with some glee that the tables had been turned, he reported to the Trustees that "we can now do what many educators have long contended should be done, concentrate upon the work of the Upper Division and graduate year, frankly recognizing in fact what is recognized in law in California—that the Lower Division is a part of secondary education."[41] Noting this separation in function and administration that was proposed for the two institutions and that "there will be no sectarian or denominational instruction of any kind given in this junior college, either directly or indirectly,"[42] Attorney General U.S. Webb informed Vierling Kersey, State Superintendent of Public Instruction, that it was his opinion that the arrangement to share facilities and faculties conformed to the requirements of law.

The advantages to Pacific were evident from the opening of the 1936 school year. Rental payments from the School District helped ameliorate the College's desperate financial situation. Furthermore, the hiring of faculty members to teach part-time for the public institution relieved the college of the total responsibility for their support. Tully Knoles had especially felt this burden; having led his band of educators into the wilderness, so to speak, he was determined that they not be abandoned. Finally after years of very real struggle, the loyal band of teachers (in 1935-36 their pay scales amounted to one half of the 1929 figures) were to be more adequately recompensed.

The advantages of the new agreement were not one sided, however. The local school district and its students also benefitted, first and most importantly from Pacific's experienced and scholarly faculty. The new college had a higher percentage of Ph.D's on its staff than any other institution of its kind in the state. Tully Knoles had chosen them, he said, because "I've always had this vast ambition—that is to see to it that on the faculty of the College of Pacific there would always be *scholars,* and at the same time very fine *teachers.*"[43] During the two years from 1934-1936 the faculty had proved to the local community that they could respond as scholars and teachers to the different needs of junior college students.

Another boon to the junior college lay in the opportunity to share with the upper division students Pacific's established campus. In a little over ten years, the trees and shrubs and lawns had been planted. The landscaping design, originally suggested by John MacLaren of Golden Gate Park, had been carried out even during the lean years thanks to gifts of plants and the careful nurturing of Santino Bava and his crew of Italian gardeners. By 1936 the campus was a green oasis on hot summer and fall days. By this time, too, the science laboratories and the physical education department had been equipped. The library's collection had grown, and junior college students who wished to live on campus shared the college dormitories. One student association worked for the interests of both student bodies and planned social and extracurricular activities for all the students.

Thus, in many ways the two schools seemed to be one. It is important, therefore, to note the distinctions between the two. The junior college program was designed to meet the needs of students who wanted general education, and of those who wanted advanced vocational courses. As early as June, 1937, the bulletin of Stockton J.C. announced that "In addition to the liberal arts and science work in preparation for senior college and university, Stockton College will offer courses in the following fields of semi-professional work:

22

General Business; Accounting; Civil, Structural and Mechanical Drawing; Electrical; Radio; Photographic; Household Science and Art."[44] These courses required new, specially trained instructors so that as the Junior College developed the almost total overlapping of faculties in the two schools was diminished. Nevertheless, almost all of the liberal arts courses continued to be taught by Pacific faculty. President Knoles and Dwayne Orton, who became the chief administrator of the Junior College, worked together to refine the complicated proportional scales that resulted in rental and salary agreements. And in spite of some inevitable disagreements during the next 15 years, the unique contract between Stockton Junior College and the College of Pacific worked in the interests of both institutions.

Once again interested friends and observers marvelled at the tenacity of the institution. Although many schools had been forced to close their doors because of what had seemed insurmountable financial problems, Pacific had once again emerged from a critical period—not only alive but stronger—thanks to the generosity and loyalty of the teaching staff and the innovative determined leadership of its administration. As had been the case earlier in its history, however, the College barely caught its breath before it was faced with another threat to its existence, World War II.

Even before the formal declaration of war in December, 1941, the draft was decimating the ranks of young male college students. And in 1942 enrollment at the College of Pacific had dropped to 447 students (from 672 in 1941-42). Obviously something had to be done, and Knoles once again embarked on a search for new programs. Application to Washington led to the College's being chosen by the War Manpower Commission as a training facility for the Navy's V-12 Program. On July 1, 1943 the program was initiated. Navy and Marine detachments came to the College for courses specializing in premedical and engineering training. During the 1942-43 school year, 545 young men participated in the government sponsored program, which brought crucial support to the College throughout the rest of the war.[45]

The contribution made by the College to the training of young men was indeed significant. That the program was enthusiastically received is apparent in the numbers of students who returned to the College after the war to complete their degrees. Another program

23

that benefitted the community at large as well as the students commenced in May of 1944, when officials of Northern California food canneries asked the college for assistance in the required testing of their products. Barthol W. Pearce, a graduate of the college, was asked to direct the new Food Processors Foundation which continued after the war to train students for work in sugar refineries, food machinery plants, cannery and preserving plants, frozen food firms, and carton and container companies. The College laboratories were used and students employed by the processors were paid an amount equal to that which they would have been paid as regular employees.

Partly as a result of the success of the Food Processors Foundation and the V-12 Program and the infusion of private and government funds, Pacific was able to liquidate the debts it had accumulated during the depression and the early years of the war. On March 26, 1946 members of the Board of Trustees, the administration, faculty, and friends gathered to celebrate the "burning of the mortgage." Another significant factor in its post-war financial solvency, however, lay in the care and conservatism of Ovid H. Ritter's financial management. After his graduation from Stanford University Mr. Ritter had worked in China for several years as representative for an American shipping company. Then in 1918, because he and Mrs. Ritter were concerned about their children's secondary education, the family returned to the United States. After working at the Bank of Stockton for ten years he became Comptroller of the College in 1930. Fourteen years later in his report to the Trustees President Knoles spoke of the "excellent job" Mr. Ritter had done for the college:

> He had to bear the terrible load of financing the Institution during the days of the depression. I do not know how he has been able to bear up under the burden, but he has, and I sincerely hope that he can be assured of easier days ahead. He is doing three men's work now. He is teaching as much as any man should teach. It is another full time job to manage the Dining Hall and Housing Auxiliaries, and still another to control the financing and accounting.[46]

In addition to these tasks, Mr. Ritter personally supervised the care of the grounds. Arriving on campus at 7 A.M. he would confer with Mr. Bava; the camellias and flowering trees that beautify the cam-

24

Ovid H. Ritter, Comptroller.

pus owe their planting to Mr. Ritter. He also played an active role in the designing of the Morris Chapel; in 1946 his ninety-two page booklet explaining the symbolic designs in the stained glass windows was published by the College. It is difficult to imagine how one man could accomplish all this and do it so successfully. Ovid Ritter's classes were memorable; he trained numbers of Stockton College's and Pacific's students in the principles of business administration. And his careful management of the finances was a critically important element in the College's emergence from the trials of the depression and World War II on a sound financial basis.

The budget he worked with was, in comparison with today's, quite small. In the auditor's report for fiscal year 1946, submitted to the Board of Trustees on September 25, 1946, educational expenses amounted to $292,070.63. Of that amount by far the largest percentage was allotted to instructional expense; 40 percent ($133,465.30) had been expended in dean's faculty salaries, and in supplies for the laboratories and library. Twelve percent had been expended for administration (salaries and supplies, President's Office, Assistant to President's office, Executive Vice President and Comptroller's

25

office and the Registrar's office). A total of $59,039.88 or 20 percent had been spent in the maintenance of grounds and buildings.

The percentage of expenditure for the instructional, maintenance and other costs shows significant variation from that shown in 1931 graphs:

Chart	Instructional	Admin.	Maintenance of Plant	Other
1929-30	75.5	10.4	10.3	3.8
1945-46	46	12	20	22

The loss in percentage in the instructional budget would be alarming were it not for the fact that a portion of faculty salaries was being paid by the junior college. The corresponding rise in plant maintenance costs must also be seen in that perspective; wear and tear on the campus had been increased with the rental of buildings and equipment to the school district. Miscellaneous costs, including student activities had also risen because of the College's subsidizing many of the junior college students' extracurricular events. These figures would, nevertheless, be a matter of concern if it were not for the fact that rental payments from the junior college amounted to $63,034 during that year—a sum which certainly contributed to the general operating surplus in 1945-46 of $91,666.18.

Another important element in the college's financial solvency lay in Mr. Ritter's careful management of its endowment and other non-expendable funds. Though this sum was relatively small ($581,172.82) it was higher, in spite of the depression and war years, than it had been in 1929-30, when it had amounted only to $314,699.98. The fact that a significant portion of these funds in 1945-46 was invested in its own income-producing properties (dormitories, dining hall, etc.) suggests potential financial weakness, but thanks to the meticulous attention paid by Mr. Ritter to these concerns, they all operated at a profit and contributed to the operational surplus mentioned above.

In fact, the Executive Vice President's concern about all aspects of the institution's budget is apparent throughout the financial report submitted to the Trustees. The expenses and income of each

26

dining hall and dormitory were analyzed and dealt with in detail. Each intramural athletic contest (both football and basketball) is listed, so that the Trustees could see for themselves the cost ratios of that program. Other extracurricular activities analyzed in the report included the a cappella choir, the little theater and the debate team, which was implicitly chided for spending $17.81 more than its income! Altogether, it is evident that Ovid Ritter exercised close personal supervision of every detail of the budget, and that he managed, thereby, not only to retire the debt but also to operate the institution with a profit.

He was assisted in this difficult work by the Board of Trustees, whose members generously supported the work of the College. In their election lay the primary formal connection between the College and the Methodist Church, because thirty members were elected by the Northern California-Nevada Conference of the church and six members were elected by the Southern California-Arizona Conference. Generally speaking, however, the Board was self-perpetuating; President Knoles and the members themselves recommended the replacements for deceased or retiring trustees and the church's election was a matter of form rather than the exertion of real control over the school. Nine members of the board were Methodist clergymen; one of these, Dr. James C. Baker, was the presiding bishop of the area. Not all of the members of the board were Methodists, however. Jewish membership, though uncommon, was not unknown and members from other Protestant denominations played a significant role.

At the time Robert Burns became President of the College, O. D. Jacoby was President of the Board of Trustees. Active in the banking circles of the San Francisco Bay Area, and a concerned layman in the Methodist Church, Mr. Jacoby had served on the Board for twenty-six years before he assumed its leadership in 1940. He had participated in the decisions to move the college, and to divest itself of the lower division, and brought to those critical discussions financial experience as well as a knowledge of the broad economic implications of the innovations Dr. Knoles urged. Mr. Jacoby perceived the function of the Board to be the questioner of new developments but felt strongly that trustees should not interfere with academic affairs of the college. Actually, none of Dr. Knoles' major recommendations was vetoed by the Board, whose members held the President in respect for his Christian dedication, his academic leadership and his conservative financial demands.

Another function of the Board, Mr. Jacoby believed, was to assist in fund raising, both through their own personal gifts and through their contacts with other benefactors.[47] In fact, a large proportion of the gifts to the college had come through the Trustees' work of publicizing the college's aims and needs. Many of them traveled some distance to attend meetings; thirteen members came from Southern California, over two hundred miles from the campus; sixteen members came from the Bay Area and other communities within about one hundred miles of the campus; seven members were residents of Stockton. One is impressed with the generosity of these men and women (five women were serving as Board members in 1946) who frequently interrupted busy schedules for the time-consuming general meetings of the Board and its committees. Trusteeship is often a thankless task, for Board members are frequently the scapegoats when unpopular decisions are made. In fact, dangerous divisions between the faculty and the trustees can arise. President David Starr Jordan of Stanford once said that "There are two universities, one as seen by the faculty, the other as seen by the Board. I try to ride both horses, as it were. They will someday coalesce, but I may fall between." [48] The situation at Pacific was different, partly because of the dedication of the Board to the religious and academic aims of the college, and partly because of the unifying leadership of the President. Tully Knoles, an experienced horseback rider, managed to ride the two horses in tandem.

The administrative staff on campus which assisted President Knoles and Vice President Ritter was comparatively small; each person, therefore, played a crucial role in the life of the College. Robert Burns had worked in various capacities for the college between the time of his graduation in 1931 and the Fall of 1946, first as a fund raiser, then as alumni secretary, recruiter of students, registrar and from 1942 as Assistant to the President. Even before he became President, his contributions to the College were manifold and significant; he was, therefore, familiar with all aspects of its administration.

Robert Burns worked closely with Ellen Deering who had begun her work in the registrar's office in 1926 after serving in the same office at her alma mater, Chico State College. Largely thanks to her efforts the emergencies created by the sudden influx of junior college students in 1935 and V-12 students during the war were handled smoothly and efficiently. Throughout all those difficult years of depression and war, her office served the College not only as registrar but also in the admission of students and their placement in jobs after graduation. Yet Miss Deering managed the threefold task with a minimum of help and a maximum of efficiency. And in spite of all these demands on her attention, she took a warm personal interest in students—many of whom have continued to correspond with her after her retirement in 1969—following thirty-three years of unselfish, competent work for the college. Ellen Deering continued her active interest in the University, its alumni, staff and students until her death in 1977.

The Deans of the College, of the Conservatory and of the School of Education shared with Dr. Knoles the governance of the academic life on the campus. Like him they divided their time between teaching and administering, and like him each one made a unique personal contribution to the academic life of the College. Fred Farley, Dean of the College, had first come to Pacific in 1918 as professor of Ancient Languages. A man who shared President Knoles' interests in philosophy, scriptural study and history, he was a true philologist, and students who participated in his Art of Language Courses still speak with enthusiasm of his inspired teaching, his wide-ranging intellect and his gentle sense of humor. Chapel services frequently were enlivened by his extemporaneous translations of scriptural passages, and the poems he wrote to celebrate great occasions were informed with a quiet wisdom and polished wit. Dr. Farley was a respected and beloved figure on the campus; he played a vital role in the maintenance of academic standards and faculty morale during times of crisis.

The liberal arts college of which Dr. Farley was Dean had always been the core of the institution. From its inception, the educational philosophy of the faculty and administration was based on belief in the necessity of educating young men and women in the liberating western cultural tradition. The 1946 catalogue described the objectives more specifically:

The college was founded upon Christian and co-educational principles. The purpose of the program of liberal education is to make men free by assisting college students through the acquisition of knowledge in achieving an attitude of self-criticism and of world-mindedness, of being tolerant yet at the same time having definite convictions leading to action benefitting both the individual and the group and consistent with American ideals. Throughout the years, it has maintained these principles, stressing the development of personality and character, along with high scholarship and broad culture. Although the institution is non-sectarian, it endeavors to stimulate interest in spiritual life.[49]

Statistics can only serve as partial proof of the success of the College in achieving its objectives; nonetheless the numbers of degrees awarded during the period of Dr. Knoles' presidency is impressive. Although requirements for the degrees were rigorous, 2,128 bachelor of art degrees were awarded between 1919 and 1946, and 254 masters degrees. In 1946, sixty-seven faculty members were teaching courses in twenty-one major departments, ranging from Ancient Languages to Zoology. Dr. Farley's task as Dean of this college of liberal arts required that he maintain the academic quality of the course offerings. That he fulfilled that requirement well during his twenty-one-year tenure is apparent in the respect with which the college was held when Robert Burns became President.

Another of the "old-timers" on the campus, Dr. J. William Harris, had resigned from the deanship of the School of Education in 1943 after 33 years of splendid service to the College. Dr. Marc Jantzen succeeded him and had become an important figure in the administrative staff by the time Robert Burns succeeded Dr. Knoles. A descendant of German Mennonites who had emigrated from Russia, Marc Jantzen spent his boyhood on a small farm in Kansas. Soon after he finished high school, he began what was to be a life-long teaching career in a small one-room grade school not far from his home. Alternating teaching winters and studying summers, he finished the work for his bachelor's degree at Bethel College in 1934. Then, as he was completing his doctorate at the University of Kansas in 1940, he was interviewed by Dr. Knoles "during a train layover."[50] Although their meeting was brief, the

President said later that he was impressed with Dr. Jantzen's "strong jaw." He evidently also convinced Dr. Knoles of his capability as teacher and administrator because the President asked him to come to Pacific as Assistant Professor of Education and Director of the Summer Session. Thanks to his unbounded energy, Dr. Jantzen was able to continue in those roles even after he became Dean, a position which required innovative leadership as well as intelligent administration of existing programs during the post-war years of teacher shortages.

The School of Education had, since its elevation from departmental status in 1923, been one of the mainstays of the institution. Recognized by the California State Board of Education on January 10, 1924, the School was authorized to issue recommendations for elementary, secondary, and administrative credentials. Hundreds of teachers from all over the state had received their training at Pacific during the years between 1924 and 1946 when President Burns took office. Many of them had achieved positions of distinction: two were college presidents, two the chief administrators of junior colleges, and thirteen were school district superintendents. Through its training young people to be teachers the School of Education's service to the community was indeed outstanding.

In addition, the presence of the School, with its well trained faculty, increased general local consciousness of modern teaching techniques. The extent of this interest can be measured in the numbers of teachers who attended summer sessions to update their skills. In 1946, 708 students attended summer school classes covering a full range of subjects and taught by eighteen visiting and twenty-eight resident faculty. By far the greatest number of offerings were in the field of education. In addition to the standard courses required for the credential, courses such as Workshop in Air Age Education were included in the list of offerings—an opportunity for teachers to explore "the significance of air transportation" by studying "global weather and weather forecasting together with important new concepts of distance and direction"[51] with field trips to United Airlines facilities and Oakland airport. Science teachers could also take advantage of the Pacific Marine Station at Dillon Beach where Dr. Alden Noble taught classes in ecology and marine biology. Teachers concerned with speech correction were able to participate in a special program combining course work with actual treatment of children with speech disorders—a program of great benefit both to the teachers and the children of the community who were involved. Altogether, the campus of the College was a busy center of continuing education during the summer.

Another division of the College which made a tangible contribution to the cultural life of the area was the Conservatory of Music under the leadership of Dean John Elliott. A graduate of Northwestern University, his credentials had been so impressive that his predecessor, Charles Dennis, hired him sight unseen in 1927 to be Professor of Piano. John Elliott, a fine musician, performed in concerts throughout the area, winning new friends and supporters for the Conservatory's programs. He consistently pleaded the Conservatory's cause with President Knoles and the Coordinating Committee and managed in spite of the financial crises to strengthen the faculty and curriculum at the school of music, which was noted as one of the finest on the West Coast.

In addition to the training of professional musicians and teachers, the Conservatory served the community as a cultural center. Students and faculty alike performed in live and radio broadcast concerts every Tuesday evening. Individual recitals, as well as the performances of the band and orchestra entertained the local community and stimulated increasing interest in fine music. The oratorios performed twice a year by the chorus and a cappella choir were playing to packed audiences by the time Robert Burns (who had been a member of these groups when a student) became President of the College.

Most of the concerts were performed in the Conservatory building, which in addition to studios, classrooms, practice rooms and offices contained an auditorium with a seating capacity of 1,200. Classes in the liberal arts and sciences were held in the other two large classroom buildings (Weber Hall and the Administration Building, now Knoles Hall). The department of Bible and Religious Education was housed in the classroom annex to the beautiful Morris Chapel. Except for the gymnasium, all of the classroom and residence buildings on the campus were of uniform neo-gothic design; their red brick walls and slate roofs brought distinction to the small college in the central valley, which had become known throughout the west as one of unusual beauty.

Altogether it was a distinguished institution that President Burns inherited from his predecessor Tully Knoles—a college noted for its able leadership, its scholarly and devoted faculty, its friendly and beautiful ambience. In spite of multiple and manifold difficulties it had managed not only to survive through the first ninety-five years of its existence but to excel in the field of higher education. Hundreds of students had benefitted from their training there and become loyal alumni. During the coming years new challenges would confront Pacific, but the College was firmly established in 1946 in its home in Stockton. President Robert Burns and Chancellor Tully Knoles could face the future with a justifiable confidence and optimism.

Chapter Two

D<small>URING THE</small> next twenty-four and a half years as President of the College and later the University of the Pacific, Robert Burns was to face a variety of formidable challenges. The years from 1946 to 1971 were tumultuous ones in the world of American higher education. Although the College was located in a relatively quiet community, Pacific was not unaffected by the revolutionary changes that occurred as a result first of the broadening base of college enrollments thanks to the GI Bill, later the rush to improve scientific or engineering training in the wake of Sputnik, and finally the student and faculty disturbances of the 1960s. Robert Burns' leadership was a factor of critical importance in Pacific's weathering those storms, so that the institution emerged in the 1970s as the University its founders had so optimistically hoped it would be at its inception.

Like Dr. Knoles, Robert Burns spent his childhood in the Midwest, in southeastern Missouri. Flat River was (and still is) a small town of about 4,000 population; its distinction lies in the fact that it is at the center of the lead mining district in that part of the state. Taking advantage of this alternative form of employment, John Luther Burns left the family farm early and went to work for the Federal Lead Company, a division of the Guggenheim controlled American Smelting and Refining Company. An able carpenter and builder, Robert Burns' father soon became foreman of the maintenance division of the mines. His mother, Stella de Grant, was an accomplished piano player and continued to be the piano teacher of the community even after her marriage to John L. Burns. On July 26, 1909, she gave birth to Robert Edward Burns, the couple's only child, because, they said later, "he was such a handful."[1]

His cousins, Mary Burns and Ruth Whitner House, also remember him as a bright, lively, mischievous little boy who enjoyed teasing them when they were imitating their mothers' tea parties with their tiny china tea sets. He teased his mother, also, pumping too fast or too slowly while she was playing the organ for the church services, pretending all the while not to hear her whispered

The Burns' home in Missouri.

directions. He liked visiting his grandfather de Grant's farm where in the summer time the watermelon patch yielded its warm red juicy fruit to the children. He also enjoyed riding his grandfather's horses, alarming onlookers by the blithe self confidence which led him to take sometimes foolish chances. "On one occasion, Bobby was going too fast on the horse toward a barn door with a low clearance. So Bobby grabbed the top of the door and let the horse run on into the barn." To calm his grandfather, who had watched, terrified, as the horse galloped into the barn, he announced with great aplomb that he need not have been concerned. "I learned the trick by watching Wild West movies!" [2]

A life-long humorist and tease, Robert Burns spoke often of "the school on practical joking which [he] received early in life" with his numerous cousins and his father as tutors.

My father had played a number of successful tricks on me. It was my turn. I heard him say at breakfast that after work he was going to repair the metal roof on a barn in the back yard. That day I connected a wire from my radio broadcasting set which packed a real electrical wallop. As he was astride the top of the roof, I started sending out electrical messages which caused him to hunch up and down on the roof. I would quit, he would start to get down but then a series of shocks would force him back to the gable. After a while and when I figured enough was enough, I made a bee-line for town and stayed there for a couple of hours until I was sure his temperature had lowered. In those days part of the entertainment was found in such activities.[3]

The Burns' white clapboard tree-shaded house was not far from the meandering river and the swinging bridge, a short-cut escape for boys running away from irate fathers.

All was not fun and games, however, because the educational system provided vigorous training in the three "R's." Flat River was blessed with excellent schools because the mining companies, in their efforts to attract competent workers to the out-of-the-way community, encouraged the school system to pay premium salary rates to its teachers. The school buildings, too, and the equipment were unusually fine, far better than most such towns could boast. The superior quality of the schooling and the emphasis on education can be seen in the fact that two of Bobby's Flat River playmates also became university presidents—Norman Topping of the University of Southern California and Paul Leonard of San Francisco State University.

Another important formative factor in his life was the Methodist Church, which was located across the street from the Burns' home. Later he wrote: "I got religion early. It included attendance at Sunday School, morning church service, the Epworth League in the afternoon, evening church service, midweek prayer meeting, plus any social picnics, etc. The church under these conditions was a great social, educational and religious experience."[4] It was to be an experience which also was to be of permanent significance, for Robert Burns was an active Christian layman throughout his life.

When he was about ten years old, "another influence of large proportion appeared on the scene."[5] The mining companies, interested in recreation as well as education, offered to erect a YMCA building if the community would support the organization. "Overnight a new social, educational and religious force entered the community."[6] The building housed an indoor swimming pool with a diving board, and a fully equipped gymnasium along with a room for ping pong, pool tables, and other games. Y leaders organ-

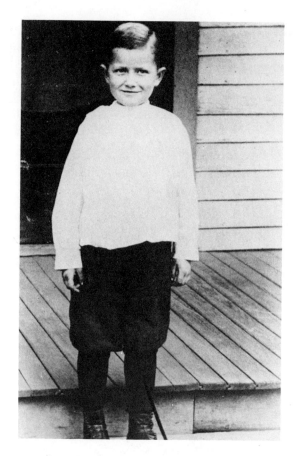

Robert E. Burns growing up in Missouri.

ized athletic games and camping and hiking expeditions. "Participation," Robert Burns remembered later, "became a way of life." [7] Together with the school and the church, the Y was a great "creative force" in the life of the future president of the College of the Pacific. "Any young person having the advantage of this grand service was lucky indeed," he wrote. "How fortunate I feel to have been to have a good family, good church, good schools and the experience of the YMCA movement in its heyday." [8]

All these activities combined to keep Flat River, small as it was, a busy, stimulating environment for the young people growing up there during the early decades of the century. It is difficult to imagine that any of them had time to indulge themselves in boredom. Nevertheless, the news that John Burns was to be transferred to the Company's plant in California occasioned considerable excitement in his son. "It was a radical move for us, but a great turning point in my life. The influence of moving to a state like California with all its dynamism, cannot be underrated."[9]

The family moved first to a small town near the plant in Selby and then subsequently to the larger North Bay community of Richmond, California, where Robert Burns attended high school. A history teacher there, Carol Frederick, took an unusual interest in her energetic young student and urged him to join the debate team. Here he gained his first experience in an art that was later to prove invaluable; he learned to speak before groups of people and gained considerable poise and presence of mind under Miss Frederick's tutelage. Her personal significance can be seen in the fact that he continued throughout his life to correspond with his former high school teacher, "whose influence went far beyond the confines of the classroom."[10]

In addition to school work, Robert Burns sought part-time jobs to earn spending money.

> A boy usually tried to do some work for pay. In Richmond the first was a job on Friday morning and evening at a fish market (it always took me three or four days to get the smell of fish off my hands) and Saturday delivering meat at the adjacent butcher shop. In my fourth year in high school I got a job in the Shoe Mart selling shoes, specializing in the Women's Department. Selling women's shoes is an art—it is vexing, perplexing and requires one to develop as much patience as you can imagine. This skill came in handy as it helped me work my way through college.[11]

While a student at the College of the Pacific, Robert Burns worked part-time for the J. C. Penney Co. at that "vexing, perplexing" job of selling women's shoes.

Of greatest significance, though, in his life as a high school student in Richmond, were his activities at the YMCA. Here his leadership ability was first recognized; he was elected president of the Hi Y Club and later of the Northern California Older Boys'

Conference of the Y. It was during a meeting of this Conference that he made a critical decision.

A great turning point in my life was my decision about college. There was never any decision about whether or not I should attend but where I should go. It was rather natural to do what most college-bound graduates of Richmond High School would do—attend the University of California at Berkeley. My parents thought this the proper choice. However, two things about this bothered me considerably. One was the size of the University—a factor which just did not square with my idea of an ideal situation. Second, and more important, was the negative image which I had received by the haughty attitude of the University and its representatives. Every so often people from the University would speak before the Richmond Union High School student body and extol the glories of the great University of California until it seemed to me to be overbearing. This seemed to me to shout through contacts with many others from there likewise. If the old scriptural reference 'The meek shall inherit the earth' is true, the University of California will not own much real estate. I will venture to say that some of the present difficulties of the University stem from such poor public relations as this—setting itself up as the "greatest, invincible," etc.—no institution is that good.

One weekend a High School Y.M.C.A. Conference was held on the campus of the College of the Pacific. When I arrived there I fell in love with the place. It was literally love at first sight. The collegiate gothic buildings covered with ivy and its size seemed more like a college to me. My discussion group was led by Dr. Fred L. Farley, Dean of the College, who was master before groups. And the religious orientation of the college helped. This did it for me. I went home and started a campaign with my parents to go to Pacific.[12]

"In perspective," he concluded, "this probably was the most important decision of my life."[13]

He liked the smallness of the school, its "personal quality." And although Robert Burns was the only one of the 255 entering freshmen to come from Richmond, he was soon to make new friends.

One of his outstanding characteristics throughout his life was his straightforward, easy-going friendliness—a quality that was certainly nurtured at Pacific where he delighted in the fact that "we knew students and staff intimately" and where "faculty members frequently entertained students in their homes."

As early as December in his freshman year, he was beginning to make a name for himself on campus. A front page headline of the student newspaper, the *Pacific Weekly*, proclaimed the fact that "Burns and Brinson Speak on Modern Advertising: The Fresno Debate."[14]

Forensics was an important activity on campus. As the catalogue announced:

> Enthusiasm for Debate is a tradition at Pacific and every encouragement is given by students and faculty. Positions on both freshman and varsity teams are won in open tryouts. Special individualistic training is given both men and women students in the various forms of public speaking. Every effort is employed to make this valuable training in thinking upon one's feet practical.[15]

Robert Burns, therefore, gained invaluable experience during the four years he participated in debate at Pacific, and learned skills in public speaking that would be extremely useful during his years as recruiter and president of the College.

Furthermore, the research required led the students into intensive study of contemporary issues. Among other resolutions, Robert Burns debated the question whether "The Installment Plan of Buying is a Danger to U.S. Prosperity" with the Oxford University team, and whether "All Nations Should Disarm" with Stanford University. Debating, therefore, constituted an extracurricular activity that contributed significantly to the overall educational experience of the participants. Participation in forensics also offered opportunities to travel and to meet students from other campuses, to gain a broader view of collegiate life. Then, during the year Robert Burns was the President of the Far Western Debating League, he formed even closer relationships with leaders from other colleges, and gained what was to be profitable experience in intercollegiate organization.

Robert E. Burns as a freshman at Pacific.

Partly because of the attention he received in debating, Robert Burns was one of the four freshmen who were invited to join Rhizomia, one of the three fraternities on campus. Like its older brother Archania, Rhizomia had been founded in the early years of the college's history as a literary society. And although the social activities had by this time become their most important function, it is interesting in the light of subsequent developments to learn of the importance attached during these years to the weekly literary meetings. Attendance at the meetings was required, and fines were levied if members could not respond to the roll call with a quotation from the writer assigned for that evening. After the roll call a passage from the Bible was read and discussed; then freshmen were called upon for brief impromptu speeches. These were followed by the major presentation of the evening—a longer, prepared speech or debate about current issues on campus and in the world at large by upper classmen. The meeting concluded, finally, with a sometimes trenchant critique of the evening's presentation by a senior member. Altogether, the literary meetings were a serious endeavor, one which contributed to the learning experience of the members and which balanced the more lighthearted social activities of the groups.[16]

42

Another student activity in which Robert Burns was active from the inception of his collegiate career was the YMCA, which offered students, according to the student handbook "the opportunity to develop themselves in the field of religion." [17] Meetings were held every Tuesday morning, and in addition to organizational work the members heard speakers from local churches and the faculty. When he was President of the Y during his junior year, Robert Burns initiated a series of talks by prominent professional and business-men. For example, he invited Guard Darrah, then the District Attorney, to speak to the group about "The Moral Obligations of a Lawyer to his Community."

Members also attended the annual week-long Y conference at Asilomar, where college students from all over the state gathered to hear Christian leaders and educators like David Starr Jordan, the former President of Stanford University. Robert Burns attend-ed the conferences every year he was a student at Pacific and spoke later of their profound significance in the formation of his adult values. The meetings included "Discussion of campus prob-lems, exchange of committee methods, Bible study that grips life, and the college men's Christian Citizenship program," in addition to "sympathetic vocational counsel, intercollegiate and internation-al friendship" and a "variety of invigorating recreation." [18] They were stimulating, busy days which, according to the student hand-book Robert Burns helped to prepare in 1929, "have come to be regarded as high spots in the year's program." [19] Like other groups, the participants at the annual conference recognized Robert Burns' unusual capacity for leadership and elected him President of the Pacific Southwest Student Council of the YMCA. In that capacity he attended the national meeting of the student Y—making the first of his numerous transcontinental trips to the meeting in New Jersey in August of 1929.

Besides serving its own members as an ethical and educational stimulus, the collegiate YMCA at Pacific also served local churches. Groups of students, including Robert Burns, would visit the Prot-estant churches in town and in the surrounding countryside with informal programs of musical entertainment, talks about Christian values and discussions with youth groups about the problems fac-ing young people. As a result in 1930 when the college was begin-ning to face the severe drop in enrollment, and as Robert Burns was becoming more and more concerned about college-wide problems, he suggested that the college itself initiate a program of student deputations. It was to be a program of critical importance in the college's survival, the major tool in student recruitment. And it began in the spring of his junior year—thanks to Robert Burns' energetic and innovative work in the YMCA.

It is scarcely surprising, in the light of all the associations he formed through the Y and debating and music (he sang in the A Cappella Choir and in the College Quartet), that he was elected to student body offices. People who knew him at the time speak of his extraordinarily large circle of friends, his genuine concern for them, and his refusal to engage in gossip. But the fact that he was elected president first of his sophomore class and then, by a resounding majority, president of the whole student body, indicates that students not only liked him but also perceived in him leadership qualities that lent weight to his candidacy. Robert Burns was unusually energetic and dependable; he attended the nitty-gritty, often time-wasting committee meetings as well as presiding over the more glory-ridden major gatherings. And he had an innate gift for organization, for analyzing the task to be done and then delegating the work. During his junior year, for example, in addition to his work with the Y, he was chairman of the International Week Organization Committee. Together with the other members of this group he planned a week long event which brought Christian Missionaries from many areas of the world to encourage students to commit themselves to international brotherhood and to an end (long before the civil rights movement brought this issue to the attention of the country at large) of racial prejudice. Under Burns' leadership the program was extended to the whole community of Stockton; the International Banquet welcomed costumed participants from many of the ethnic groups which composed Stockton's cosmopolitan population. Debates and classroom discussions were held with the speakers. Even during the years of the depression, when American eyes were turned toward domestic problems, Pacific students were being invited to observe a broader view, and student leadership was largely responsible for the success of the program.

As important as all these activities were, both in his own formation and in the college at large, it would be a mistake to neglect the

Dr. Gustavus A. Werner   **Dr. George Colliver**   **Dr. Fred Farley**

classroom's effect on Robert Burns' thinking and future career. Thanks to the stimulus of the extracurricular educational organizations and to his classes, his scholarship and his interest in academic subjects increased steadily during his four years at Pacific, contrary to what might be expected given all of his other time-consuming pursuits. His grade point average showed significant improvement—so much so that he was accepted for graduate study in history after he completed the B.A. degree in that subject.

The influence of some of his teachers—especially Professors Knoles, Farley, Werner and Colliver—was of great consequence in his development. As a freshman he was a student in Dr. Knoles' class, College Man and Society, which was required of all entering students. Once a week the freshmen and new upper classmen would gather to hear the President lecture on current events. Dr. Knoles brought to these classes his background in history, economics, sociology and philosophy in a wide-ranging extemporaneous commentary. His lectures were so informative that by public demand they were broadcast over the radio to the community at large. Far more important to Dr. Knoles than the factual content, however, was the opportunity the class afforded him to influence the value structures and the basic academic points of view of the young people in his classes. Dr. Knoles believed that Christian higher education had the responsibility for "teaching character" as well as stimulating the intellect. And after a year of such meetings with the President, students were well grounded in the Christian and scholarly philosophy which was the cornerstone in the College's sense of purpose. College Man and Society thus served as a major unifying force on the campus, and Dr. Knoles was indeed the *pater familias*—whose formative influence was felt by all the students.

If Dr. Knoles was the somewhat awesome, stern father figure on campus, another of the quartet of professors Robert Burns cited as influential in his life, Dr. Fred Farley, the Dean, might be likened to a kindly uncle. More poetic and lighthearted than Dr. Knoles, Dr. Farley spoke frequently at YMCA gatherings. As member of the executive committee and student body officer, the future President of the College worked closely with Dean Farley in all aspects of student discipline and governance. Later he spoke gratefully of the Dean's gentleness and wisdom in handling student problems.

Robert Burns' religious understanding was most directly affected by Professor George Colliver from whom he took Old and New Testament History, another class which was required of all students. Dr. Colliver's dramatic explications of Biblical themes helped to soften the onus of requirement, however, and in spite of themselves students assimilated some of his enthusiasm for the scriptures. His influence on Robert Burns can be seen in the latter's lifelong concern with the social implications of the Bible, the living out of the Gospel message through work for others. Dr. Colliver was a firm believer in the "social Gospel," and he encouraged students to work in such programs through the local churches, especially in the Chinese Christian Center, for which he assumed a particular responsibility.

The last of the four professors cited by Robert Burns, and probably the most influential during his student days, was Gustavus Adolphus Werner who, until his death in 1966, continued to act as Burns' mentor in the fullest sense of that word. Dr. Werner was an ordained minister, and shared the deep religious convictions of the other three, but he balanced their sometimes transcendent intellects with an earthiness, an infectious sense of humor. Known affectionately as "Ole," Dr. Werner had come to this country from Sweden when he was eighteen years old and had earned his B.A. degree under Dr. Knoles' tutelage at U.S.C. The two kept in touch during the years Professor Werner served as a minister in South America, and after he returned to this country he joined the faculty of the College of the Pacific, first as a part-time instructor, and later, after he earned his doctorate in history at the University of California, as professor of history.

Later he became the Dean of the Summer Session, and although Stockton is known for its high summertime temperatures, he managed to attract large numbers of visiting faculty and students. In fact, the summertime revenues frequently made the difference between deficit and profitable operation of the college. His major work at Pacific, however, was not as an administrator but as a teacher.

Ole Werner was primarily a great teacher, and he taught by entertaining. Whether speaking to a class or to a group of businessmen, he had a marvelous knack of striking an attention-getting note of levity, and, on the basis of this rapport, obtain a friendly hearing for his ideas. He was a great raconteur, using this talent both to tell stories and to dramatize history.[20]

As a result of his teaching, many students were stimulated to pursue graduate study in history, as was Robert Burns. Dr. Werner was also a canny judge of character and prophesied when Burns was still an undergraduate that he would one day be a college president. (The student promised to send for his professor should that event come to pass and astonished Dr. Werner on the morning of his inauguration as President of the College of the Pacific by sending a taxi to bring him to the ceremony!)

None of these men who so profoundly influenced Dr. Burns and the other students during their time at Pacific was a research scholar, though they all possessed keen minds and earned their doctorates from Harvard, Stanford and other major universities. Their primary interest lay in teaching. Each of them was humane, and vitally interested in the young people in his classes. They were men of integrity and Christian idealism who, in conformity with Dr. Knoles' educational philosophy "impressed *themselves* upon the students . . . and their work had a carry-over into the *lives* of the young people."[21] Many of them played a role in forming the mind and values of Robert Burns. They also aroused in him a lifelong fascination with higher education in general, and the College of the Pacific in particular. His masters thesis was dedicated to "President

Knoles and the faculty of the College, who have succeeded in building a fire under my heart which has caused me to love my alma mater beyond measure." [22]

His work in the interests of the college had, in fact, become an all-consuming concern by the time he was a senior and he faced with some dread the prospect of graduation. He received with delight, therefore, the invitation of Lyman Pierce, of the fund raising firm of Pierce and Hedrick, to set up a Bureau of Public Relations for the College. Mr. Pierce, according to Burns:

> . . . was probably the best known man in his field at the time, having developed the "whirlwind" type of campaign while he was General Secretary of the Washington, D.C. Y.M.C.A. and on graduation day, June 6, 1931, he came to the campus and offered me a job to help set up the organization. He also selected an outstanding student and a good friend, president of the senior class, J. Henry Smith, Jr. This was like manna from heaven. Here was a job but more than a job. Here was a golden opportunity to give everything I had for my alma mater. We set up offices in Stockton and in the Phelan Building in San Francisco. We prepared brochures to tell the story. We started roaming the state to seek out support. The valuable part of this experience was the art of raising money. It would come in good stead. For a while I accompanied the old master, Mr. Pierce, on interviews but then one day he said that I should take over and he would listen—like a mother bird pushing her young offspring off the limb of a tree. The first interview was difficult, the second not so bad and so on until shortly, I enjoyed the confrontation with my prospect. Believing in and being enthusiastic about my cause gave me desire to ask people for support. One thing I would always say to myself "Let your cause protect your reputation." And what better cause was there in my mind than Pacific. This year under the "old master," Pierce, was invaluable and was at a school where the teacher was the best. For the experience of the year I would not take anything because it seemed like a springboard for things to come. [23]

Pierce had proposed the formation of the Bureau in a letter to President Knoles and the Board of Trustees. He knew well the College's needs and believed that long-range planning was essential. "No institution of such promise should live from hand to mouth. We should compel California in particular and generous spirited people in general to an understanding of the great opportunity which the College of the Pacific has." [24] He was confident, furthermore, that "the sum of $2,225,000 [$750,000 for new buildings, $200,000 for debt retirement, and $1,300,000 for additional endowment] called for by your suggested Ten Year Program is attainable during the next 10 years." [25]

During the succeeding months the Bureau of Public Relations conducted promotional meetings with community groups (service clubs, chambers of commerce, etc.), church groups and YMCA's, alumni members and high schools. Four thousand public relations booklets were printed and circulated and 429 attorneys received a letter and forms for codicils from Dr. Knoles, urging that they suggest to their clients a bequest to the College. Letters were also mailed to 400 Methodist ministers and 1,700 alumni. By June 1, 1933 over 500 individual interviews had been arranged with potential givers. The activities of the Bureau had, in fact, amounted to the "siege" that Lyman Pierce had recommended to the trustees, but donors were scarce in the midst of the depression and the results were, to say the least, disappointing. The contributions had not even amounted to the $16,000 necessary to cover the costs of the program.

In June of 1932, the Board of Trustees voted not to renew their contract with Pierce, Hedrick and Company. They decided at the same time, however, to continue the program on a diminished scale, under the leadership of Robert Burns, who was hired directly by the College. Because one aspect of the program had been successful, the number of potential students contacted led to a threefold increase in the attendance on Visitors Day. Although the institution had not been relieved of the dreadful necessity of relying almost wholly on tuitions for yearly operations, at least the enrollment for the next fall was better than had been anticipated.

In addition to fund raising and student recruitment, Burns soon took charge of the alumni and placement offices. "The main idea was to incorporate as many of the outside contacts [as possible] in one office." [26] On trips to communities all over Northern California, then, this young man of all trades would arrange meetings with local alumni, interview potential donors and students, speak to whatever church group would listen, and hope for a luncheon club talk, because the tours were impelled more by youthful hope and optimism than by the promise of a travel allowance sufficient to cover any more than the cost of gas for his car.

Frequently, meetings were arranged with high schools and small groups of music and drama students would accompany Burns on these forays into the countryside. They would board the old Chevrolet sedan the college provided and travel throughout the valley and into the far corners of the state to present assembly programs for the high schools, sometimes as many as three or four a day. The programs were extremely well received; these were the days before television had sated young people's appetite for good entertainment. And they provided Robert Burns with a chance to address the students on the great educational opportunities awaiting them at Pacific.

Arthur Farey, who had returned to his alma mater as assistant in public relations in 1932, worked closely with Burns in planning the programs and accompanied the expeditions as master of ceremonies and director of the dramatic presentations. Farey had graduated in 1929 with a degree in religious education and speech and he shared his colleague's fervor and enthusiasm about the College and its mission. He, too, was a jack of all trades; he assisted De Marcus Brown in the theater, working as manager and publicist. He was also an instructor in the Speech Department and brought to the College its first formal instruction in radio broadcasting. An able dramatist, his comical dramatic reading of Mark Twain's story, "Jumping Frog of Calaveras" was frequently a highlight of community gatherings as well as the deputations programs. His creativity is apparent in the pageants he wrote—to commemorate the history of Methodism, the history of the College of the Pacific— and his work with the students on the deputations teams assured the fact that they were unusual events and fine entertainment.

In 1933, another new arrival on campus made the work of the deputations teams significantly easier. Amos Alonzo Stagg, the world renowned football coach of the University of Chicago, was forced to resign because he had reached the mandatory retirement age of 70. A group of alumni suggested that he be invited to come to Pacific and after a discussion with Dr. Knoles in Chicago the "Grand Old Man" of American football agreed to assume the position at the College of the Pacific which Coach "Swede" Righter had recently resigned. Stagg had been football coach at Chicago for 41 years and had been promised that he could remain as long as he wished. Therefore, when the University notified him that the usual retirement age of 70 would be applicable in his case, he and the football fans in the midwest received the news with some dismay and anger.[27] The blow was soon softened, however, by the numerous offers for coaching positions which poured into his office. Some of these were from prestigious schools offering the coach higher salaries than he had earned at Chicago. But the meeting with Dr. Knoles convinced the "Old Man" that he wanted to come to Pacific, not because of the salary or the fame of the place, but because of its Christian commitment and the challenge it proposed. He repeated to Dr. Knoles the statement he had made forty years earlier when President Harper asked him to come to Chicago: "After much thought and prayer, I feel decided that my life can best be used for my Master's service in the position you have offered," and added, "In the same spirit I will come to Pacific."[28]

To the newsmen who were astonished that the most famous man in American football had decided to come to the small unknown college on the West Coast, Stagg issued the following statement:

It means considerable financial sacrifice for me to take the job, as I can earn more elsewhere. Money, however, has never influenced my decisions, nor my purpose in life and, of course, in this decision it has not had influence...It wasn't the California climate that influenced my decision. It was the missionary spirit...My forbears were all pioneers. I think I have some of their iron in my blood.[29]

Like the faculty members who had come to Stockton nine years earlier, Stagg was moved by the pioneering missionary spirit. To the task of coaching he brought his invaluable experience in the tactics of football and in the inspiration of young men. "Winning," he said, "isn't worth the while unless one has something finer and nobler behind it. When I reach the soul of one of my boys with an idea or an ideal or a vision, then I think I have done my job as a coach."[30]

And to the struggling college he brought international renown. As President Burns later commented:

The uninitiated cannot understand the importance of this event. Football had a great hold on the colleges at the time. Mr. Stagg was a world figure in sports, standing for the highest principles possible. In this he was unwavering. This news focused attention on Stockton immediately but more particularly made Pacific known internationally. To be perfectly honest, Pacific was hardly known within a 100 mile radius— now it was international and Mr. Stagg, as a life member of the Football Rules Committee, commanded so much respect that large schools such as U.S.C. and Notre Dame would give him a game for the asking. This provided revenue. His name attracted players. The sum total of it all was to lift us to a new level and we had a chance to take off from there. I have often wondered if this could have happened with any other man in America—probably not.[31]

For fourteen years Amos Alonzo Stagg lent his skills as well as his fame to the College of the Pacific. His presence on campus made the job of promoting the interests of the College a less arduous one, for much of the groundwork was done by the newspapers.

Robert Burns, though, was never one to sit back and let things happen. If anything, Stagg's presence on campus spurred him on to even greater efforts. During the first year of his marriage to Grace Weeks he was off on his traveling junkets throughout the state a total of thirteen weeks. But she had known of his devotion to the college; they had first met in the fall of 1930 when he was so caught up in YMCA and college activities. The student body president found time that year, however, to date the delicately beautiful young student from Stockton. And during the following years the two were frequently seen together at the events all students at that time attended—the exchange dinners, theatrical productions, conservatory concerts. Entertainment budgets were limited, but there was an abundance of things to do on the busy campus. On October 6, 1934, Dr. Knoles married the attractive young couple in the Presbyterian Church in Stockton.

All of his journeying in the interests of the college had not dampened Robert Burns' delight in travel. The honeymoon trip he planned took them by train to Galveston, Texas, where they

**Robert and Grace Burns on their
wedding day, October 6, 1934.**

boarded a ship for a cruise through the Carribean and up the east
coast to New York. They traveled through New England, then on
to Cleveland where he was a delegate at the annual YMCA conference, and finally home. If his bride had not been completely
aware of the extraordinary dynamism, the indefatigable energy of
the man she was marrying before the wedding, she came to know
it well on this whirlwind honeymoon trip.

Fortunately, Grace Burns shared her husband's excitement about
the College of the Pacific, and the activities on campus kept her
occupied during the long weeks he was away. They entertained
frequently when he was at home, and she quickly learned the art of
being a gracious hostess—an art that was to serve her in good stead
in her life as wife of the President of the College. Together they
planned the house his father built for them the following year near
the College. Later his father, who had retired from the American
Smelting Company, built them a cabin near his own at Lake
Tahoe, and they spent their autumn vacations there. In December
of 1941 they adopted their daughter, Bonnie, and in 1944 their son
Ronald. Like many young couples they were soon caught up in the

excitement of parenting—a natural extension of their interests in young people.

After his graduation from college, Robert Burns joined the Y in downtown Stockton, and was quickly named to the Board of Directors of that organization. The downtown Y was in desperate straits at the time. One of the earliest in California, the Stockton Y's building was old and in bad condition; it had been condemned, and the organization was too debt ridden to finance the needed repairs. It seemed for a while that they must discontinue operations. But Robert Burns and two other young men, Ernie Segale and Bill Morris, made a pact that they would find a way out of the dilemma. Together with other Board members and the Board President, B. C. Wallace, they found a dynamic new executive secretary, Ralph Pederson, to manage the activities of the Y. And after he arrived, Robert Burns suggested a new program that "turned the tide." [32]

Little was being done at that time by the public school system in the field of adult education. Burns suggested, therefore, that the Y embark on a program of adult classes and leisure time activities. Board members liked the idea but were troubled by the lack of funds to hire instructors; nevertheless, the young man whose life had been so profoundly affected by the Y during his childhood and collegiate days was not to be daunted. He managed to communicate his enthusiasm for the program to his friends on the college faculty, and they volunteered to teach classes free of charge. The program was an immediate success and brought hundreds of new members into the organization who then supported the fund drive. Enough money was raised to retire the debt and repair the sagging building so that it could meet the code requirements that had threatened to close it.

The work at the Y was demanding and, together with his church membership (Robert Burns was an active member of Central Methodist Church), brought his energetic leadership into the community at large. His first loyalty, however, was always to the College. In 1936 the title of Registrar was added to the already long list that followed his name. He wrote of the new assignment later:

> Charles E. Corbin, a long-time and devoted staff member, Registrar and professor of mathematics, resigned from the

duties of Registrar. Normally the assignment would have gone to Miss Ellen Deering, who was an expert in the field and knew the work at Pacific thoroughly. However, typical of her unselfish attitude, she thought I should be the candidate and promptly made such representation to President Knoles. This suggestion he accepted and I promptly added this title to my portfolio. For a time I had so many titles and different responsibilities that to unscramble them would have presented some difficulty.[33]

As the Associate Registrar, Miss Deering took care of most of the detailed work of the office, but at the same time Robert Burns became familiar with the workings of that vital center of the College's administration.

After the agreement with Stockton Junior College was signed, there was less pressure on the fund raising aspect of his multifaceted work. Burns vigorously pursued his goals in that area, however, soliciting donations from alumni and friends of the college to eliminate the debt that had accumulated during the early 1930s, to raise endowment and for new projects. The first of these was the chapel, which had been a much longed for but unrealizable dream since the college had moved from San Jose in 1924. The thrice weekly chapel services were held, of necessity, in the Conservatory Auditorium which scarcely provided the kind of sacred atmosphere that a real chapel on campus might afford. Nor was there a quiet center that could draw students and staff to quiet prayer.

In his 1938 outline of objectives to be achieved by the 1951 centennial celebration of the College, President Knoles spoke to the Trustees of the importance of such a chapel.

> A medium sized auditorium of churchly design to be used for religious services is very much needed. I have the faith to believe that somewhere in our constituency there is a family that would like to build such a building [which] would give a religious atmosphere that is hard to get at present.[34]

Responding to this appeal, Mr. and Mrs. Percy Morris donated $30,000 to the fund. And the board accepted the challenge of raising the additional $130,000 necessary for the chapel and a religious education wing with unusual alacrity. Dr. U. A. Christensen was assigned to work closely with Robert Burns in the campaign which, as he said later, "was one of the easiest and yet most satisfying I ever attempted." [35]

The cornerstone of the new building was laid on December 14, 1941, just seven days after the attack on Pearl Harbor which propelled the United States into World War II. Fortunately the materials for the chapel had been ordered and for the most part delivered before the emergency had required that all building materials be used in the war effort. On April 19, 1942, the completed Morris Chapel was dedicated. Bonnie Burns was the first baby to be baptized in the beautiful new religious center, a fitting distinction since her father had worked so effectively to raise the funds for its construction. Between the time of Dr. Knoles' address in 1938 and the laying of the cornerstone in 1941 all the monies had been donated, in spite of the financial alarm caused by the spreading conflict in Europe.

World War II was to precipitate other crises, however, on the campus and in the community. The draft decimated the male student body, and for a while it seemed possible that the College might have to close. The opposite phenomenon occurred, however, in the quiet agricultural city of Stockton, which was suddenly inundated with thousands of service men, stationed at military camps nearby. Robert Burns was appointed to the board of directors of the local U.S.O. and brought to that position the insights gained through his many years with the Y. He was an active member of the hastily formed U.S.O. organization, attended the time-consuming weekly meetings, and helped arrange entertainment and hospitality for the droves of young men who were far from home and on their way to the Pacific front.

Because of the numbers of young men who were called into the armed services, the ranks of the local clergy were diminished. Dr. James C. Baker, presiding Bishop of the Methodist Church and member of the Board of Trustees of the College, was concerned about the churches without ministers in the area. Well aware of Robert Burns' strong religious convictions and his ability as a speaker, Bishop Baker asked him if he would serve as acting pastor of the Escalon Methodist Church. Burns evidently accepted with typical enthusiasm this added responsibility and after having been granted the Local Preacher's License began serving the people of Escalon and later those of Brentwood as minister of the Gospel. He and Grace and the baby would travel the twenty miles to the little farming community on Saturday afternoon to attend meetings and spend the night at the parsonage. He preached at the Sunday services and then met with the young people of the parish. It was this latter activity he enjoyed the most, as did the students; many of them later matriculated at the College of the Pacific because of his influence in their lives. But his preaching and other work were well received also; the young couple would return home Sunday afternoon in a car laden with farm produce.[36]

Unfortunately, the College to which he was so devoted could not survive on such expressions of gratitude to its staff. By the fall semester of 1942 the financial plight of the institution was so severe that the Board of Trustees decided to relieve Burns of his tasks as alumni secretary and recruiter and assign him to "full-time service on the campaign to raise funds."[37] To his title of Registrar was added the title "Assistant to the President." His first step in this new campaign was to design a public relations brochure which announced to the College's friends that "The College of the Pacific will not close its doors, and is determined to service democracy in war as well as in peace." Appealing for the $25,000 needed for the current year, the folder suggested that "an investment in the College of the Pacific represents the highest type of patriotism for the present and builds Christian statesmanship for tomorrow."[38] It was an appeal well designed to meet the wartime state of mind, and soon donations were coming to the assistance of the College. The campaign was so successful, in fact, that a year later Robert Burns' salary was increased (to the lordly figure of $4,200 a year), and for the first time he was allotted the services of a full-time secretary!

In addition to the gifts of money he procured for the College, his meeting with Samuel H. Kress resulted in his gift to the chapel of the organ and a valuable fifteenth century painting, "The Assumption of the Virgin" by Calisto Piaza Da Lodi. In the process, his conversations with that great collector aroused Burns' own interest in fine art. He was blessed with remarkably good taste and a gift for driving a shrewd bargain; for the rest of his life he took a great delight in collecting fine clocks and art works.

In a statement that reveals his eclectic approach to new possibilities for his alma mater, he reported Mr. Kress' gifts to the

Trustees, with the hope that this would be "the beginning of other gifts from that source." Then, after the announcement of other monetary gifts, he "explained at length his idea of [relating to] the history of The Gold Rush, as well as the possibility of a Foundation for Food Processing, and the possibility of the College becoming a center for the Veterans Bureau to care for the education of returned war veterans." [39] One idea after another tumbled forth, at a rate that leaves one breathless even at this distance. It is tempting to conjecture about the initial reaction of the traditionally conservative Board of Trustees to this pell-mell recitation. In the course of events, however, they assented to all these projects suggested by Dr. Knoles' persuasive Assistant. And it is clear that his presence at the Board meetings immediately injected vibrance and innovative thinking in that gathering of the College's most steadfast supporters.

His idea that the College should find a way to exploit, to relate to the enthusiasm for Gold Rush history, was rooted in his own fascination with that subject. On his travels for the College he had visited towns up and down the length of Highway 49, the historic road that connected the gold mining towns in the California foothills. There, he delighted in talking to old timers and history buffs, to teachers and students who lived in those areas and shared his fervor; so he began to search for "an old miner's shack," a place that his father could help him rebuild which would enable him to spend weekends in the Mother Lode. In February of 1945 he could shout "Eureka;" he had discovered his "shack"—an old commercial building in Columbia which to many would have appeared impossibly rundown. But Robert Burns approached the project with his typical sanguinary vision. It was an optimism which was subsequently justified; the Burns' house in Columbia was to become the site for innumerable weekend brainstorming sessions. During his presidency, Robert Burns would gather small groups of administrators and staff members for days of intensive discussion at Columbia—a fitting place to mine for ideas.

The interest in history which had been implanted during his collegiate years also bore fruit in his master's thesis on the history of the College. The extensive research he completed for this work gave him valuable insights on the background of his alma mater; and in his analysis of the trials and tribulations of those early years of the College, one can see that he had learned the importance of the fund raising aspects of the administration. Special attention was paid to the Reverend Greenberg R. Baker, who worked as fund raiser in the late 1860s and whose appointment was "lucky for the school indeed." [40] Rev. Baker, who "was ideally suited for the responsibilities of a fund raiser," was "a fine looking man and inspired confidence everywhere he went...forgetting self and plunging into the fray...he raised over $9,000 his first year in cash and in pledges which was considered near to the miraculous." [41] Baker was also "the moving spirit in launching the ambitious project," the life-saving move of the College from Santa Clara to San Jose.

The thesis also praises President Bannister whose success, Burns wrote, resulted from his being "a jack-of-all-trades." President Knoles evidently agreed with his young assistant in this definition, because when Burns suggested to him that he take some time off to complete his Ph.D. in history, Dr. Knoles discouraged him. The man known as the "scholar President" had evidently reached the conclusion that the task of future college presidents would be more all-encompassing—that the chief executive would be required to handle the myriad practical, mundane aspects of higher education which he abhorred. In the multitude of tasks he assigned Robert Burns during the fifteen years the young man had worked for the College, one can see a course of training which would prepare the kind of successor Dr. Knoles had in mind.

It is scarcely surprising, therefore, that the President so strongly recommended that the Assistant·he had groomed for the post be named the President of the College of the Pacific. Dr. Knoles had for some time been acutely aware of his own shortcomings in the financial operations of the College; the 1931 Methodist survey report had severely criticized what they perceived to be "the dual administration" of Pacific. Mr. Ritter was an extremely able business manager, but because he had complete charge of the finances of the College, he sometimes made decisions which affected the academic life of the institution—decisions which, according to the survey report, should be made by the President himself. Therefore, the authors recommended: "There is a need for an administrative officer whose vision embraces both the educational and financial aspects of every question. It is only such a person who can give sound advice to a board of trustees on matters of policy." [43]

Dr. Knoles had also been criticized because of his reluctance to ask people for money for the College; more than once he offered to resign so that the struggling College might have the benefit of a more aggressive fund raiser as president. The Board never accepted these offers; they recognized better than Dr. Knoles himself the fact that indirectly he *had* acquired monetary support for the College. The respect in which he was held throughout the state, his renown as a public speaker had won for Pacific innumerable generous friends. He was convinced, however, that in the future the College's President would have to be more actively and directly engaged in that aspect of administration. During his informal discussions with the Trustees prior to that momentous meeting in 1946, he voiced that conviction and pointed out to them Robert Burns' successful experience in that area.

The Board assented to his recommendations, but the fact that they did so with some reservations is clear in their insistence that Dr. Knoles continue to work closely with the new President. The resolution passed by the Board stated that insistence unequivocally: "We are exceedingly anxious to have the full benefit of [Dr. Knoles'] counsel, advice and direction...We are not in any sense thinking of allowing him to retire from the life of the institution."[44] Their anxiety about the youth of the new President was only assuaged by Dr. Knoles' assurance that he would continue in the role the Board assigned him. He would continue to train Robert Burns for the position Dr. Knoles himself had held so ably.

Assuming the title of President, therefore, simply meant that Robert Burns moved his desk into Dr. Knoles' office, and when faculty members or staff would go to the President's office for a decision they would walk right by Robert Burns to talk to Tully Knoles. For more than two years the two of them worked side by side, though it is difficult to imagine a situation more fraught with the dangers of disunity and resentment. Fortunately for the College, although these two men were as diverse in personality and style of leadership as they were in age, they shared religious ideals and their absolute commitment to the College of the Pacific. As a result Tully Knoles and Robert Burns administered the College cooperatively and amicably. And Pacific was spared what could have been the crippling results of discontinuity during the critical post-war period.

Gradually, as Dr. Burns became more conversant with all aspects of the presidency, Dr. Knoles withdrew. And gradually Dr. Burns assumed more of the decision-making responsibility of the position—impressing the character of the College with his own very different stamp. That he was able to accomplish this feat, in the light of Dr. Knoles' olympian quality, the fact that the latter had come to personify the College during his twenty-seven and a half years as President, seems at the very least a remarkable achievement. But Robert Burns brought to the task that self-confidence, that sense of humor, that vigor and energy, that creative, practical mind which had been developing and ripening during the previous thirty-seven years of his life. He wisely never tried to imitate Dr. Knoles nor to pretend an erudition he neither possessed nor sought. He never lost sight, however, of the basic academic function of the University. It was a commitment that would be frequently tested but never broken during subsequent years in questions of academic freedom. He was also aware, however, of the need to adapt, to be flexible in other areas, and under his leadership Pacific changed and grew—into an institution of major rank among California's universities. There can be no doubt that like his predecessor he made mistakes, some of them serious ones. But neither can there be any doubt that along with Tully Knoles, Robert Burns was one of Pacific's great presidents.

Chapter Three

THE CALM and order Americans had hoped for in the aftermath of the great conflagration of World War II proved to be an illusory dream within months of VJ Day. The unleashing of atomic power in Hiroshima and Nagasaki led to the realization that mankind possessed the technology to destroy itself, and the fear of atomic holocaust became the source of uneasy anxiety underlying Americans' planning for the future. Economic problems also troubled the nation and, in fact, the whole world, as war industries retooled. Civilian consumers were tired of the shortages which had developed during the war. Returning veterans clamored for education, new housing, new automobiles and other goods—in spite of the spiraling inflation which followed the relaxation of war time price controls. And at the same time citizens of the devastated European continent looked to America for the aid they needed to restore the centers of western civilization.

Less than a year after the signing of the armistice, Winston Churchill was pointing out to Americans the vital necessity of the restoration of the Continent. In the strongest of terms he spoke to the audience in Fulton, Missouri, and to the free world, of the dangers of Russia's expansionist policies.

> From Stettin in the Baltic to Trieste in the Adriatic an iron curtain has descended across the Continent... From what I have seen of our Russian friends and allies during the war, I am convinced that there is nothing they admire so much as strength, and there is nothing for which they have less respect than for weakness...[1]

Soon afterwards Herbert Bayard Swope, Pulitzer prize winning editor of the *New York Herald Tribune,* coined the ominous term "Cold War" to describe the war of nerves being waged by the Russians. It was soon abundantly clear, therefore, that much as they might desire a return to a pre-war peacetime economy, Americans would never again be able to retire to the comfortable isolationism which had followed World War I.

In his Inaugural Address as President of C.O.P. Robert Burns reflected the tensions of the post-war period. Speaking to the gathering of graduates and friends of the college on the warm, sunny, peaceful morning of June 16, 1947, he warned his listeners of the dire possibility of World War III. "Language barriers, different legal systems, cultural differences, economic systems, religious separations all are divisive and as yet the unifying forces in the world are only very weak...Unless this trend is changed we are marching right down the rocky road to war." [2] At the same time, however, he spoke with optimism of the possibility of "thinking our way out" of the dilemma. He cited the importance of liberal arts colleges in nurturing thinkers able to formulate solutions to that emergency and the grave problems faced by the nation. He spoke, for example, of the dreadful reality of racial prejudice in the United States, "a fact of which we should be ashamed." [3] He also called for attention to the needs of the developing nations—especially those which bordered on the Pacific Ocean—the Orient and South America—and promised new academic programs which would lead to increased understanding, which would "lend themselves to the elimination of our differences and blend our cultures into the ultimate ideal of world brotherhood." [4]

These new efforts were to be undergirded, President Burns emphasized, by the same principles which had been the basis of the College's founding. He reminded his listeners that "this College was founded in the name of Jesus Christ," and that the "first formal act of its founders was to kneel in prayer and invoke the blessings of God Almighty." [5] He called for a reawakening of moral consciousness and an ethical grappling with the problems left in the wake of the atom bomb. "These days we are faced with the tragic fact that ethical and spiritual progress has lagged far behind our scientific and technological advancement." [6] Formulating new resolutions of this new crisis and of the age old problems of "war...the use of power...the use of persons, the education of the emotions" [7] constituted "the New Frontier," the President asserted. And the College of the Pacific, with its pioneering experience, was peculiarly suited to educate the new frontiersmen. "Pioneer or Perish," his address was titled, and in its conclusion he quoted the poet Browning: "A man's reach must exceed his grasp." [8] Applying this principle to the College, he insisted that "a community of scholars is bound together by a dynamic idea. They either move forward or perish. An institution becomes great by daring to dream and then bending every effort to make these dreams come true."[9]

A number of very practical obstacles, however, lay in the path of the realization of Robert Burns' dream of a "great college." Already during his first seven months as President he had faced the problems caused by the burgeoning post-war enrollment. As early as 1944 Congress had passed the Servicemen's Readjustment Act in response to the pressures of the veterans' lobby for adequate reward to the young men who had fought during the war. Warren Atherton, Stockton attorney and national president of the American Legion, had pressed for the educational benefits included in the Act, more popularly known as the GI Bill; but it is doubtful that he foresaw the revolutionary social and economic effects of the wide-ranging legislation. Millions of returning veterans took advantage of the opportunity to attend schools and training programs. By November 30, 1947, when the numbers reached their nationwide peak, 1,235,761 veterans were attending institutions of higher learning and college enrollments had jumped to more than fifty percent above their previous all-time highs. Many students were enabled to complete bachelor and, in many cases, advanced degree requirements who in pre-war America would have been limited, at best, to a high school education. The service to the nation rendered by the institutions of higher education—in adjusting to and meeting the needs of the sudden flood of students, in upgrading the intellectual and professional skills of large numbers of citizens—was incalculable.

At the College of Pacific enrollment began increasing during the school year 1945-46. By 1947 the number of students had almost doubled—from 492 in the fall of 1946 to 912 in the fall of 1947. As it had in colleges throughout the country, this sudden influx of students imposed severe strain on staff and facilities. From the outset the administration of the veterans' program had been fraught with complications; as one contemporary observer reported: "The multiplicity of forms [more than seventy] has been a subject of serious complaint by institutions since the inception of the training program..."[10] For although the initiating legislation comprised a slim nine-page booklet, over a thousand pages of regulations and interpretations had soon accumulated. Returning veterans, weary of the restrictions of Army and Navy life, were frequently frustrated by the red tape and inefficiency of the program. At the College of the Pacific many of those frustrations were averted through the efficient offices of the registrar; Miss Deering's experience with government programs in the V-12 era proved invaluable. Nevertheless, it soon became apparent that a special advisor for the veterans would be needed.

Mr. Ritter's business office also reported administrative problems. The payment to the College of the servicemen's tuition charges lagged months behind, so that the College was forced to borrow money for current expenses, and for the construction costs of setting up government surplus buildings. Quonset huts were erected on campus in 1946 and were immediately put to use for veterans housing. Two-story barracks buildings (Owen and Bannister Halls) were also reconstructed on the campus for classroom and office space, and metal buildings (called tropical huts) added much-needed space for the Conservatory program and the Department of Engineering. By October 28, 1947, President Burns reported to the Board that the value of surplus property which had been acquired by the College amounted to over $672,000. Altogether 73,420 square feet of space was added to the campus at an average cost of $3.48 per square foot—considerably less than the contemporary average of $10 per square foot for institutional construction.

Even this massive infusion of new space, however, did not solve all the College's problems in regard to facilities. From the outset of his administration President Burns expressed deep concern over the library which was housed in the former heating plant of the College (now Baun Hall) and which comprised a mere 52,000 volumes. During the spring of 1947 the accreditation committee of the State Board of Education visited the School of Education and recommended only a temporary accreditation for the Secondary School Administration Credential. In their report members of the committee informed the Board of Trustees "that the Library facilities are entirely inadequate." [11] After some discussion, the Board agreed, therefore, on April 23, 1947 "to approve the forward looking program of raising $250,000 for the first unit of a library and other purposes and that Jesse Rudkin be engaged as an assistant to the President... to carry out this work." [12]

Jesse Rudkin, like the President and Chancellor of the College, was a transplanted midwesterner. An ordained Methodist minister, he had been serving a church in Tracy in 1922 when the College initiated its fund-raising campaign to move from San Jose to Stockton and had traveled extensively to solicit subscriptions for the drive. Subsequently, he had attended classes on the new campus; so in 1947, when Dr. Burns approached him in his Grass Valley church about working as fund raiser, he was no stranger to the work of the College of the Pacific. When Bishop Baker, then a member of the Board of Trustees and presiding Bishop of the Methodist Church in California, added his urgings to those of the President, Jesse Rudkin agreed to come—for at least three years. He was actually to stay for eighteen years and to play an extremely significant role in the development of the College, as fund raiser and as Assistant to the President.

A small, rotund man, Jesse Rudkin had a remarkable faculty for making friendly contacts for the College. He was a man of indefatigable energy and traveled up and down the state, arranging meetings at which Dr. Burns and Dr. Knoles would "tell the Pacific story." Having been minister in several Northern California communities, he was convinced of the Christian mission of the College and knew how to convince others of its significance. Jesse Rudkin and Robert Burns were a remarkable team; together they raised over fifteen million dollars in gifts and pledges between 1947 and 1962.

Before he became the President, Dr. Burns had also worked as student recruiter. Given the College's dependency on tuition income, this position was one of extreme importance. During the spring of 1947, therefore, he embarked on a search for a person to serve as admissions officer and recruiter. Elliott Taylor, then Director of Counseling at Reedley College, had graduated from the College of the Pacific in 1928. Subsequently, he had spent a year in Rome and six years in Albania working for the Near East Foundation, before returning to this country to work for the same agency in New York. Dr. Burns had met him at Reedley College during his recruiting forays for the College, and during the spring of 1947, he telephoned to see if the alumnus might be at all interested in coming to Pacific as Coordinator of Veterans Affairs and Admis-

**Dr. Lloyd Bertholf,
Dean of the College.**

sions Director, the latter a job which included the recruitment of students. Dr. Taylor was understandably reluctant; he held a tenured position which promised early promotion at Reedley College; but he had fond memories of his alma mater and Robert Burns' enthusiasm for the future of the College of the Pacific was infectious. So Elliott Taylor accepted the position and returned to Stockton during the summer of 1947. From that time until 1972, when he retired, he served the College energetically and intelligently.

Another of Dr. Burns' administrative appointments during his first year in office was that of Dr. Lloyd Bertholf as Dean of the College. During his tenure as president, Dr. Knoles himself had overseen the academic life of the College. But Robert Burns never pretended to be the scholar Dr. Knoles was; he was fully cognizant of the fact that the role of "scholar president" was not one he could fill. And although Dr. Knoles continued to act as advisor in academic matters, he also urged the new President to find a younger man, a man of his own academic and Christian ideals and integrity, who could serve as Dean. Dr. Bertholf was recommended by Dr. John Gross of the Methodist Board of Education, as the man who could best fill the position.

Lloyd Bertholf came to the College of the Pacific from another Methodist related school, Western Maryland College. A distinguished biologist, he had studied with Dr. Rudolph Frisch and had to his credit numerous publications on honey bees. His credentials also recommended him to the Chancellor, President, and Board of Trustees as an active churchman. While in Maryland, for example, he had served as "a lay delegate of the Methodist General Conference, president of the Board of Education of the Baltimore Conference and Superintendent of the Church School of the Westminister Methodist Church." [13] Members of the Board hoped that he would be as active in the California-Nevada Conference, representing the interests of the College before that organization. (Of the forty-five Methodist institutions of higher learning, the College of the Pacific ranked forty-fourth in the amount of financial support from its Conference affiliate.) Dr. Bertholf fulfilled their expectations. Soon after his arrival in California, he became Conference lay leader and was a member of numerous committees. A man of warm understanding who was blessed with a dry, witty rhetorical style, he was frequently asked to address church groups about the Christian mission of the College.

Dr. Bertholf's religious commitment was also brought to bear on the internal life of the College. He interviewed new faculty members, and although there was a shortage of qualified candidates, every effort was made to secure professors who supported the College's Christian traditions. Neither the Dean nor the President wanted faculty members who would attempt to interject religious dogma in the teaching of history or psychology or physics; what they looked for were academically qualified instructors who would teach from a basic stance of Christian belief. Potential faculty members were not required to be Methodists (nor were they asked questions about their smoking and drinking habits, as had formerly been the case), but church membership was seen to be a sign of active faith and was, therefore, one of the qualifications to be sought.

Actually, some kind of religious commitment was essential, given the low salary scale. During President Burns' first report to the Board of Trustees on March 25, 1947, he expressed his concern about faculty recompense. The College was at that time paying full professors a maximum of $3,500 a year, although three private colleges of similar size (Redlands, Pomona, and Occidental) had established $5,000 maximums for the same position. "Salaries are still rising in the academic world and we find it difficult to obtain staff members at the caliber we want and keep within our present scale. There is also the danger of losing some of our present staff who are looking for a larger income." [14] On April 23, therefore, the Board adopted an improved salary scale:

Deans	up to $4,900
Full Professors	$3,900 - $4,500
Associate Professors	$3,400 - $3,900
Assistant Professors	$2,700 - $3,400

Because of the sudden enrollment increases, additions to the faculty were essential, and fortunately, in spite of the relatively low pay scale, dedicated capable men and women were attracted to Pacific. President Burns announced seventeen new appointments in 1947; fourteen in 1948.

The injection of new and youthful instructors brought fresh vitality to the College's academic programs and led to exploration and innovation in whole new areas of study. Under Dr. Bertholf's leadership, departments which had had to be abandoned during the war were reinstated and programs which had formerly been carried out on a minimal scale burgeoned into real growth. With the wholehearted encouragement of President Burns, Dean Jantzen initiated exciting experiments in course work during the summer session. Pacific was, indeed, from the outset of his administration, embarking on the pioneering effort Robert Burns had promised in his inaugural address.

Veterans' demands precipitated some of the curricular developments. Many of the older students wanted to pursue practical, job-oriented courses of study. Having gained considerable experience in the field during the war, numbers of former servicemen wanted to earn the degrees which would qualify them to meet the great demand for qualified engineers. The College of the Pacific was no stranger to the task of training such engineers. The Department had opened in 1924, and, although it was small, the accomplishments of its graduates had been distinguished. Ted Baun was one, the founder and president of the successful Baun Construction Company in Fresno; Carlos Wood, another, was a director and designer of Douglas aircraft; Eugene Root held a similar position at Lockheed. Despite this record, the offerings in engineering had had to be discontinued during the war because of shortages in staff, students and materials.

In his first presidential report to the Board, Robert Burns called for the re-establishment of the department to meet the needs of the returning veterans. He reported to the Trustees that the Engineers' Council for Professional Development with headquarters in New York, "has told me that Northern California was the most active area in the U.S. as far as civil engineering was concerned and that the engineering schools there could not produce enough engineers to meet the demand. They recommended that we re-establish our course..." [15] The Board approved his recommendation and by October of that year the President could report that "the Department of Civil Engineering is getting underway." [16] Professor Felix Wallace of the Carnegie Institute of Technology had been hired to direct the new program, and seventeen majors had already enrolled. It was a move that was to be typical of Robert Burns' entire administration; for he was quick to seize new opportunities and delighted in taking full advantage of the College's ability to move into new areas of study without the red tape-plagued delays of public institutions.

Marine biology was another area of curriculum he was to expand early in his presidency. Dr. Alden Noble, Professor of Zoology, had started taking students on field trips to Dillon Beach as early as 1933, using space rented from the proprietors of the resort. A quiet, out-of-the-way family community, located on the junction of Tomales Bay and Bodega Bay, Dillon afforded an ideal site for college students to study marine life without distractions. Cognizance of the scientific opportunities afforded by the site was also, of course, a primary factor in its selection. But it was not until 1946, when "an extended exploration of the Pacific Coast from Canada to Lower California" was conducted by Dr. Noble, "that the magnitude and range of possibilities became so impressive that it seemed necessary to assume larger responsibilities for scientific exploration of the area." [17] On the entire coastline no other location was found "which equalled that of Dillon Beach in diversity of

Dr. Marc Jantzen, Dean of the School of Education and director of the Summer Session, and Dr. Alden Noble, director of the Marine Station, work with students at the Dillon Beach facility.

habitats and consequent variety and abundance of living things." [18] This richness, Dr. Noble concluded, long before the outcry in protest to pollution of the environment, was at least "partly due to the lack of industrial or sewage contamination within many miles." [19]

The number of significant publications which had already been produced by the students and staff of the summer sessions had attracted the interest of professional biologists from other institutions. Dr. Noble was convinced, therefore, that it was time to embark on a year-round program in permanent quarters. First, he spoke with the Lawson family about his dreams for the project. As the proprietors of the small resort and major landowners in the area, the Lawsons had pursued a cautious plan of development in the area which was designed to preserve the quiet, family-oriented character of the beach. Over the years however, they had been impressed with the seriousness of the students' work and by Dr.

Noble's conviction that responsible scientific explorations of Dillon's marine life could yield significant biological findings. They reached the conclusion, therefore, that the addition of a College of the Pacific Marine Biology Research Station would not interfere with but, in fact, enhance the values of the community they sought to conserve. They deeded valuable beach front property to the College in 1948, and an executive of California Cedar Products in Stockton contributed the lumber for the construction of laboratories and living quarters. In August of 1948, the new Marine Station was dedicated "to the furtherance of biological research and the training of leadership in the natural sciences."[20] Robert Burns enthusiastically supported the new development. The Marine Station would constitute another element in that great institution he had projected in his Inaugural Address.

An entirely new program initiated soon after his inauguration was especially dear to the President's heart. As early as 1943 he had recommended to the Trustees that the College develop the California History Foundation "for the purpose of promoting more extensive study of the lusty and poignant history of California, with particular attention to the Gold Rush Days and early statehood."[21] Not only was Robert Burns himself a devoted student of California history, he was also sensitive to the excitement that would be engendered by the celebration of California's Centennial. Perceiving the opportunity such a foundation would offer the College to capitalize on that enthusiasm, he announced with great satisfaction the appointment of Dr. Rockwell Hunt to be director of Pacific's new California History Foundation.

Dr. Hunt came to Pacific from the University of Southern California. He had graduated from Napa College in 1890 (soon after it had merged with the College of the Pacific) and had served as a faculty member in San Jose before he transferred to U.S.C.'s social science department where he was a colleague of Dr. Knoles. He had subsequently served as Dean of the Graduate School and on his retirement in 1945 was awarded the title of Dean Emeritus. Like Dr. Knoles, Rockwell Hunt was an active septuagenarian—he was evidently delighted to emerge from retirement to direct the new project, for it provided him with a center where he could continue his research, writing and teaching. In turn, he lent his name to the Foundation, and the addition of this professor, who, as

Dr. Burns said, "probably knows more about the State of California than any man alive," [22] gave the Foundation invaluable prestige. Immediately after his arrival, classes in California history were announced and a program of tours established—to the California Missions, to Gold Rush towns, to Sacramento's historical sites. On March 12 and 13, 1948, the first of the annual two-day California History Institutes was held. John D. Hicks of the University of California addressed a sizeable group of students and history buffs on the subject "The California Background: Spanish or American?" The establishment of the California History Foundation under Dr. Hunt's vigorous and imaginative leaderhip was the realization of a dream for Robert Burns; he had gathered together an imposing list of sponsors from throughout the State. His well known interest in California's history resulted in his being named to the five member State Centennials Commission, along with Joseph Knowland, Willard Keither, J. W. Maillard, Jr., and John L. Knox. So his hope that the Foundation would make new friends for the College was realized immediately.

Another new program which reached beyond the confines of the campus was sponsored by the philosophy department. When in 1947 Dr. Burns challenged the faculty "to suggest creative new schemes," [23] Dr. William Nietman had taken him seriously. In the summer of 1948 the first annual Pacific Institute of Philosophy met at the Zephyr Point Conference Grounds on the Nevada Shore of Lake Tahoe. More than 100 students "from all walks of life" [24] joined Dr. Radislov Tsanoff of the Rice Institute, Dr. J. H. Randall of Columbia University and Carlos Wood, aircraft designer, to discuss that problem which had been noted by President Burns in his inaugural address "The Discrepancy Between Moral and Technological Advance." Participants declared the Institute a great success: the Socratic method had stimulated them to grapple thoughtfully with the problem at hand. Many of them returned year after year to take advantage of this opportunity to discuss questions like "Philosophy, Politics and Peace," and "Capitalism, Communism and Social Justice." The Philosophy Institute became an important cog in the wheel moving Pacific toward the greatness its President had promised at his inauguration.

One of the problems requiring thought and imaginative educational efforts which the President had cited in his inaugural was the

74

prevalence of racial prejudice. He supported Dr. Jantzen's proposal, therefore, for an Intercultural Relations Institute in 1948. Dr. Harold Jacoby agreed to direct the Institute. He had graduated from the College in 1928, had received his doctorate at the University of Pennsylvania and returned to teach at his alma mater in 1933. As an active member of the Socialist Party and as a concerned sociologist, he had taught courses in race relations throughout the 1930s. During the War, he had taken a leave from the University to serve first as director of the Japanese Relocation Center at Tule Lake and later to act as advisor for UNRRA at refugee camps in Africa and Israel. This varied experience proved invaluable in designing and administering the summer session program in Intercultural Relations—a program which encouraged in the students a better understanding of other ethnic groups.

According to Dr. Jantzen, Dean of the School of Education and of the Summer Sessions, Robert Burns actively fostered and encouraged such innovation and experiment—especially during summer sessions. As a result, Dr. Jantzen planned programs which not only included courses taught by resident faculty but also invited visiting faculty from all over the country to offer specialized course work and to inject new academic insights on campus. Workshops in folk dancing, audio-visual teaching in churches, educational radio, and college admissions, recording and registration also were offered. The classes and institutes and workshops were extraordinarily popular. Altogether over 1,500 students participated in the 1947 summer session, a figure higher than the regular year-round enrollment. Throughout Dr. Burns' administration the summer school was a mainstay of the institution; he supported its many and varied programs wholeheartedly.

Some of the most exciting and novel of these summer classes were those offered under the aegis of the Department of Speech, and during the regular school year this department was the third largest in the College. As many as five majors were offered: dramatic art, public speaking, radio broadcasting, speech correction and speech (a combination of any two or three of the more limited areas of study). The speech faculty was also involved in numerous extracurricular activities. Forensics, for example, as it had been when President Burns was an undergraduate, was one of the most respected activities at Pacific, and with good reason. In 1947, the

College debate team "defeated the cream of the crop of the nation representing 180 colleges and universities," [25] at the Pi Kappa Delta National Debate Tournament at Bowling Green University in Ohio. The Director of Forensics, Edward Betz, who had coached the team, was elected national president of the Forensics honor society at the same meeting. Both the speech department and the College could be justly proud, therefore, of its debate coach and the members of the team.

The Department of Speech also offered students an opportunity to test their rhetorical skills in a variety of activities in radio production. Soon after the College's move to Stockton, regular broadcasts on the local radio station KGDM were aired from a campus studio which had a direct connection with the station. The studio was also the site for the first of the College's classes in radio, taught by Art Farey. Then in 1937, John Crabbe joined the faculty to organize a full course of studies in radio broadcasting; subsequently the "first radio production major in the West" was established. After the war, when the Federal Communications Commission set aside a group of frequencies on the FM band for educational stations, Pacific submitted an application. The problem of financing such a project was a formidable one, John Crabbe reported later, but "President Burns gave unstintingly of his time and effort in this campaign." [26] As a result, at seven o'clock in the evening on September 22, 1947, the first broadcast from Pacific's new FM station KCVN was broadcast, with messages from President Burns, Art Farey and Trustee George Wilson, as well as performances by music and drama students. The radio facilities were housed in a quonset hut and consisted of two studios, four control rooms, two offices, and a news room with press wire facilities. These were augmented by an army surplus van equipped with a portable transmitter; consequently, broadcasts from the Philosophy Institute at Tahoe, and from the Marine Station at Dillon Beach could be aired on KCVN. Altogether the value of the facilities for radio broadcasting was appraised to be $75,000.

John Crabbe responded in the *Pacific Review* to the question: "Why should Pacific be so vitally interested in Radio?" He cited the need for radio broadcasters who were not only trained in the technical aspects of the profession but also had a strong liberal arts education. He also wrote of the "social obligation" of collegiate broadcasting, its responsibility "to stimulate the industry," and, finally, he informed alumni that "where programming can be flexible and program content designed to meet the needs of the classroom, as in the case of KCVN, a broadcast station can provide a great service on the local educational level."[27] Robert Burns, "whose financing leadership made KCVN possible,"[28] shared Mr. Crabbe's sense of purpose, and he was undoubtedly also aware of the radio station's capability of taking "the Pacific story" to numbers of radio listeners.

The Pacific Theater, a division of the Speech Department, also was a means of publicizing the College. In fact, during the 1930s the director of the theater, DeMarcus Brown, was second only to Amos Alonzo Stagg in making Pacific's name familiar throughout California. He was not only a man of great talent and energy (he taught classes in the art department and in the speech department—a total of sixteen units), he was a man with unusual directorial skill. His student actors and actresses presented finished performances, to packed houses, of classical repertoire as well as modern productions. Several members of his troupe went on to achieve distinction in the professional theatrical world: Jo Van Fleet and Lois Wheeler among the most notable. His directorial skills also benefitted innumerable other student performers, of course; for, as he was aware, "the student who has had the advantages of training and participation in drama has a sureness, an inner poise, and a broadened outlook."[29]

In addition to the large scale productions on the Conservatory stage and in the Greek amphitheater (built by DeMarcus Brown and volunteer students), the department also sponsored numerous student-directed performances in the studio theater. Located in the basement of the Conservatory, the "studio" was the scene of academically essential but less popular plays from dramatic literature. Together with the major productions, these studio theater plays had an important educational value for the performers, the College and the community at large. For DeMarcus Brown recognized the obligation of the theater "to produce a type and style of play of definite literary quality, supplying entertainment for a distinctly intellectual audience." He was convinced that "as a means of developing taste and appreciation of fine creative work, there is nothing so forceful as the drama."[30]

77

Theater had been recognized for a long time to be a significant aspect of the summer program, but in 1945 exciting new possibilities were suggested. Charles Segerstrom of Sonora, Trustee of the College, informed Robert Burns that the Fallon House Hotel and dance hall in the Gold Rush town of Columbia, was for sale. Dr. Burns immediately perceived an opportunity for expanding the College's programs and set to work raising the five thousand dollars necessary to purchase the land and buildings. He was successful, and in July of 1945, to celebrate Columbia's being made a state park, the first theatrical production by the College of Pacific players entertained the audience with a series of "olios" at its Fallon House Theater.

It was apparent even then, however, that the building needed extensive repair. Arthur Farey, who directed the performance, was so concerned about the sagging floor that he himself purchased lumber and reinforced the most dangerous areas. A subsequent examination revealed that even partial restoration would cost the College thousands of dollars—far more than it was willing or able

Establishment of a speech clinic by Dr. Howard Runion in 1948 added a new dimension to the College.

to spend. Robert Burns was undaunted, however; he suggested to the Trustees that the property be deeded to the State and urged the State Parks Commission, in return, to restore the building and then lease it to the College for the summer theater program. The transaction was a complicated, troublesome one—a less determined college president would surely have abandoned the project. Ultimately, though, on March 20, 1947, President Burns' persuasive ability coupled with his persistence succeeded in overcoming a myriad of obstacles. The State agreed to his plan for the restoration of the building for use as the College's summer theater, and the property was transferred to the State of California. A reinforced concrete foundation was constructed; steel girders and cross ties strengthened the walls; dressing rooms and a stage were built; and electricity and hot and cold water lines were installed.

All of the reconstruction was carefully planned so that the original style of the building would be preserved. Today, the wallpaper approximates the peeling shreds on the old walls, and the proscenium arch decorations are a replica of the window's interior framing designs. Special efforts were required in the preservation of the ceiling, so that it would be the same as it was when "Jim Fallon laboriously designed, painted, cut and adhered the appliques onto the peeling tongue and groove . . . The State managed this difficult procedure of preservation by actually lifting the ceiling in its entirety by jacks while the walls under it were being straightened and buttressed." [31] The building itself, then, provided an interesting backdrop for the College's first production, in 1949, of Augustin Daly's melodrama, "Under the Gaslight." Crowds of summer visitors to the State Park enjoyed this and the four other plays in that summer's repertoire. Summer theater at Fallon House soon became an integral component of the multi-faceted program offered by the College's drama faculty: DeMarcus Brown.

Another of the Speech Department's courses of study which reached out to serve the community, the speech correction program, was also expanded during the early years of President Burns' administration. Speech correction classes had first been offered at the College in 1937, when Dr. Roy C. McCall joined the faculty. Gradually other courses were added as the need for this kind of professional training became evident; the major in speech correction was instituted in 1939. Coincident with the development of course work was the development of the College's speech clinic—in which faculty members and graduate students worked with children and adults in the effort to overcome handicaps in speech. In the summer of 1945 the first residential clinic was held; students and parents lived in one of the fraternity houses and worked full-time with the psychologists and speech therapists. The program was an immediate success—beneficial for both clients and training clinicians; it became an annual component of the summer program. Dr. Howard Runion, who succeeded Dr. McCall as chairman of the speech department and speech therapy professor in 1948, immediately perceived the possibilities inherent in the summer residency and in the school-year clinic to exploit all the resources of the college for the children's benefit. He initiated a proposal to expand the speech clinic and to integrate the various clinical services offered by the College.

President Burns, who was himself aware of the significance of speech in personal and professional development, supported Dr. Runion's proposal; he moved at once to find benefactors for the integrated program. Presentations before local service clubs, pointing out the vital community service performed by the clinic, had already resulted in continuing generous donations. Sizeable injections of capital, though, were required to fund the projected expansion and integration of the program. Fortunately, Dr. Burns' conversations with the Rosenberg Foundation were fruitful; the Foundation agreed to make an initial contribution of $30,270 to the project. As a result, new faculty members were hired, and courses in audiomentry and lip reading were added to the curriculum so that the clinic could help deaf and hard-of-hearing children to improve their speech.

Dr. Runion was aware that children with speech handicaps were sometimes also troubled with psychological and educational problems. His plan for integrating the clinics made it possible for weekly discussions to be held between faculty members and student clinicians so that the best combination of clinical services might be brought to bear in each individual case. The psychology department administered tests and developed a system of "play therapy." The School of Education sponsored a reading clinic. Lawton Harris of the religion department encouraged the learning of movement skills and cooperative effort with folk dancing. And

DeMarcus Brown at Fallon House Theatre in Columbia State Park.

many young people were helped with art activities directed by Dr.
Runion's wife, Bess. In effect, all the resources of the college which
might be applicable were brought to bear in the effort to aid
individuals who experienced difficulty communicating in speech.

The Conservatory of Music also initiated a therapeutic program
during this period—a revolutionary one, for their program in
music therapy was the first in the West. Wilhelmina Harbert, of the
Conservatory faculty, had initially become aware of the healing
quality of music during and after World War I. "During a year
spent overseas [playing piano concerts] in hospitals, rest areas and
improvised recreation halls, she began to note the power of music
in the emotional adjustments of people under great stress." [32] The
experience stimulated her study, with her physician husband, of
the physiological and psychological bases of human behavior.
There was very little formal literature at the time in the area of
music therapy; it was necessary, therefore, that she herself "create
techniques based upon as sound psychological principles as possible." [33]

Mrs. Harbert joined the faculty of the Conservatory in 1937, but she continued with her volunteer work at the Stockton State Hospital. She had had some difficulty convincing the staff there of the therapeutic value of music. Soon, though, her Friday musicals became popular events among the recovering patients. Then, one afternoon, a hospital attendant brought Leroy, "who had been sitting for months in complete silence." [34] His case was considered hopeless; his only activity was to play his saxophone. Mrs. Harbert started to play the introduction to the piece of music in his music case, "Nola," and to her surprise, Leroy joined her at the right time and they played it through.

> The tone quality which Leroy produced was unusually good. He not only seemed to grasp the melodic line and the rhythmic pattern, but he was sensitive to the accompaniment as well. During the interludes he would play the melody and then with apparent ease switch to his solo part. Although there was no verbal communication between us, I felt a real musical conversation had taken place. As soon as the number was finished he silently put away his saxophone, placed the music in the case, closed it quickly, and ignoring the applause from the audience of patients was led back to his cottage. [35]

The incident "made a deep impression" on Mrs. Harbert, although the hospital staff tried to discourage her efforts. It was "silly to waste time on Leroy. He would never talk anyway, so why bother?" [36] She patiently continued. Four months later, her perseverance was rewarded. Leroy joined the group singing "in a thin weak voice." [37] Gradually Leroy emerged from his catatonic schizophrenia; he joined the hospital chorus, the orchestra and the folk dance group. The hospital staff was finally convinced; music could indeed open the door to reality in some patients for whom nothing else was effective.

During the years of World War II Mrs. Harbert not only continued her professional work at the Conservatory and her volunteer activities at the State Hospital, she also commuted to Mills College where she taught a course on the use of music in therapy programs to government trainees in Occupational Therapy. All of these experiences laid the groundwork for her proposal in 1946 that a musical therapy program be introduced at the Conservatory. Dean

Elliott concurred and President Burns heartily supported the innovative program. Students were soon attracted to the new course of studies which included, in addition to formal course work, field experience with the mentally ill, the mentally retarded, and the physically handicapped. The inter-clinic plan brought them also into contact with the hard of hearing and speech handicapped. Through both individual and group activities in body rhythms, voice production, singing and playing instruments, hundreds of young people in Stockton have overcome their handicaps or learned to cope with them through the work of the musical therapy students from the Conservatory. Together with the other clinical services the musical program has not only trained professionals in these vital areas of treatment, it has also served a vital healing function in the local community.

The needs of the whole San Joaquin-Sacramento Valley were cited in the proposal for another of the College's post-war curricular innovations. The Board of Education of the Methodist Church had been allotted a portion of the $25,000,000 Crusade for Christ Fund which it, in turn, was to disperse to its affiliated theological schools, colleges and universities. None of these monies was to be expended for programs already in existence; the fund was to be used solely for the establishment of "distinctly new educational projects." Robert Burns immediately perceived this challenge to be the potential source of new educational opportunities for the College. In the shifting California post-war scene, Pacific's President saw emerging a critical need for Christian social and educational leadership. He cited the official state estimate which projected a population of eight million for the great interior valley, "Pacific's area," within two decades. He proposed, therefore, that the College be granted $33,000 for the establishment of the Christian Community Administration Major, "for the training of social leadership with Christian principles."

The Board of Education accepted the proposal, "one of the most significant projects stimulated by the Crusade for Christ apportionments."[38] Frank A. Lindhorst, with degrees from De Pauw University and Boston University School of Theology, graduate study at Harvard and the University of Chicago, and extensive field work in Christian education for the Methodist Church, came to direct the program. Together with Dr. Colliver, he developed a course of study which included formal study in the religion department. But the Christian Community Administration major, like the Inter-clinical services, also pioneered in the development of inter-departmental cooperation. The School of Education and the Department of Speech developed special educational and audio-visual courses. The Business Administration Department constructed a course leading to Goodwill Industry management. At the heart of the curriculum, however, was field work, since "it affords the organization experience to which the student can relate the various theoretical and practical studies he is taking."[39] Cooperative arrangements were made, therefore, with various local agencies; Pacific's students were soon at work assisting church groups, the YMCA and others to expand and enrich their programs.

Students responded with considerable enthusiasm to the innovative educational opportunities offered at Pacific; President Burns' business acumen and his educational vision immediately bore fruit in the expanding enrollments. But it would be a mistake to assume that the College's only attraction lay in its academic life. For the first couple of years after the war, to be sure, the presence of veterans did have a dampening effect on the social life on campus. They were not only older in years than the average college student, their participation in the most destructive war in history had aged many of them prematurely. They were impatient to "get on," to glean as much from the educational process as they could and then to find the security of a settled job and home life. Having survived the rough and tumble world of army and navy camps, they were sometimes contemptuous of traditional collegiate activities, which they perceived as childish distractions from the business of getting an education. The student newspaper, the *Pacific Weekly*, reflected the younger students' dismay at these attitudes. In an editorial plaintively headed "What's Wrong?" the student writer asked:

> What's wrong with the school spirit at Pacific?
> What has happened to the old razzle dazzle and hubba hubba of former years?
> Can it be that there are so many veterans in school that no one cares about what happens to the spirit and enthusiasm of getting an education?[40]

Attendance at rallies and parades and bonfires was notably diminished during the years immediately after the war—and it was correspondingly difficult to find a place to study in the library.

Gradually, however, social life on campus returned to normal. Dances were held nearly every weekend; these boy-meets-girl events were, without doubt, among the most popular of social occasions. Some of the most famous bands in the country played for them: Stan Kenton's band was brought to the Civic Auditorium for the Homecoming Dance; Les Brown entertained the costumed dancers at the Mardi Gras with his "Sentimental Journey" and "I've Got My Love To Keep Me Warm." Local groups of musicians, often made up of students from the Conservatory, played for the less formal affairs like the dance for the annual Sadie Hawkins Day when, according to the *Pacific Weekly*, "The fella shrinks in the shrubbery" while "the gals flock and stalk and prey like hawks." [41]

The girls did, indeed, participate joyously and sometimes raucously in this annual respite from conventional restraint; though compared with more recent student "happenings," Sadie Hawkins Day was quiet and orderly. As did most other public and private institutions at the time, the College enforced strict parietal rules—especially for the girls. Young women living on campus were required to check in at their dormitories before 10 P.M. on weekdays and lights had to be turned off half an hour later. On weekends they were allowed to stay out until midnight; if they returned late, they were "campused"—confined to their rooms except during class hours and meal times and not allowed to participate in extracurricular and social activities. The dress code forbade girls to wear pants, except in their rooms or in the gym. Even being seen in public with curlers or pin curls in one's hair was punishable. And the hand book warned against trying to cover up such infractions with long coats or scarves!

Student participation in formulating these regulations was nonexistent. No one, including the students themselves, expected that there should be any. Student government, which consisted primarily of the Executive Committee of the Pacific Student Association and the Associated Women Students organization, did not question the right of the College to regulate the students' social activities. The Executive Committee dispersed the student body dues to student organizations and to the athletic program. They discussed such campus problems as the lack of enough pep songs, or whether or not the football squad could keep their jackets.

Their most important activity during this period lay in their fund raising drives for the student union. Until it opened in the fall of 1949, the only gathering spot for students was the small, inadequate "cub house," across from West Hall, which was sponsored and managed by the Associated Women Students. Although the student fund drive was unsuccessful, the administration was forced by the seriousness of their efforts to recognize the need. Arrangements were made with local business concerns to finance the construction of a bookstore, a barber shop and a coffee shop in the area west of West Hall. The new student union building was soon a popular gathering place. It provided a center where students from on and off campus could meet and eat and smoke (the latter activity forbidden on campus except in certain designated locations).

The student newspaper, the *Pacific Weekly*, also served as a unifying force on campus. The tone of the paper had changed considerably from that of Robert Burns' student days. There were fewer reports of scholarly and religious talks by the faculty. Nevertheless, the paper was a vital organ, informing students of concerts, theatrical and social events, engagements and weddings, changes in administrative staff and faculty. Reports of club meetings took up a great deal of space, for clubs proliferated on campus during the post-war years. In addition to the eight national honor societies in journalism, biology, social sciences, etc., students formed a photography club, a radio club, a home economics club, etc.—in effect a club for every student interest.

By far the most popular portion of the newspaper, however, was the sports section. Although more than two full pages of the *Weekly* were devoted to sports every week, a poll of readers, reported on February 17, 1948, confirmed that a great majority wanted even more articles about athletics. This interest in the newspapers's sporting coverage reflected an enthusiasm for intercollegiate sports which pervaded almost the whole student body. Basketball, swimming, water polo, baseball and track events drew remarkably large attendance. The major intercollegiate athletic activity, however—the one that attracted large crowds from the community as well as students—was football. Preceding these autumn contests elaborate, noisy rituals were held, rallies and bonfires which aroused feverish enthusiasm for the games themselves. Pacific was not alone, of course; collegiate football, especially in those days before the proliferation of the professional sport and television, was the favorite spectator sport of thousands of Americans.

The coaching of Amos Alonzo Stagg had lent the College's football team unusual prestige and fame. He absolutely insisted on amateurism; although the College did award tuition scholarships to athletes so that Pacific would be on a par with free public institutions, he forbade any other support or payment to his players. As a result, the College seldom fielded the championship teams which other more generous, less idealistic schools were able to recruit. Nevertheless, Mr. Stagg's players were ably coached; they always performed respectably and sometimes surprised the pundits of the sporting world by defeating one of the "big" teams. Thanks to Mr. Stagg's reputation, the College of the Pacific team arranged contracts to play important schools like U.C. Berkeley, Stanford, U.S.C., and Northwestern, and the contracts were generally lucrative ones; except for the two coaching salaries paid by the College, and a modest subsidy from the student association dues, football paid for itself.

But by the fall of 1946, Mr. Stagg's age was affecting his coaching ability. Though Tully Knoles had promised the "Grand Old Man" a lifetime appointment, he concurred in the decision to ask Mr. Stagg to reduce his responsibility for the team by becoming the football advisor, and deputed the new president to break the news to him. Years later Robert Burns wrote of the difficulty he had performing that task.

> After fourteen years of service [at Pacific], Mr. Stagg was now 84 years of age. The majority of the football team felt he should be put in an advisory capacity. It was decided to ask him to do this. It was my first official act after being elected President. At 9 A.M. the following morning, I told him of our decision but he refused to be an advisor...Considering the previous confrontation with Robert Hutchins at Chicago and Mr. Stagg's passionate desire to "wear out" rather than "rust out," I would consider this a prime item on which to cut one's administrative teeth.[42]

Undaunted, Mr. Stagg removed to Pennsylvania where he joined his son Amos Jr. on the coaching staff at Susquehanna University.

Lawrence Siemering, who had been assistant coach, was named to succeed Mr. Stagg. For three subsequent years the College of the Pacific fielded remarkably successful football teams—partly owing to Mr. Siemering's coaching, but in great measure because of the inspired quarterbacking of Eddie Le Baron. He was relatively small but also lithe and intelligent; spectators delighted in watching the way he darted out of the hands of opposing linemen to pass the ball to a teammate. He broke several records during his collegiate career and went on to play for the Quantico Marines and the Washington Redskins and the Dallas Cowboys after his graduation. While Eddie Le Baron was competing for Pacific, students and local football fans were assured of colorful, exciting, well played games. Crowds overflowed the small Baxter stadium on campus; several games had to be played in neighboring Lodi's "Grape Bowl."

Students and townspeople, therefore, began to urge that a larger stadium be built on campus. And many of the Trustees, alarmed at the suddenly increased cost of the sport (after Mr. Stagg's resignation, the practice of offering potential players room and board as well as tuition was initiated), became convinced that with better facilities, the crowds of spectators would once again make the game self-supportive. In fact, one of the trustees predicted that football profits would help the College to diminish the debt which had accrued since the war. Nevertheless, some of the other members of the Board were reluctant to support such a costly addition. President Burns also hesitated. On a trip East in January of 1950 he called a special meeting of college presidents to discuss with them the question of expanding Pacific's program of intercollegiate football. They all agreed that because of Stockton's location and C.O.P.'s status as an old, established institution and other factors, the College would be wise to embark on a growing intercollegiate football program at this time. Their counsel, together with the Stockton Chamber of Commerce's assurance of its fund raising assistance, convinced the Board to accede to the plan. Groundbreaking ceremonies were held on April 20, 1950, and on October 21 of that year the new Pacific Memorial Stadium was the scene of the Homecoming Game. Thirty-two thousand spectators listened to dedication speeches by such personages as Governor Earl Warren, General Albert Wedemeyer, Admiral R. J. Rogers, and actor Dick Powell. They also watched the football game, "a dazzling, hair-raising, spine-tingling thriller" in which Loyola defeated Pacific by a score of 35-33. The defeat was "a bitter capsule," but "the magnitude of the total Pacific achievement during this memorable weekend made it possible to swallow even this."[43]

It could be argued, of course, that the critical need of the College for better library facilities should have taken precedence over its need for a football stadium. But to do so would be to ignore the fact that funds for library construction were much harder to raise than funds for the athletic facility. Furthermore, everyone believed that contributions would cover most of the building cost of the new stadium which would, in turn, produce more income than it required. No one guessed that the sale of scrip—even after it had been augmented by Trustee Lowell Berry's generous contribution—would fall as far short of paying for the new facility as it did. Nor did anyone foresee that the advent of televised professional football games would diminish local enthusiasm for collegiate football to the extent that it did.

President Burns himself was sensitive to the question of priorities. In an interview for the *Stockton Record*, he urged local citizens to remember the academic significance of the library.

> Most of the people of the community are well aware of the stadium drive and we are glad to see it making such good progress. We most certainly want the stadium drive to succeed, but we must not underestimate the importance academically of a new library and what it will mean to the future of the college.[44]

The commitment of the faculty to the new library had already been proven. Altogether they had pledged $20,000, to be withheld from their comparatively low salaries. And subsequently, Mr. Irving Martin, Sr., publisher of the *Stockton Record*, acceded to Dr. Burns' urgings and agreed to contribute the munificent sum of $125,000 to the library, which would be named in his honor. The campaign for the library was then well on its way.

The generous gift of Mr. and Mrs. Osro Sears made possible another new academic facility. Stimulated by the success of the

Christian Community Administration program, their challenge grant of $30,000 was soon matched with funds donated by other churchmen who were grateful for the fresh, enthusiastic leadership provided by the graduates of the program. The new building, Sears Hall, to the north of the Chapel, was dedicated at the annual Methodist Conference Meeting in June, 1950, and valuable new classroom and office space was ready for use during the busy summer session.

President Burns had taken an active personal role in all the developments of the College, academic as well as financial. It was he who had challenged the faculty members to expand their existing programs and to initiate imaginative new ones. But he also had assumed the responsibility for finding the monetary support necessary to fund them. Traveling up and down the state, he spoke two or three times a week to church gatherings, and to meetings of Rotary, Kiwanis, Chambers of Commerce, Women's Clubs, Farm Bureaus, Bankers' Institutes. He addressed them on a variety of topics: reporting on his European tour in 1948, encouraging their awareness of California's Centennial celebrations in 1949, 1950, and 1951. But always he concluded with a message emphasizing the critical role played by the College of the Pacific in training young ethical leadership for the nation as well as the State of California.

His membership in the state's Centennial Commission enabled him to make new contacts for the College. He was also active in the group which sought to save the South Grove of the Calaveras Big Trees, and he was elected chairman of the Stockton Chamber of Commerce Committee for development of industrial and financial expansion in the local community. He personally interviewed the prospective donors he met in the course of these wide-ranging activities. His ebullience as well as his perseverance, during these early years of his presidency, resulted in innumerable new supporters for the College.

It was, to say the least, a physically and emotionally exhausting schedule, which finally caught up with him in January of 1950. He was in New York to interest foundations in the work of the College, when suddenly he had to be taken to the hospital with hemorrhaging ulcers. He recovered from the nearly fatal attack only after numerous blood transfusions. (Through the San Joaquin

County Blood Bank undergraduates of the College, including members of the football team, donated blood to his credit.) His doctors insisted on weeks of complete rest, but he was back at his desk by the end of March and was immersed at once in the planning for the Centennial observances of the College to which he was so totally and wholeheartedly dedicated.

Throughout the 1950-51 school year he and Dr. Knoles and members of the faculty accompanied "Centennial Caravans" throughout the state—speaking to large meetings of alumni and friends of the College about its heritage as well as its prospects for the future. In addition, special centennial observances were held on campus. Dr. Howard Hanson, dean of the Eastman School of Music and formerly Dean of Pacific's Conservatory, was guest conductor and composer for a two-day Centennial Festival of American Music. Dore Schary, film producer, at a special pre-curtain convocation, addressed the audience of the centennial theatrical production—the West Coast premiere of "Sing Out Sweet Land." A new chapter of Phi Kappa Phi was established on campus during ceremonies presided over by Dr. Rufus B. Von Kleinsmid, Chancellor of the University of Southern California. The whirl of events attracted nationwide attention.

On June second the year's week-long culmination of the observance was opened when one hundred runners, in relay, carried a torch lighted by Governor Warren in Sacramento to the campus in Stockton. Subsequently, Dr. Malcolm Eiselen delivered the first Annual Faculty Research Lecture, speaking to his colleagues on "The Religious Dynamic of Six Great American Statesmen." On Friday, "Tully Cleon Knoles Day," three prominent philosophers from the East Coast delivered lectures on topics relating to Dr. Knoles' concern about "America's Moral Foundations." Finally Dr. G. Bromley Oxnam, distinguished American churchman and former student of Dr. Knoles, addressed the graduating seniors, their families and friends of the College during the Commencement Ceremonies. The College had every reason to be proud of its academic heritage; the commemorative celebration was of remarkably high scholastic caliber.

As interested as he was in history, especially in the history of his alma mater, President Burns might well in his centennial addresses to alumni have emphasized the past laurels of the College. He certainly did not neglect the historical developments, but he saw them more importantly as promises for the future. He projected a second century for Pacific during which it would continue to emphasize the performing arts as well as the traditional study of liberal arts. In pursuit of its goals, the College would "maintain its great heritage of academic freedom" and at the same time, commit itself even more strongly to its ideal of a Christian and personalized education. In conclusion, as he had done in his inaugural address, the President promised that Pacific would draw on its pioneering experience to move into new areas of study. "The College of the Pacific," he reminded his listeners, "as a private college, has no state controls, deals with less red tape, never worries about the whims of legislatures or politicians. It is free..." [45]

During his first five years as President, Robert Burns had already taken advantage of that freedom to develop new programs and new facilities for the College. He had demonstrated a genius for perceiving opportunities for Pacific; this, coupled with his phenomenal energy, his enthusiasm, and his ability to make new friends for the College, had resulted—even during these first few years—in exciting new growth. During the next two decades, which saw unprecedented growth in American higher education, the College of the Pacific was indeed fortunate in having as president a man who matched the times.

Chapter Four

THROUGHOUT HIS presidency, Robert Burns was a consistent and able defender of the principle of academic freedom. In fact, his commitment to that controversial principle was so unswerving as to be surprising, given his sensitivity to the necessity for favorable public relations and fund raising. It was, nonetheless, one of the most notable characteristics of his administration. In spite of all kinds of pressures brought to bear—by wealthy donors, both potential and actual, and occasionally by anxious members of the Board—Dr. Burns' clear perception of the importance of presenting all sides of the question led him to the courageous support of that vital and essential precept in education—intellectual freedom.

His dedication to this principle was apparent even during the perilous period of McCarthyism when Dr. William Nietman invited a Marxist scholar, as well as a traditional capitalist, to address the Philosophy Institute in June of 1950. The *Pacific Review* description of the Institute promised "a direct, clear cut, no-punches-pulled investigation" of the two systems. Dr. Charles Norman argued the case for capitalism, while the case for Marxism was presented by Dr. Herbert Phillips of Seattle, who had been dismissed from the faculty of the University of Washington the year before because of his Communist Party membership. A panel of three other philosophers for whom "the sanctions of social justice are religious," were there to comment on and question the principle speakers.

The fear of communism, which had become so prevalent during the years immediately following the war, led a number of local citizens and friends of the College to object, and object strenuously, to what they perceived to be an alarming incursion of Communist doctrine. But in spite of the threats of withdrawal of monetary support, Robert Burns lent the project his unequivocal support. Like Dr. Nietman, he believed that the "overall result of this out-in-the-open attack on the critical and touchy communist-capitalistic controversy" would be "to send those who attend the Institute back to their daily tasks with new insights for strengthening the American way of life." [1]

93

The invitation to Dr. G. Bromley Oxnam to address the centennial commencement gathering was further evidence of the administration's commitment to academic freedom. Dr. Oxnam was, to say the least, a controversial figure. Nationally known churchman and Bishop of the Methodist Church in New York City, he was also the target of anti-communist crusaders like Mrs. Elizabeth Dilling, author of *The Red Network*, because he had abolished compulsory military training while president of De Pauw University. Dr. Oxnam was subsequently to confront McCarthy himself and to publish the account of that confrontation in the volume, *I Protest*.

As early as 1951, however, he perceived the grave threat to American freedoms posed by the McCarthy-bred hysteria. The graduates and their families gathered in the sun-soaked Baxter Stadium heard his chill warning.

When fear and faction become decisive in determining national policy, the craven and the partisan take the helm, and the ship of state is lost in the storm. Research and reflection, two of the chief contributions of the college, are basic essentials to the formulation of course in crisis. Men who seek to limit free inquiry and deny men the freedom necessary to discover the truth that frees; men who demand thought control and regimented conformity in the name of patriotism; men who would destroy our civil liberties, silence the prophets, turn out the lights in laboratory and classroom, are subversive in the most sinister sense of that term, since they are destroying the foundations upon which the free society rests.[2]

At the College of the Pacific, inquiry, research and reflection, those "basic essentials" *were* carried on in an atmosphere of freedom, in spite of repeated questioning.

Again in 1952 the principle was threatened. Some members of the Board of Trustees were distressed because a number of the college's professors had openly endorsed Adlai Stevenson's candidacy in a newspaper advertisement in the *Stockton Record*. Several Trustees complained to the President that such partisan political activity on the part of faculty members was inappropriate. The issue was potentially an explosive one. Dr. Knoles himself had been among the signers of the newspaper statement in favor of Stevenson; neither he nor the professors involved were likely to accept passively a ban on political action. In his treatment of the issue President Burns demonstrated not only his commitment to scholarly freedom but also his developing strategical skills. The question appeared last on the agenda of the December 12 meeting after a full day of complex financial discussions. The Board agreed, therefore, without the lengthy heated discussion which might have occurred, to assign President Burns the task of wording a resolution to be addressed to the faculty.

By January 22, 1953, when the issue was brought before the Board meeting again, emotions had cooled and the statement adopted was relatively mild in tone. "As a Board of Trustees we wish to go on record against any staff member, or group of staff members, giving endorsement to a political party issue or speaking in behalf thereof, if he implies in any way that this represents his staff relationship to the College of the Pacific rather than his doing so as an individual." At the same time, however, the resolution strongly affirmed this right to act as individuals. "The College of the Pacific believes in and defends academic freedom. There has never been an instance in our one hundred and one year history when we have muzzled our teachers. These teachers have the same right to personal opinion and its public expression as assured to any other citizen."[3] This was a statement acceptable to the faculty. Once again the storm had been weathered, but it was not to be the last such tempest. Disputes regarding academic freedom arose over and over again during Dr. Burns' presidency. His tenacity, his courage under fire, his firmness in defense of the principle drew the praise of every accrediting committee that visited the college.

Partly owing to this dedication to the freedom necessary for scholarship, partly because he saw to it that faculty salaries were raised year after year, partly because of his friendliness and accessibility, President Burns generally had the support of the faculty. Only once during these early years did a controversy arise that was potentially divisive. Fearing the drop of enrollment which the draft for soldiers for the war in Korea threatened, Dr. Burns recommended that the College apply to the government for an ROTC unit on campus. When he first broached the subject to the Trustees, however, he acknowledged that there might be some difficulty associated with such an establishment because "church related colleges have rarely encouraged ROTC programs on campuses."[4] And as he anticipated it would, the proposal did indeed arouse considerable furor amongst the college's religious constituency. A petition signed by 25 religious education majors objected to the unit, and a number of ministers wrote letters in opposition. Many faculty members were opposed—especially when it was discovered that the Air Force insisted that the program be compulsory for all male students.

The Board voted in favor of applying for the unit, but at the same time they recognized the importance of faculty support. Mr. Berry's motion, therefore, that the action be "subject to the approval of the majority of the faculty" was accepted. Nothing as controversial had been discussed by the academic community at Pacific for years, and the faculty meeting proved to be an emotional one. Both proponents and opponents of the program debated forcefully. When the vote was counted the majority of the faculty voted in favor of establishing the ROTC unit. In the end, however, the opponents of the program were satisfied. The Air Force instituted the training unit on another campus.

The problem of declining enrollments was solved by two other developments, the first of which was beyond the control of the College. President Truman ruled that college students would not be drafted to serve in the Korean conflict; so the great flight of students from the halls of academe which had occurred during the second World War was no longer a threat. As a matter of fact a number of young men who probably would not otherwise have entered college did so in order to avoid being drafted.

The second development, however, did result directly from decisions made by the college's administration. During the first few years of the association with the public junior college, relations between the two schools had been mutually supportive. Administrators of the two schools, Tully Knoles and Dwayne Orton, who had designed the unique contractual agreement, worked amicably together. The overlapping faculties also contributed to a sense of unity. Perhaps most important, however, was the fact that the arrangement was in the best practical interests of both colleges. A number of events during and after the war, however, tended to vitiate those unifying factors, and Pacific began to consider the possibility of reestablishing its lower division.

In 1942 Dwayne Orton resigned his position as Chief Administrator of the junior college to become the Director of International Business Machines Corporation's educational division. After his departure, none of the subsequent Stockton College executive officers was as committed as he had been to maintaining and developing the experimental model. Nor did they support his overriding emphasis on liberal arts training. More and more the junior college in California was being called upon to meet all kinds of educational needs for vocational training as well as the preparation for upper division college work. The community of Stockton was not unlike the rest of the state in desiring a new, more extensive educational role and identity for its junior college, and the Board of Education as well as the administrators of the junior college reflected that changing attitude.

In 1944, therefore, the school district purchased 43 acres across the street from the College of the Pacific campus with the intention of developing its own facilities. After the war, surplus buildings were erected on the site, and by the spring of 1947 classes were being held on the new campus. It was originally planned that the new buildings would be used primarily for the new vocational classes, but it soon became apparent that given the great post-war crush of veteran students that space would also be needed there for the traditionally academic subjects. This move, in itself, need not have upset the status quo. Both schools needed more classroom space, and the campuses were adjoining.

Another concomitant development, however, contributed significantly to the separation of the two schools. In 1948 the Stockton School District initiated the 6-4-4 plan, wherein the juniors and seniors in high school joined the junior college students in the new facilities across from Pacific. This new arrangement caused considerable confusion. Although the intermingling of lower and upper division college students on the Pacific campus had proved to be beneficial to both, the addition of the younger high school students led to discord. College students resented the high school students' "invasion" of the new student union, the inclusion of the younger students in extracurricular activities. In 1949, therefore, the unified student association was divided so that there were two organizations: one for the high school and junior college students of Stockton College, another for the students of the College of the Pacific.

The divisiveness extended to the faculty. The new teachers brought in to teach the high school curriculum and the college's vocational courses frequently did not share the educational interests of the senior college liberal arts faculty. More important, as their teaching load was increased, the junior college faculty had less and less time for the joint meetings which once had served an important unifying function. The addition of younger students also added significantly to the faculty's counseling load. The College of the Pacific feared that its portion of faculty time and teaching energy would proportionately diminish as more and more was required of professors at the junior college.

Many of these problems could have been worked out had the two sides to the agreement been really desirous of continuing the agreement. But as early as March 28, 1950, President Burns spoke to the Board of the worsening relationship between the two schools "which is giving us much concern at the present time. We are dealing with a cantankerous school board and a new and difficult administrator. It is now coming to the point where there is little more than a rental of facilities." Dr. Knoles confirmed that judgment: "relations between the two schools have reached a place where cooperation is almost impossible."[5] Clearly, the junior college was no longer committed to the coordinate structure.

Pressures on Pacific to reestablish its lower division and to terminate the experiment were also mounting. Alumni were unhappy with the arrangement. Most students from outside the local school district could not attend Stockton College unless their own districts agreed to pay a tuition fee. Although Pacific had been granted the right, in 1946, to recommend 100 outside students without the requirement, many students who desired a continuous four-year education at the College were denied admission to the junior college. Alumni were understandably distressed when their sons and daughters, though academically qualified, could not take advantage of the full four years at Pacific which they had enjoyed.

Further impetus toward the reestablishment of Pacific's lower division was provided by two external agencies. On October 20, 1950, Dr. Burns reported to the Board that Victor Schmidt, Commissioner of the Pacific Coast Conference for Athletics, had ruled that Pacific was "not living up to the rules of the P.C.C.," because Stockton College sophomores played on Pacific's athletic teams.

All intercollegiate athletics activity for the spring of 1951 was cancelled, therefore, "as pressure is being placed on the independent colleges not to play us."[6]

Even more alarming was the refusal of the American Chemical Society to accredit the College's chemistry major.

> After careful consideration of all the data in our files pertaining to the College of the Pacific, as well as a careful study of the information which you supplied last summer concerning Stockton College, the Committee voted to withhold approval. The principal reason for taking such action at this time was the fact that the present organization of the College of the Pacific cannot permit the Department of Chemistry to retain proper control over the calibre and scope of the lower level courses and training, nor provide the indispensable comparison of junior college transfers with lower division students trained by the department. The Committee does not believe that these circumstances are conducive to a program of adequate strength.[7]

The President feared that other accrediting bodies might assume the same stance toward the College's programs. The College of the Pacific's experiment with innovative educational structure had, thus, finally been required to face the obstacle so many other experimental programs had found. And like those others it was forced to conclude that it is difficult, if not impossible, to vary the traditional pattern of educational structures unless a host of other related bodies (professional accreditation committees, athletic boards, etc.) are similarly committed to the experimental model.

These arguments in favor of reinstituting the freshman and sophomore classes were, to say the least, persuasive. Added to them was the ever present need for more students and tuition income. On November 10, 1950, Dean Bertholf reported to the Board that the results of his study indicated that approximately fourteen new teachers would be necessary in a reestablished lower division for 200 freshman and 100 sophomores. The cost of the additional staff would amount to about $82,500; income was projected at $123,675. The last hurdle had, therefore, been surmounted—that of the financial feasibility of the new program. The Board voted unanimously "to ask the administrative officers to proceed to or-

The Burns family at home during the early years of his administration.

ganize the freshman and sophomore years at the College, limiting the number to about 300 students."[8] And in October of 1951 President Burns informed the Board that the financial condition of the College was indeed healthier than it might have been, thanks to the enrollment of 202 new freshmen and 68 new sophomores.

Stockton College continued to rent classroom space on the Pacific campus and a number of faculty members were shared by the two institutions for many years. But for all intents and purposes, when the lower division at Pacific was reestablished in September of 1951, a singular experiment in American higher education was ended. Some mourned its passing. They were those who believed in the principle which had rationalized its foundation: that general education should be completed by institutions wholly devoted to the

100

President Burns and his wife, Grace, enjoyed escaping from the pressures of the early years of his administration to their retreat in Columbia.

broad educational needs of junior college students, so that the upper divisions of colleges and universities could dedicate their efforts to specialized training and graduate work. Such is the European pattern which Jordan of Stanford and Lange of the University of California had urged and which Orton and Knoles had implemented at Stockton College and the College of the Pacific. An appraisal of that fifteen-year experiment suggests not that the idea was proved faulty but rather that when the practical underpinnings of economic necessity were removed, the experimental model was no match for the traditional American pattern of higher educational structure: community colleges geared to meet the multifaceted vocational as well as academic needs of the local students; and liberal arts colleges designed to lead their students through a traditional four-year curriculum.

The administration perceived at once that Pacific needed to reestablish its sense of identity as a four-year liberal arts college. At their 1951 fall meeting President Burns announced to the Trustees that thanks to the generosity of Ted Baun a faculty retreat was to be held in Volcano. There, away from the daily pressures of work with students, the administrative staff and faculty members would discuss long-range aims of the college. They would attempt to reach a consensus of opinion on the College's place and function in the world of higher education—the meaning of its identity as a Christian liberal arts college.

The meeting was held on February 21 and 22, 1952 and was "a great success" according to the participants. In addition to the broad general issues, faculty members discussed and made concrete decisions in regard to the curriculum. They agreed with undergraduate and alumni opinion surveys that "the present structure of required courses at Pacific is burdensome, especially in certain major fields."[9] Consequently, social science requirements were reduced from twelve units to eight, the physical education requirement was reduced from four full years to three, the swimming test required for graduation was eliminated and the two-unit requirement in fine arts was altered to read either music or graphic art instead of both. The group also recommended that the Curriculum Committee study further changes in the requirements, so that the multidisciplinary requirements would amount to thirty-nine units and the major study requirements forty units. Then students would have as many as forty-three units in electives, and their general liberal arts background would be developed.

Given the fact that general faculty meetings are frequently bogged down in endless discussions of trivia, the very real accomplishments of this and of subsequent retreats were remarkable. Probably the most important result of these gatherings, though, was intangible. Throughout his administration, Tully Knoles had referred to the faculty and staff as "the Pacific family;" in his role as *pater familias* he held the family together and guided it through its pioneering efforts in Stockton. As Chancellor during the first years of Robert Burns' presidency, he had continued to perform that unifying function. Gradually, though, Dr. Knoles began to withdraw; by 1951, after five years in office, Robert Burns was firmly in charge of the administration. His style of leadership, together with the changing times, demanded new forms if that valued sense of family community was to be kept intact, and the annual faculty retreats were significant factors in the achievement of that goal. Throughout the 1950s, although the administrative staff as well as the faculty changed and grew in numbers, the "Pacific family" continued to be a distinctive characteristic in the life of the College.

Robert Burns' efforts to develop unity were not confined solely to the college's own community, however. He also sought ways to encourage leading citizens in the Valley to identify with the aims and goals of Pacific. A great deal of that work he accomplished informally, through his membership in Rotary, the Masonic Lodge, the YMCA, the Methodist Church, and other civic groups. His enthusiasm, his energy, his lively wit, his genuine friendliness made him a welcome presence in all sorts of "extracurricular" societies, and the contributions he made to the community at large through his activity in these groups were substantial. It was in great measure because of his tireless work on the State Park Commission that Asilomar, an invaluable piece of real estate which private developers wanted, was instead acquired by the state park system. The facility which Robert Burns had so enjoyed during collegiate YMCA conferences was preserved for use of all the people of California.

Robert Burns' first and consuming loyalty, however, was always to the College of the Pacific. He constantly sought ways to imbue others with his enthusiasm for the College, to make them aware of its needs. During the spring of 1953, he initiated a program which would bring some of the leading citizens he had met through his wide ranging activities outside the College more directly into contact with the school itself. He announced the establishment of the Pacific Associates, "to bring into the Pacific family people throughout the West who believe in the Pacific program and who will actively lend their counsel to planning and stimulating Pacific progress." [10] Small groups of Associates met with departments whose programs were of especial interest to them "to suggest ways in which department projects can best be related to the needs they serve and also how resources may be developed." [11] In addition, biennial meetings of the whole association were held, at which the President reported on the College's present development and its needs for future advancement. Faculty members also addressed the group on some pertinent topic. The program had very pragmatic aims: the attraction of prospective students and new donors. But at the same time, it served a significant educational function, updating the academic awareness of the Associates by bringing them into immediate contact with the educational process on campus.

Until this time, for many local citizens, the sole contact with the College had been through athletics. Soon after building the new stadium, however, enthusiasm for intercollegiate sports had begun to decline. As television spread the fame of professional football and basketball, the crowds who once stood in line to watch the college games diminished. Numerous colleges discontinued intercollegiate athletics because they considered it too costly and irrelevant to the educational task. Articles by such leading sports figures as Robert Ruark (author of "College Football Idiocy") and Bob Mathias ("I'm Through With College Football") lent fuel to the criticism of intercollegiate football.

In the midst of this furor President Burns spoke in defense of the game—so forcefully that a digest of his speech before the San Francisco Advertising Club was printed and widely distributed by the Tidewater Associated Oil Company. He acknowledged that certain "excesses" were scandalous, but also insisted that the positive qualities of football deserved attention. He praised its "ruggedness," which prepares the player for the competitive, individualistic system in which we live. Life in America, he reminded his listeners, "is not all a game of drop the handkerchief." He also described football's beneficial effects on the college at large, citing its function as a safety valve for obstreperous youthful energies.

For Robert Burns, however, the game's greatest value lay in its unifying function. He described collegiate life as it had formerly been when students had lived in small dormitories, had eaten in the same dining hall, taken the same courses with the same professors. "They had a common social and intellectual experience." He contrasted the resultant sense of commonality with contemporary college life in which "curriculum has been diversified" so that "few study the same courses or sit under the same professors." Campus social life had also been fragmented as the number of students increased, so that "there are many who graduate who have never had a broad common experience, or have never met each other up to Commencement Day." Only at the football games, in the rooting sections for their home teams, do modern college students come together. "Football," Dr. Burns concluded, "has become more than a spectacle; it has become a symbol...Actually if you want to look at it on a higher level, football has become the spiritual core of the modern campus." [12]

His experience in the 1930s, when Amos Alonzo Stagg came to Pacific, had convinced him of the public relations value of the game. The problem lay in the fact that spectators, so necessary if the costly sport was to pay for itself in fame and dollars, prefer winning teams. Colleges and universities across the country, therefore, had difficulty restraining ambitious coaching staffs, overzealous alumni and fans from violating the code governing amateur sports. Pacific, itself, had not been immune to such problems. Jerry Kirsten, the graduate athletic manager, resigned his position with the College because he believed the President had failed to reprimand one of the coaches strongly enough for an alleged infraction of the rules. Yet in spite of these difficulties, Robert Burns supported intercollegiate sports. He was convinced that "if the administrators of colleges worked together," the "excesses" could be eliminated. Already such cooperation "had succeeded in shortening spring practice and freshman competition in the Pacific Coast Conference." [13]

Dr. Burns was also convinced that cooperative action could benefit colleges in that essential task of fund raising. As a result, in addition to his work cultivating individual friends for the college, in addition to his speaking engagements and work in a multitude of organizations and commissions, in addition to his administrative duties at the College, he was among the first to urge the other independent colleges in Northern California to form a new organization, to band together for at least a portion of their fund-raising drives. He believed they could make a stronger case if they appeared together before large corporations and impress them with the significance of independent schools in providing the companies with the skilled workers and executives they needed. At first he hoped that Mills College and Stanford would join the effort, but in the end the organization (California Independent Colleges Foundation) was composed of seven Catholic schools and the College of the Pacific. Some of the Trustees were dubious about the value of participation in such a religiously unbalanced association, but Dr.

Burns persuaded them to support the College's membership. It would provide an *entree*, he was confident, to the executive offices of San Francisco corporations.

As one of the first presidents of the Foundation, Dr. Burns was soon at ease with the sisters and priests who directed the other colleges in the Foundation. He was surprised and sometimes amused to discover that the Catholic Church was not the monolithic body he had thought. He spent many days in San Francisco moving with them in pairs from one appointment to the other, pleading the cause of independent colleges, cajoling new donors, winning corporate support for liberal arts education. Mary Murphy Bertrand, then the general secretary of the Foundation, remembers his returning to the small office after a morning of such encounters, stretching out a line of straight-backed wooden chairs with a telephone book under his head, and falling sound asleep. Then, at the end of twenty or twenty-five minutes, he would awaken, completely refreshed, ready for an afternoon and evening of more meetings.

Dr. Burns' concern about independent higher education also led him in 1952 to accept membership on the Board of Trustees of the American Academy of Asian Studies. He was attracted as well by the program of the Academy; in his inaugural address as President of Pacific, he had spoken of the importance of developing better understanding with the peoples of the Orient, which was the central focus of the Academy's work. Louis P. Gainsborough, San Francisco importer and exporter, had founded the school in 1951. He, too, was convinced of the urgent need to build intellectual and cultural bridges with the East. By the spring of 1952, when the first meeting of the Board of Trustees was held, he had gathered together a small faculty and graduate students were already attending classes.

The Academy's major goals and its approach were described in its bulletin:

> The basis of all Asian life is spiritual and philosophical. It permeates the whole of Asian culture, entering into the smallest details of life to an extent which people born and bred in the modern West can hardly realize.
>
> For example, to attempt to study the Islamic countries without full courses on the Koran and the Prophet Moham-

med is as absurd as trying to understand American History in total ignorance of the principles of democracy. The same applies to studies in the Hindu and Buddhist areas.[14]

In addition to the emphasis on philosophical and religious studies, classes in Asian languages, in art, drama, music and the dance were offered because these cultural areas "come next in importance as fields of study for the understanding of the mentality of Asian peoples—playing a role at least as significant as radio, television and the cinema in modern America."[15]

Its founder hoped that the Academy would become "a nucleus for the expansion of Asian Studies" because he was shocked at the dearth of Asian programs in American colleges and universities. The program did indeed attract considerable attention, but by the fall of 1953 it had become apparent to Mr. Gainsborough and to the Trustees of the Academy that it would be strengthened—in its appeal to both students and donors—if it were affiliated with a larger institution. The school had a small but effective faculty; in addition to visiting Asian scholars the staff included such well-known personages as Rom Landau, English journalist and specialist in Islamic studies, and Alan Watts, internationally famous scholar and writer on Zen Buddhism. The staff taught for the Academy at a considerable financial sacrifice; however Mr. Gainsborough hoped to broaden the financial base to improve salaries and to gain accreditation through a merger with an older, established school.

He proposed to Dr. Burns that the Academy become affiliated with the College of the Pacific. Both men were sanguine about the potential benefits to each institution such an arrangement promised. Nevertheless, considerable discussion ensued. Mr. Gainsborough had to convince his staff that the Academy would remain autonomous in its control of "faculty appointments, courses, attitude, methods of teaching, etc." At the same time, Dr. Burns had to reassure his Board that the College would have "no financial obligation to the Academy." On April 6, 1954 the agreement was signed. The Academy continued to hold its classes in the four story mansion it had converted at 2030 Broadway, in the Pacific Heights district of San Francisco. But from that date, its degrees of Master of Arts and Doctor of Philosophy in the field of Asian Studies were awarded by the College of the Pacific, and a description of the

Academy's programs embellished the College's catalogue.

President Burns promised to help with the Academy's fund raising campaign. The immediate goal was for a minimum of $20,000 a year for three years to cover the deficits of the operation. With his typical energy and optimism, he outlined a program which called for an approach to the business concerns and steamship companies which had direct contact with Asia. Then the various ethnic group organizations, Asian consulates (and through them, their governments), the membership of the Council of World Affairs and other groups of internationally minded people were to be asked for support. Before much time had passed, however, it became apparent that the academy's needs had been underestimated, and that it was more difficult to raise funds than had been anticipated.

In 1956 an outside consultant, Mr. W. B. Simpson, was brought in to study the Academy's curriculum, staff, and administration. In his detailed, incisive report, he suggested two reasons for the lack of widespread public support of its programs. First, the Academy's emphasis on psychology and philosophy "is both a source of strength and weakness;" a source of strength because "it is in these aspects of Asian culture that the need for understanding Asia is perhaps the greatest, and that the contribution of Asia to our own way of life is most valuable." The report praised the Academy's pioneering work in these vital areas. At the same time, however, the emphasis constituted a source of weakness because these areas of study are not only "suspect in the minds of the general public" but also "come in for abuse" by more traditional Western scholars. [16] The Academy's staff was also accused of proselytizing.

> Compounding these difficulties in being fairly appraised by the public, the approach emphasized in some of the studies at the Academy maintains that Asian philosophy and psychology cannot be adequately appreciated with the detachment of a clinical technician—some amount of experimental involvement is essential. This approach tends automatically to be interpreted by many as one of religious involvement... [17]

All these factors contributed to the association of the Academy with the esoteric, and combined to form real barriers to the kind of public relations which would attract wealthy donors.

The consultant recommended that the Academy seek a better

balance in its programs by adding lecturers in the history, geography, sociology, economics and politics of Asia. Such additions, however, would entail considerable cost. Neither Dr. Burns, nor Mr. Gainsborough, nor the staff of the Academy were able to secure enough individual gifts and Foundation grants to subsidize the operation, to improve salaries, to expand the library, and to broaden the curriculum as the consultant recommended. Nor did President Burns or the Board of Trustees of the College believe that Pacific could underwrite the program; it had been clearly stated at the outset of the affiliation that Pacific would not be financially responsible for the Academy. The College's Board decided, therefore, to terminate the agreement on July 1, 1959. To continue the affiliation without the essential improvements, they feared, might jeopardize Pacific's own accreditation as a graduate school.

Another move during the early 1950s to expand the College's curriculum was more successful. In fact, the development of the School of Pharmacy constituted one of President Burns' finest accomplishments. Yet the inception of the idea might almost be called accidental. Jesse Rudkin was playing golf one day early in 1951 with a prosperous retired pharmacist, Jacob Rehfus. Like Dr. Burns, Mr. Rudkin seized every opportunity to find new donors for the College; almost at once, therefore, he began talking to his golfing partner about Pacific, suggesting that Mr. Rehfus donate money to support the work of the College. Mr. Rehfus evidently bridled at the suggestion. "The College of the Pacific doesn't have a School of Pharmacy and isn't training the pharmacists we need so badly here in the Valley. You develop a School of Pharmacy. Then I'll contribute." [18]

Later, Jesse Rudkin recounted this conversation to the President, but both of them were preoccupied at this point, trying to raise the money for the new library so desperately needed by the College. The idea lay dormant for about a year, until Dr. Emerson Cobb broached the possibility again. In 1948, when Dr. Cobb had come to Pacific, a mere fifteen students were enrolled in chemistry. His vigorous leadership had led to an improvement in facilities and an increase in enrollment, but he continued to look for ways to improve the department. Reasoning that pharmacy students were potential chemistry students, he suggested a plan to Dr. Burns for developing the project. Once again the conversation took place informally; the two men were on a hunting trip. President Burns, relaxed and unhurried, listened attentively and granted Dr. Cobb a different kind of hunting license: permission to look for moral and monetary support for a School of Pharmacy.

Dr. Cobb began by discussing the idea with local pharmacists. Angelo Sanguinetti, Leon Happell and Edna Gleason were among those with whom he conferred at this preliminary stage. They confirmed Mr. Rehfus's judgment that California's two existing pharmacy schools (one at the University of Southern California and the other at the University of California, San Francisco) were not training enough pharmacists. Especially needed were young graduates willing to locate in rural areas and in the burgeoning communities of the Central Valley. These local pharmacists were convinced that the profession would contribute monetary support to such an undertaking. They persuaded the President of the California Pharmaceutical Association to conduct a survey to determine the need for an additional pharmacy school in California, so that they could focus attention on the proposal at professional meetings of pharmacists.

John D. Crummey served as President of the Board during early discussions of the School of Pharmacy, from 1952-1953.

The Committee's report on the results of its survey were discussed at the meeting of the Northern California Pharmaceutical Association meeting in July, 1954. The survey of existing pharmaceutical educational facilities had led the study group to the

Dr. Ivan W. Rowland, second from right, was welcomed to the campus in 1956 by (from left) Leon Happel, Stockton pharmacist, Martin Winton, Fresno pharmacist, and President Burns.

conclusion that they could not be expanded sufficiently to meet the need for pharmacy students in the next decade. Dr. Burns, Dr. Cobb, and Mr. Sanguinetti were also present at the meeting to present their plans for a School of Pharmacy at the College of the Pacific, which had been recommended by the pharmacists' survey as an institution with the right location, with the necessary preliminary physical facilities and staff, and with the interest in developing such a school. The representative from the established schools countered these statements. He argued defensively but eloquently before the assembled pharmacists, assuring them that California's pharmacists were well served by the two established schools and that no new institutions were needed.

A pharmacist from Fresno, Mr. Martin Winton, responded at once, and with some feeling. He told of registering work opportunities at the two schools and then waiting for as long as five years before finding assistant pharmacists who would come to the Valley. He moved that the Association give immediate encouragement and support to the College of the Pacific in the development of a new School of Pharmacy. Mr. Winton spoke so forcefully that the motion passed unanimously. (Even the representative of the older schools had to admit the strength of the arguments presented.) Mr. Winton then pledged his personal interest in the plan with the first monetary contribution, $1,000. Mr. George J. Filpi, Mr. William E. McCown, Mr. Edward J. Burke, and Mr. Louis Shoneff, partners in the Valley Wholesale Drug Company in Stockton, were among the other early supporters of the project. A few months later, after being assured that the facility would have adequate space (the junior college would no longer be using classrooms in Weber Hall) and that the program would pay for itself through tuition income, the Trustees of the College voted to establish the School of Pharmacy at their meeting (March 22, 1955).

Dr. Burns and Dean Bertholf immediately set out to find a dean for the School. They traveled extensively and among others, interviewed the dean of Idaho State University's School of Pharmacy. Dr. Ivan W. Rowland had not applied for the job, but had been recommended by local pharmacists, a number of whom had had to go as far away as Idaho for their training. Dean Rowland hesitated to take the position. The School of Pharmacy at Idaho was one of the strongest in the West—with new facilities and an excellent faculty. He had visited the College of the Pacific and was disturbed by the fact that pharmacy classes would share the only science facility on campus with the College's chemistry and biology departments. But President Burns asked him a troubling question when they met in July at the School of Pharmacy in Pocatello:

> You don't want to sit here in a place like this. How will you ever know whether you're worth anything or not if you sit here in the shadows of the two deans who have preceded you? That history has already been made; this is all to be done here. If you come to Pacific and establish a School of Pharmacy, you'll know in short order whether you've got what it takes or you're a dismal failure. It's the challenge of a lifetime.[19]

After their conversation, Dean Rowland was unable to dismiss the challenge from his mind.

Robert Burns had the uncanny sense of the good executive for choosing the right man for the job and then finding ways to get that person to the College of the Pacific. On numerous occasions he telephoned reluctant or hesitant appointees in the midst of the academic year. "How is the weather back there?" he would ask, and then proceed to describe the balmy warmth, the blue skies, the blossoming camellias outside his California window. In Dr. Rowland's case, it was not this invitation to sunny California but rather the challenge which constituted exactly the right approach. A month after the interview, late in August of 1955, he capitulated; when Dr. Burns called to ask for his decision he accepted the position as Dean of the new School of Pharmacy.

Clearly the President had known whom he wanted for the post; and in the end his energetic, intrepid pursuit was successful. He risked a good deal in waiting for the Idaho Dean to accept the position; the pharmacy program was begun in September of 1955 with sixteen pre-pharmacy students and without its Dean, who arrived in February of 1956. That the President's choice had been a sage one is indicated by the phenomenal success and growth of the Pharmacy School. Within four years the enrollment had reached a peak of 250 students.

But the success of the professional school is also the product of the President's openness to new ideas, his willingness to give Dr. Cobb the green light to go ahead with the project, and finally his decisive action when the program became feasible. Robert Burns was an opportunist—not for himself but for the College. When an opportunity presented itself to add to the strength and prestige of Pacific, he seized it. Some of these ventures, this pioneering of new territory, led to dead-end trails for the College, as did the Academy for Asian Studies. But in the School of Pharmacy Dr. Burns discovered a highroad which not only led innumerable students to serve the State of California as pharmacists, but also the College of the Pacific to expand in the area of professional education.

In spite of all these distractions, both Dr. Burns and Jesse Rudkin had worked throughout the early 1950s to raise funds for that badly needed facility, the new library. The Trustees and the administration were notable for their fiscal conservatism; construction of the $400,000 building was not begun until the money was in hand. That goal was reached early in 1954, and in September of 1955, the Irving Martin Library was ready for the use of students and faculty. It was a great day for the academic community; for the first time, the College housed its library collection in a building specifically and solely designed for that purpose. Accrediting committees which visited the College that fall took due note of the improvement and praised the new facility.

The plural "committees" is used with some reason; as a matter of fact, the College was inundated by groups of accreditors during the last months of 1955. The Visiting Committee of the Western College Association, the Survey Committee authorized by the University Senate of the Methodist Church, the Committee on Accreditation of the California State Board of Education, and the Engineers' Council for Professional Development studied the College's facilities and programs that fall. All but the last (because of the small staff and limited curriculum of the Engineering Department) recommended that the College be accredited and praised the improvements which had been made since the last visits of their respective bodies. Of the reports made by those accrediting teams, that of the Methodist group was by far the most extensive and intensive in its analysis of the College's strengths and weaknesses. Like the 1931 survey, the *Report* issued in January 1956, contains striking evidence of the continuing educational concern of the Methodist Church, its determination that affiliated institutions achieve the highest possible standards.

The *Report* is 209 pages long and its thirteen chapters analyze all aspects of the College's operation: its history and aims, its administration, the faculty and curriculum, the library and the rest of the physical plant, the student body and personnel services, "religious cultivation," the business management of the College, and finally, its public relations and finance. Altogether the document is remarkable for its critical balance; while not minimizing the problem areas, it nevertheless registers high praise for many facets of Pacific's academic, social and religious life. It commended, for example, the accessibility of the chief administrative offices, and the "friendly and helpful" informality which characterized the relationships between the President, the faculty, and the students. It recommended, however, that the faculty be given more formal opportunities to study and affect educational policy.

The survey team was impressed with the low turnover and high morale of the faculty, in part attributable to the "sound" and "cooperative" relationships between the faculty and "the deans'

114

offices, the library, the business office, and the maintenance office."[20] In the questionnaire filled out by faculty members, respondents also "commented especially on the full measure of academic freedom the faculty enjoys."[21] The *Report* commended the Board of Trustees and the administration of the College for its protection and furtherance of free inquiry because "Not only is intellectual freedom for faculty and students essential in an educational institution whose purpose is to seek, to teach and to speak the truth; it is the very foundation of democratic government."[22] On the other hand, the College was criticized for the low scale of faculty compensation, and the *Report* particularly recommended that more generous provisions for retirement be arranged.

While praising the educational achievements of the faculty, the survey team strongly urged the administration to strengthen the liberal arts, the general education curriculum offered by the College. They questioned the value of certain graduate programs and some of the College's vocational courses and specialized curricula. It was suggested that proliferation in these expensive fields (e.g. engineering, pharmacy, business administration) could lead to a weakening of that central core of the College's offerings in the liberal arts. The *Report* acknowledged that these programs had been initiated to attract students, and it noted with favor the fact that Pacific had not suffered the degree of enrollment decline so many schools had. At the same time, however, the visiting scholars questioned whether or not the College's staff had a clear vision of its function as a liberal arts institution. The curriculum of the Department of Religion, they recommended, could also benefit from a reexamination of goals and a paring of the many small, expensive courses.

The survey team was favorably impressed with the new library but unfavorably impressed with the students' failure to use the new facility. This factor, coupled with relatively low median scores on national tests for students, led the committee to urge as strongly as possible that academic standards be enhanced by raising admission and graduation requirements and by strengthening the College's intellectual atmosphere. A better sabbatical program was recommended, so that faculty members could keep abreast of new developments in their disciplines and explore new interdisciplinary methods of teaching. But the *Report* also cited the importance of extracurricular activities—more effective use of the chapel services could contribute to a heightened intellectual awareness on campus, as would attendance at the College's unusually fine theatrical and musical performances.

The criticisms of the College's academic life reflected not only the opinions of the visiting scholars but also the responses of alumni and students. The questionnaires revealed additionally that these groups agreed with the survey team in seriously questioning the College's expenditures for intercollegiate athletics, especially football. Contrary to the President's view of the sport, a good deal of "strong student opinion" had been expressed that "the present football program is more divisive than unifying, and that the College is not in fact keeping the program under control."[23] The survey committee concurred in this "widely held" opinion. "While not opposing intercollegiate athletics, the survey committee does reject the interpretation of the president that the College would be as deeply involved financially in a limited intercollegiate program as in the present big-time effort."[24] Citing the tremendous cost of the wide-flung travel schedule and the annual expense of so many full athletic scholarships, the *Report* asked whether the money expended every year for football (more than $150,000 in 1953-54) might not be better spent in improved faculty salaries, etc. "The survey staff is unanimous in its judgment that the current football emphasis is dangerous and inappropriate to an institution like the College of the Pacific."[25]

The *Report* included high commendation for the generally improved financial condition of the College. Although critical of some aspects of the business management (the investment of endowment funds in dormitories, the lack of a centralized purchasing office, etc.), the survey staff praised the improvements that had been made in accounting records and in the planning of the budget. The visitors expressed astonishment at the remarkable increase in gifts and bequests to the institution—from $175,334 in 1950-51 to $726,138 in 1953-54. Complimenting the President on this achievement, the survey team stated its belief that Robert Burns "by training and aptitude is unusually well qualified for work in public relations and finance." This was in marked contrast, they noted, to the situation in many private colleges "where the chief administrative officer is either blind to the necessity for a good public relations program or lacks skill in presenting the financial needs of the college to its constituency."[26]

President Burns could indeed be proud of the financial support he had gained for the College. As a result of his indefatigable enthusiasm for his alma mater, the College had reached a position of financial strength unknown in its 104-year history. The Survey *Report* concluded, nevertheless, with the warning that the endowment fund must be increased substantially if the College were to survive hard times. Although new dormitory facilities were recognized as being vitally and immediately needed, the writers urged the Board of Trustees to delay other building plans until the goal of sufficient endowment had been reached. The *Report* recommended strongly, in fact, that future growth (in students, in curriculum, in faculty) be limited and that the College instead consolidate and strengthen its already existent programs—especially in the liberal arts. As the only church-related liberal arts school in the Central Valley, the College should fulfill its singular function and avoid moving into competition with larger public and private institutions.

Altogether, the recommendations of the Methodist Survey Committee are remarkable for their insight and evince a great deal of careful and deliberate research. But the conservatism of their concluding recommendations is curiously at odds with the times. Were the visiting scholars unaware of the pressures to be exerted on college enrollments by the phenomenal post-war "baby boom?" Especially in California, the impetus toward growth would be almost irresistible. They seemed to fail also to take into account the inexorable growth in costs and the corresponding need of the College for more students, more tuition income. Perhaps most importantly, however, they were mistaken in their appraisal of the College's leadership. Even a cursory examination of events, of new buildings, of organizations joined, of people contacted during the first nine years of Dr. Burns' presidency should have led them to the realization of his phenomenal energy, his singleminded, absolute commitment to the College's aggrandizement. The Survey team might as well have told the tide to stop rising in the Delta as to tell Robert Burns to limit his dreams for the College of the Pacific.

117

Chapter Five

ON FEBRUARY 25, 1957, 600 friends of the College and its President gathered at the Stockton Civic Auditorium to celebrate the first ten years of Robert Burns' administration. Governor Goodwin Knight was there to pay tribute to Burns' contribution to the State of California, and Senator Alan Short, a Pacific alumnus, presented Dr. Burns with a congratulatory resolution from the State Senate. Chancellor Knoles spoke of the difficult challenges which the President had already faced: the sudden explosion of enrollment following World War II; the corresponding decline during the early fifties; the transition to the full four-year curriculum. "The difficulties he will face in the next ten years," the Chancellor predicted, "are the problems of expansion."[1]

Speakers referred to Dr. Burns' service to the community of Stockton, his membership in professional, service, religious and educational organizations. Everyone acknowledged, though, that "first and last he is Bob Burns of Pacific." The President agreed. "After all," he said, "the College has been my life, and I must confess my decisions revolve around the advances of this institution and what it stands for in California life. I live it and breathe it, and I know of no higher purpose to which I could devote my time."[2]

He praised Jesse Rudkin and the development staff for their aid in garnering millions of dollars in gifts for the college—gifts which had made possible the erection of fifteen new buildings and the inception of many new projects: the Pacific Marine Station, the School of Pharmacy, the Fallon House Theater, the California History Foundation. The importance of these new developments was indicated by the fact that during the first ten years of Dr. Burns' presidency, enrollment had climbed by fifty percent. Even greater growth was projected as the students from the post-war "baby boom" came of age. He informed his listeners that "Pacific may have to spawn a new college or colleges if private church-related higher education is to keep pace with dynamic Northern California."[3]

Having been a member of the first group of travelers to tour post-war Russia during the summer of 1956, the President was aware—even before Sputnik was launched—that the Russians were moving into a position of scientific and technological superiority. "The United States may be falling behind educationally," he warned. To meet this challenge independent schools like Pacific, "which have produced some of the most revolutionary changes in education," would explore new ways to bring knowledge to the students. As a Methodist college, Pacific was determined to meet high intellectual standards and at the same time to communicate "moral and spiritual values" to its students.[4]

Just a few days before this honorary event, the faculty retreat had been the scene of discussions on how to achieve the goals enunciated by the President. Seven committees which had been formed to study the Methodist survey *Report* submitted their recommendations to the faculty at large. That the report had served as a provocative stimulant to careful examination of problems is indicated in the detailed, specific responses to the questions it raised. The Committee on Aims, Control and Organization, for example, responded to the *Report*'s criticism of the "vague" statement of goals with the following summary of the objectives of the College:

> That the aims and objectives of the College of the Pacific be summarized as follows:
> a. The College of the Pacific is a private, coeducational college offering work on the undergraduate and graduate levels. Its courses of study are designed to provide (a) a comprehensive liberal arts education, and (b) pre-professional and professional education in selected fields. We believe that this dual program is academically and socially desirable and ought to be maintained.
> b. The College was founded on the Christian faith, and is dedicated to Christian principles; and although related to the Methodist Church, it welcomes students of all religious faiths. It seeks to keep close contact with the churches, believing that much help can be derived by both the college and the churches from such contacts.
> c. Emphasis shall be given to quality in academic program, scholarship, and selection of student body.

d. Our immediate policy should be to strengthen the College's present educational program and to upgrade its present plant, faculty, staff, salaries, and financial foundations. This should take precedence over expansion into new curricula, programs, and activities which will retard the realization of these purposes. This does not preclude expansion into any new desirable area as soon as ample resources are available to establish and maintain a high quality program.

e. The College should remain a comparatively small institution having classes of small enrollment, where most students live on campus, thereby deriving values typical of the small institution.

f. An appraisal of the present total resources of the College suggests that we should aim for a well-balanced student body of about 1,750 full-time students. This figure is necessarily tentative and should be the subject of further careful study.

g. The College believes in a friendly mutuality between students and faculty, and in a salutary program of student activities.[5]

It is interesting to note that as early as 1956 the faculty perceived Pacific's role in "professional education." The Committee also agreed with the *Report's* suggestion that the Dean of the College be made the chief academic administrator—to eliminate the sometimes competitive relationship between the Dean of the College, the Conservatory, the School of Education, and the School of Pharmacy.

The group urged, furthermore, that the structure and function of faculty committees be examined, "with an eye to reducing the number and simplifying..."[6] It is apparent, however, throughout the summary of recommendations, that although the faculty desired fewer committees, they wanted more participation in the decision-making process of the College. The study committee on the faculty proposed "that new departments and new schools may be established, and old departments and old schools may be abolished only after such proposals have been discussed at a general faculty meeting called only for that purpose."[7] The Curriculum and Instruction Committee affirmed that principle even more strongly, recommending "that a new curriculum may be added to the present program of the College only after careful study and consideration by the *faculty* have shown that the proposed curriculum is feasible in terms of academic status, staff, prospective enrollment, and financial resources."[8] The Committee on Financial Management recommended that a new committee composed of elected faculty members and administration appointees, be established "with the responsibility of studying building requests, priorities, and opportunities to purchase property adjacent to the campus and recommending action through the President to the Board of Trustees."[9]

The faculty's determination to affect policy is also reflected in the nine pages of specific recommendations regarding curriculum, faculty status, student counseling, and other areas of concern. The Committee on Faculty urged that "administrative duties and responsibilities be more specifically defined and published."[10] Another sign of the growing desire for a more formalized relationship between the administration and faculty can be seen in the proposal that if reports and recommendations of a committee are sent to the appropriate administrative officer, "a *written* reply be returned by him *within a reasonable time* to the committee indicating that the administration has read and acted, favorably or unfavorably."[11]

Challenged by the Methodist Survey Team to raise academic standards, the faculty responded with specific proposals relating to probationary status, admission and graduation requirements. They recommended a restudy of grading standards and the requirements for directed or independent study. Development of more effective use of the library was high on the faculty's priority list, as was improvement of counseling procedures "looking toward the stronger motivation of students for scholarly achievement."[12] To assure their own competence, the faculty urged that the College promote a study of its liberal arts objectives and a periodic reevaluation of the graduate program and specialized instructional activities. They urged the administration to encourage faculty research projects.

The discussion of these questions, in itself, led to the accomplishment of one of the goals sought by the survey team. President Burns subsequently reported to the Trustees that faculty morale was "at an all time high, due in part to the survey and the resulting study of our College problems."[13] Even more importantly, the

122

survey served generally as a gadfly, a goad to higher achievement. Many of the events in the development of the College during the following years can be seen as direct responses to the recommendations in the Methodist *Report.*

The Faculty Club (an informal organization which arranged social gatherings two or three times a year) invited the Trustees to "an evening of fellowship" on March 25, 1957 to discuss the faculty's response to the survey. In its membership and its leadership the Board had experienced considerable change during the ten years Robert Burns had been President of the College. At the March 1952 meeting John D. Crummey had succeeded Olin D. Jacoby as President of the Board. But ill health forced Mr. Crummey to resign in November of 1953. The College was sorry to lose his guidance. "His life-long devotion to the Church, his world-wide philanthropies, his connection with the business interests of his denomination and his abundant social graces qualified him as a dependable and able administrator in a Christian college." [14] Another active churchman, Ted Baun, then became the President of the Board. In fact, church membership was an important qualification for Board membership. As a result, the Trustees shared many of the faculty's concerns, their Christian values, and it was not difficult for the two groups to reach general agreement on the educational principles proposed by the Methodist survey team. At the April 23rd meeting of the faculty, Dr. Bertholf announced that many of their recommendations had been accepted by the Board and that others had been sent to appropriate committees for further study and implementation.

A sign of that acceptance lay in the fact that before the Department of Engineering was elevated to the status of the School of Engineering, the faculty discussed the change. After being assured that the move would not engender any new costs and that it was being made primarily to satisfy the engineering accreditation board, the faculty assented to the name change, and in June of 1958 Dr. Burns announced the development. To head the new School, Dr. Adelbert Diefendorf, retired Dean of the School of Engineering at the University of Utah, was appointed. The engineering classes had already been moved into what had formerly been the library building. Dr. Burns recommended to the Trustees that this building be named Baun Hall, in honor of their President.

A graduate of the Class of 1927, Ted Baun was one of a number of successful alumni of the engineering program at the College of the Pacific: he had established the Baun Construction Company in Fresno. Both he and his wife, Alice, shared continuing affection for and loyalty to Pacific. Their three children (two of whom, like their father, were engineering majors) attended the College. The Bauns had been generous not only in their monetary gifts but also in the hours and hours spent in meetings for the benefit of the College. In fact, Ted Baun's friendship, his counsel in practical matters, his integrity and Christian faith were to be of vital and influential significance throughout Burns' life. The two worked well together, and Dr. Burns' recognition of the honor his colleague deserved can be seen in the naming of Baun Hall. For the fledgling School of Engineering, it was surely a good omen that one of Pacific's own engineers should be so closely involved with the College's development.

The formation of the engineering school, though it was accomplished in accordance with the Survey's proposal that the faculty discuss new developments, was nevertheless another step away from the concentration on the liberal arts which the survey team strongly recommended and toward university structure. So was the appointment in April of 1957 of Dean Bertholf as Academic Vice President to coordinate the work of the separate schools. The *Report* had been quite clear in delineating the choices to be made.

1. If the institution chooses to develop the close knit, relatively simple organization of the "college," the deans of the specialized schools should be made responsible to the dean of the college....

2. If the institution chooses to develop along the university lines toward which it is now tending an executive dean should be named to whom the dean of the college as well as the deans of the specialized schools will be responsible.[15]

Although the Academic Vice President continued to act as dean of the college, the nomenclature clearly reflected movement toward university structure.

Dr. Bertholf was not to hold the title for long. In October of 1957, Dr. Burns announced that Pacific's new Vice President had been elected President of Illinois Wesleyan University, and that

124

Dr. Bertholf would leave in July of 1958 to assume his new position. Both the faculty and the administration were sorry to see him leave. As Dean, he had encouraged the faculty in its fledgling attempts to participate in the decision-making process of the College. A devout Christian, Dr. Bertholf had founded the Faculty Christian Fellowship on campus, a group which met weekly for prayer and discussion of the College's Biblical heritage. The faculty trusted him as an honest, humane, scholarly leader—a man whose sense of humor frequently de-fused potentially explosive arguments.

The Methodist constituency of the College would also miss Lloyd Bertholf. As Lay Leader in the Conference he had established warm relationships with ministers and laymen throughout Northern California and Nevada. As a result, the Conference had voted significant increases in the amount of its annual contribution to the College. And prominent churchmen, convinced of the importance of the College's work through their association with Dr. Bertholf, became extremely generous in their support of Pacific as the only Protestant, church-related school in Northern California.

Dr. Bertholf had ably demonstrated the importance of the position of Dean of the College and Academic Vice President. Careful attention was given to the selection of his successor. In compliance with the Methodist Survey's suggestion, committees delegated by the Board of Trustees and the faculty held meetings to discuss the qualifications to be sought in the new administrator. Dr. Samuel Meyer, who like Dr. Bertholf was highly recommended by the Director of the Methodist Board of Education, evidently fitted the description. Later, Dr. Meyer remembered his first conversation with Dr. Burns:

> I was the Dean of Central Methodist College in Missouri, and one evening as my wife and family and I were having dinner the telephone rang. The voice at the other end of the line said, "This is Robert Burns and I'm President of the College of the Pacific. Our Academic Vice President is going to leave us to become President of Illinois Wesleyan University. Would you have any interest in being considered for the position of Academic Vice President at the College of the Pacific?" [16]

"Well, I really had no interest in being considered for anything right at that moment,"[17] Dr. Meyer recalled. He had only been at Central College for three years. It was his undergraduate alma mater, and the town in which it was located his home town. After years of teaching and research at Emory, Tennessee and Florida State Universities, he had returned to Central fully expecting to spend the rest of his professional career there. But Dr. Burns was persuasive, and "the possibilities were intriguing."[18] Dr. Meyer agreed to a meeting with the President in Chicago and subsequently to a meeting with the faculty and trustee committees in Stockton. A few days later Robert Burns telephoned Central's Dean again—this time to offer him the job.

Dr. Meyer accepted. He had been impressed with Dr. Burns' description of the role which he envisioned for the future of the College, and the concern which he had expressed about improving the academic life of the institution. The new Academic Vice President arrived in Stockton in June of 1958, ready to plunge into his new duties. For although he and Dr. Bertholf shared Christian values and intellectual interests (both were biologists), the two men were at opposite poles in personality and style of leadership. Unlike Dr. Bertholf's gentle persuasiveness, Dr. Meyer's manner was dynamic, and sometimes brusque. He brought to the position a critical intelligence which was to be an essential factor in strengthening the faculty. He and Dr. Burns agreed that "the measure of an institution's greatness is the measure of the greatness of its faculty."[19]

The new Vice President enlisted the help of students in the "pursuit of excellence," and the students responded with considerable enthusiasm. Sixty-seven seniors and five juniors met with twenty-two faculty members representing all departments at a Columbia retreat to discuss "teachers who are echoes of the text, student attitudes and study habits, campus conditions influencing study."[20] Although they agreed that disgruntled students should "talk to faculty members instead of going back to their living groups and complaining about them,"[21] the student representatives circulated teacher rating forms which Dr. Meyer promised would be "studied carefully."

Teaching effectiveness was, in fact, the first qualification Dr. Meyer looked for in new faculty members. But the Academic Vice

126

President also believed that research is "the normal and natural outgrowth of good teaching," so he encouraged all faculty members to engage in continuing study. In the course of his first general faculty meeting in the fall of 1958 he suggested that "some faculty members seek out small colleges to escape competition." Such a refuge would not be available at Pacific, he warned, for "we can not fail to add to our intellectual stature by study and research." [22]

Dr. Meyer believed that Pacific had an "unique opportunity in fulfilling its role as an institution emphasizing not only academic quality but at the same time academic and spiritual values." [23] But he did not include active church membership as one of the essential qualifications in new faculty appointments, as his predecessor had. When the Trustees asked Dr. Bertholf the question "How does our church relationship make us different?" he had replied that "It is in the attitude of our teachers toward religion. Faculty may react in three ways: 1. No relation to religion. 2. Distinctively religious. 3. Christian in presentation. We expect our faculty to be on levels two or three." [24] Insertion of dogmatic, unrelated religious material in their lectures had always been actively discouraged; nevertheless, faculty members had the primary responsibility—through their dedication to teaching, their openness and friendliness toward students, through their personal integrity, and their participation in religious activity—of communicating the Judeo-Christian heritage and value system to the students. To reinforce that religious orientation of the faculty, friends of Bishop Tippett had established the annual Tippett Lectures in 1956 so that each year a distinguished scholar delivered an address on religion and higher education.

By the late 1950s, however, many members of the Pacific family who had upheld this tradition, who had in fact embodied it, had retired or were deceased. Mr. Ritter and Dr. Farley left in 1953. Herbert Jonte, whose annual geological study trips to Death Valley had for decades been a highlight of the College's year, retired in 1957. Dr. E. E. Stanford, the nationally known scholar in biology, retired in 1959, as did Wilhelmina Harbert, the founder of Pacific's music therapy program.

The whole community was shocked and sorrowed by the death of Dr. George Colliver in December of 1957. Generations of Pacific students acknowledged the significance of his Bible classes in the formation of their spiritual values. Delivering the eulogy, Chan-

127

cellor Knoles remembered Dr. Colliver's outspoken defense of social justice and his condemnation of bigotry and prejudice. Soon after the College moved to Stockton, a Ku Klux Klan-style cross had been burned near the campus, and an anonymous caller had threatened worse damage if Dr. Colliver were not fired. Neither the President nor the religion professor was intimidated, though; for over thirty years, even apathetic students were aroused by his teaching. Not long after his death the Colliver Lectures were established—to continue his work.

The community mourned *en masse* two years later when Dr. Knoles died. The Chancellor had played such a critical role in the College's history. His bold, intelligent leadership during his twenty-seven years as President, his popularity as a public speaker, his profound faith, had molded the character of Pacific. Even after his resignation from the presidency, his influence had been considerable. As Chancellor, Tully Knoles personified the spirit of the Methodist school he had nurtured through the difficult years of the move from San Jose, the depression and World War II. Many friends of the College perceived in his passing the end of an era.

In some aspects of the College's life they were correct. By the fall of 1959 the faculty appointments to replace retiring or deceased members of the Pacific family were bright young Ph.D.'s—whose religious affiliation was no longer a factor considered in their hiring. Instead the College depended on the courses offered by the religion department, the Anderson Y, which had traditionally been the focus of Christian social action and recreation on campus, and on its new Director of Religious Activities, to sustain the religious traditions of the College. Thus, what was to become a revolutionary change in the basic ethos of the College was generated by policy decisions effected coincident with Dr. Knoles' death.

Yet it was not just the religious life of the campus that was affected by the change. Shared belief in the Protestant tradition, along with joint participation in church activities, had constituted a major factor in the unity of the faculty, their loyalty to the whole College. But from this time on the bright young secular scholars who came to Pacific were to owe their primary loyalties to their academic disciplines—history, English, psychology, etc.—and not to the institution as a whole. Never again would the term "Pacific Family" be as apt a description of the relationships between mem-

128

bers of the Pacific community. The death of its patriarch Tully Knoles can, therefore, be seen as symbolic of the beginning of the end of the sense of extraordinarily close kinship which had previously characterized associations within the institution.

It would be a mistake, however, to read into these changes solely College of the Pacific phenomena. The movement toward secularization and specialization was apparent in many schools and colleges. Nor was there a sudden, abrupt deterioration of the faculty's sense of unity. For a number of years the older faculty members, those who had experienced and enjoyed the family community, outnumbered the new additions to the staff. Furthermore, some important executive positions were accorded during the late 1950s to loyal members of the "Family." A case in point— when John Elliott resigned as Dean of the Conservatory, J. Russell Bodley was appointed to the post. The new dean had received his bachelor degrees in music and art from the College when it was still in San Jose. Subsequently, he studied for a year in France and at the Eastman School of Music, where he earned his Master's degree. But he had spent the rest of his professional life at Pacific as professor of theory and choral director—a position he continued to hold even after he became Dean because his talented singers attracted much favorable attention to Pacific. The concerts they performed at Christmas and Easter drew standing-room-only audiences, and their singing at the College's weekly chapel services imbued those assemblies with a beauty and grace unusual in student gatherings.

When he was an undergraduate, Robert Burns had sung in Mr. Bodley's quartet and in the college choir. Later he had traveled with them on his recruiting forays. The President was well acquainted with the capability of the professor and singing master. He was genuinely pleased, therefore, when the search committee, after considering a number of applications, determined that Russell Bodley was the best man for the post. During his ten years as Dean, the Conservatory continued to fulfill its role in music education for its students and in aesthetic education for the entire campus community.

Another promotion from within the ranks of the Pacific family took place when Robert Winterberg was appointed Business Manager on June 15, 1957. (Later, he became financial Vice President.)

129

Dr. Robert R. Winterberg
Financial Vice President

Like Dr. Burns, Robert Winterberg went to work for the College immediately after he had received his degree from its Business Administration Department. He had worked under Mr. Ritter, and after returning from Korean War service had been Assistant Business Manager under Dr. Dale. He was, therefore, thoroughly familiar with the College's financial operation. That experience, together with the fact that he was an active Methodist layman and "a man of the highest moral character," [25] made it easy for the Trustees to affirm his nomination by Dr. Burns. For the remainder of his presidency Dr. Burns depended on Robert Winterberg for the efficient and intelligent management of the College's business affairs and for that tireless dedication and loyalty to Pacific's cause that Robert Burns himself personified.

The work of the financial administrator had become increasingly complex since the early years of Robert Burns' presidency. The following chart shows the increases in enrollment, income and expenses between 1947 and 1958.

	Equated Full-Time Enrollment	Total Educational Income (Excl. Gifts) (1000s)	Instruc. Expense (1000s)	Total Educational Expense (1000s)
1947-48	740	506.7	306.3	638.9
1948-49	940	593.2	406.1	835.3
1949-50	959	664.7	386.0	805.2
1950-51	887	598.2	366.8	840.4
1951-52	970	692.5	404.6	820.0
1952-53	862	614.6	363.7	820.9
1953-54	860	646.4	367.3	853.2
1954-55	926	897.9	492.7	1,073.7
1955-56	1,233	995.2	578.5	1,197.1
1956-57	1,278	1,095.8	705.8	1,345.9
1957-58	1,391	1,254.6	801.6	1,525.9
1958-59	1,534	1,511.8	930.0	1,766.1

The value of campus assets had increased from $1,600,000 to $6,100,000, but indebtedness had also increased—from $80,000 to $2,524,992. It had been incurred primarily to cover construction costs of the twenty new buildings on campus. This jump in the level of indebtedness disturbed some of the older, fiscally conservative Board members. But Mr. Winterberg pointed out that several of the new buildings were income-producing and that their mortgages were self-liquidating. The largest sums had been borrowed to build new residence halls.

No one doubted that the College needed new student living quarters. Even the Methodist Survey, which had generally urged a policy of endowment increase rather than more bricks and mortar, had strongly urged the College to build new dormitories. The residence halls, the *Report* pointed out, were overcrowded and were scarcely conducive to the quality of study which the College should demand. The Board, which had already recognized the

131

Largest residence hall on campus is named in honor of the late Regent Mrs. Grace A. Covell, one of the most generous benefactors in the history of the College.

need, moved quickly. By the fall of 1956 South and West Halls had been joined, providing space for eighty more girls.

Even this addition, however, had not satisfied the College's increasing need for new residences. An important element in its attractiveness lay in its friendliness, the fact that most students lived on campus. Early in 1957, therefore, the Trustees applied for a government loan to build a new dormitory to house 400 girls. The new building, the largest on campus, was ready for occupancy in

September, 1958. It was a critically important addition to the College's facilities, enabling 210 men to move into South Hall from the quonset housing, which had always been considered inadequate and temporary. Anderson Dining Hall then became the men's dining room, and the dining hall in the new residence hall—later named in honor of the generous Trustee, Grace Covell—was the dining hall for women. Thus, for the first time on Pacific's campus there was sexually segregated dining for the residents of the dorms. To counteract what the staff feared would be a serious deterioration of table manners among the men, numerous exchange dinners were planned.

Further pressure on the budget was exerted by faculty needs. The College had received a Ford Foundation Grant in 1956 of $279,600 to endow salary increases. But early in 1958 the newly organized American Association of University Professors Chapter presented the Trustees with a study showing that Pacific's salaries were still far below those at equivalent institutions. As he described the next year's budget at the Board's June meeting, Dr. Burns explained that it was based on a projected enrollment of 1,500 (full time equivalent) and "an intermediate salary raise." If the enrollment surpassed the 1,500 figure, the President recommended "that a little higher salary increase should be given." [26] After some discussion, the Board voted in favor of the budget with the salary increment. It was the first time that salary increases were tied directly to enrollment increases. One can see in the unprecedented action the inexorable pressure toward growth that accompanied inflation.

The College appealed to its alumni for help in improving faculty salaries, and that group responded more generously than ever in its history. The ground work for the new dynamism had been laid in 1957 when meetings were held throughout the State to develop a new framework for the Alumni Association. A twofold proposal emerged from the discussions: first, that the Alumni association sponsor educational and social events; and second, that it encourage alumni giving to the College. The first goal was to be accomplished through the maintenance of the alumni office to promote and coordinate alumni activities, class reunions, Homecoming Day in the fall, Alumni College in the spring, and the summer camp at Silver Lake. The fourteen local clubs were to play an even more significant role in maintaining contact between the College and its alumni. Though primarily social, such clubs could also serve an educational function by inviting speakers from the College to address their meetings. "By this means we will be creating an extension of education, and though an alumnus may be quite removed from the classroom atmosphere, he can still participate in further learning through stimulating programs of his local alumni club." [27]

No membership dues would be charged henceforth, and all alumni would receive copies of the *Pacific Review*, published ten times a year. Instead of annual dues the alumni would be asked to contribute to the annual Alumni Fund. To administer this new financial program, an Alumni Fund Council was elected, and Rev. Donald Smiley of the Development Office was appointed Executive Director. By the spring of 1958 the Council had already sent letters to all the alumni and giving during that year was considerably higher than before. Encouraged, they embarked on an even more ambitious program for the following year. Monroe Hess, co-chairman of the Council with Marlitt Stark, challenged the Trustees at their October meeting to donate $1,000 for every percentage point of increase in the number of donors to the Fund. The Trustees accepted, and in October, 1959, an elated Alumni Council announced the results of the campaign. Over 300 volunteer workers had combined their efforts to achieve this goal, and their personal contacts with individual alumni had borne fruit. Participation had "soared from 6.2 to 26.4 percent, the total number of givers from 450 to 1,710 and the gross gift from $5,955 to $14,750." [28] The increases won a $20,000 bonus from the Trustees.

These results were encouraging in that they suggested a more dynamic program for the alumni would indeed result in more giving to their alma mater. But the results should not have been surprising. A statistical study of the graduates from 1925-1950 had indicated that alumni had fond memories of their student days at Pacific. Eighty-five percent of the 1,106 respondents had said they would choose the College again. Furthermore, large numbers of them (89.7%) contributed regularly to charitable enterprises. The task of Pacific's fund raisers, therefore, was simply to call to their attention the College's needs; it was made easier by the fact that so many alumni lived close to the College. In fact, the study had reaffirmed the importance of the College's role in educating young people for leadership positions in its own region. Over seventy percent of Pacific's graduates lived within a hundred mile radius of the campus. Their vocational choices were shown to be wide-ranging:

Education	34.9%
Business	25.6%
Homemaking	19.7%
Professions other than Education	14.0%
Graduate Study	5.1%
Unemployed	.4%
Retired	.2%

Nineteen Pacific graduates held significant positions in local government in Stockton.

The questionnaire which had been sent to alumni was based on one which had already been circulated by the editors of Time-Life. As a result some interesting comparisons could be drawn between the responses of college graduates in general and Pacific alumni. Given the religious affiliation of the College, the results studied most closely by its faculty and administration were those which measured values. Ninety-two percent of Pacific's graduates (as opposed to 82.6% of the Time-Life group) disagreed with the statement that "Religion has little to offer intelligent people today." Some other questions reveal less directly religious but nevertheless related value judgments of Pacific's alumni. (The following figures register the percent of respondents who agreed with the following statements.)

	Pacific	Time-Life
Over the next decade we must try to make the standard of living in the rest of the world rise more rapidly than in our own country.	83.8	57.5
Deep ideological differences between countries are reconcilable.	76.7	58.4
All Americans—Negroes, Jews, the foreign born and others—should have equal opportunities in social, economic, and political affairs.	93.2	80

	Pacific	Time-Life
Agitators and troublemakers are more likely to be foreign born citizens than native Americans.	83.9	53.4

Pacific graduates also registered strong affirmation of the importance of personal integrity and community responsibility. They showed much stronger disagreement with the following statements than did the Time-Life group:

	Pacific	Time-Life
If we allow more immigrants into this country we will lower our standard of culture.	86.1	69.3
Foreigners usually have peculiar and annoying habits.	90.1	67.5
Children of minority groups or other races should play among themselves.	94.6	86.1

No effort was made in the study to determine whether the attitudes were the result of the college experience; however, the faculty and administration of the Methodist College with its strong traditional emphasis on the "social Gospel," could well be pleased with this reflection of its graduates' values. [29]

The religious affiliation of the College had been, in fact, among the most important factors in the graduates' choice of Pacific. Forty-two percent of the respondents had been raised in Methodist families, 46.4 percent in other Protestant denominations; ten percent were Catholic, nine-tenths percent Jewish, and six-tenths percent "other." Other reasons cited by graduates as significant factors in their choice of the College were its convenience of location, academic standing, "the friendliness of campus living" and small size.

In these descriptions of their rationale for choosing Pacific, the alumni in general mirrored the reasoning of the President of the College. Robert Burns, the first Pacific alumnus to become President, spoke frequently of the significance of the College's academic life, its religious training, friendliness and smallness in the formation of his own values. All of these factors continued to be important, in fact—leading to his decision to stay at Pacific. In 1958 he was offered the presidency of Ohio Wesleyan University, and the Executive Directorship of the National Council of Christians

136

and Jews. Both jobs would have offered significant increases in salary, but Dr. Burns rejected them. His loyalty to his alma mater was all-encompassing; he was determined to lead Pacific into a new era of greatness.

At the same time, he was concerned that the values of personalized education which had so affected his own life not be lost. As it became more and more apparent that unprecedented numbers of young people were seeking a college education and that a significant portion of these desired the kind of academic milieu which Pacific offered, the question was raised frequently among faculty and administration of the optimum size for the College. The recommendation of the faculty after their study of the Methodist Survey was that the figure 1,750 be projected as the maximum enrollment. President Burns and the Trustees had agreed. But toward the end of the decade, more and more highly qualified students were clamoring for admission. That phenomenon, together with the inflationary pressures on the fiscal solvency of the institution, led its President to seek new resolutions of the problem.

As early as 1957 Dr. Burns had suggested the possibility of establishing new colleges at Pacific. By December of 1958 his concept of the new institution was more precise. At the meeting of the Board of Trustees Dr. Burns spoke of his concern that private church-related colleges would be "handling a lower and lower percentage of college students as the State institutions grow." [30] He suggested that the best way for Pacific to counter that trend would be "to establish another small related college of liberal arts, having the same administrative staff, and perhaps using some facilities jointly, much in the manner of Oxford University." [31] The new institution would require unusually high qualifications for admission and instruction would resemble the tutorial system of English universities. There would be a minimum of athletics and activities. At the same time he recommended that the Trustees consider buying the forty-three acre Stockton College campus for the new development. (The community college was hemmed in on all sides; and since it was anticipating additional growth, the Stockton School Board was looking for a new location.) Contiguous acreage across the Calaveras River might also be available. A Faculty-Trustee Committee on the Future of the College was delegated to study the idea.

137

On April 30, 1959, in keeping with the faculty's recommendation on policy making, a meeting of the faculty was called solely to discuss the new proposal for the institution's growth. President Burns opened the meeting with his statement that the biggest decision in the history of Pacific had been the decision to move from San Jose to Stockton. "The decision whether or not to purchase the Stockton College campus, and what use would be made of it if it were purchased could easily be the second most important decision."[32] He suggested two alternatives for the use of the new space should it be available: first, an enlargement of current programs; and second, the establishment of the new liberal arts college.

Considerable discussion ensued. A number of faculty members urged that instead of adding a new college that the institution raise funds for expansion and improvement of its already existing programs. But President Burns replied that it would be very difficult to stimulate interest for a mere expansion of facilities. "We must have something to sell which will stimulate the imagination—we must be visionary." Several of the faculty expressed the concern, however, that a new liberal arts college would necessarily compete with the College of the Pacific for students. Dean Betz recommended that "the sister institution" be different—an upper division and graduate school. Professor of Art Richard Reynolds suggested moving the School of Education and the Graduate School to the new area. Mr. Evans asked whether it might be possible to establish "a school of technology, which would not compete with our present offerings." But Dr. Burns was sure that there would be no difficulty in filling both institutions. The Director of Admissions, Elliott Taylor, reported that enrollment in State colleges was expected to double by 1965 and double again by 1970.[33]

Practical questions on finance were also raised at the meeting. The four million dollar estimated price tag on the new campus seemed reasonable, but when would the inadequate science facilities in Weber Hall be improved? When would an addition to the overcrowded library be built? Dr. Burns replied that in many instances, at Pomona, for example, more than one institution "instead of dissipating resources, increases those available." He assured the faculty that needed improvements on the Pacific campus would not be neglected. The meeting was adjourned, however, with a

138

President of the Board of Regents, Ted F. Baun, and his wife, Alice, at left, traveled to England with President and Mrs. Burns to study the "Oxbridge" system as a model for the new Cluster Colleges.

number of questions still pending. Further study by the Faculty-Trustee Committee would be necessary before the faculty as a body would assent to the new plan.

President Burns wanted to visit Oxford and Cambridge to study at first hand their system of allied colleges, and he asked the President of the Board to accompany him. Ted Baun was hesitant; he suggested that Sam Meyer go instead since he was the chief academic officer of the College. But Dr. Burns was adamant; he wanted the leading representative of the Trustees to experience with him the "Oxbridge" way. The two traveled to England, therefore, in September of 1959. They stayed in guest rooms of the colleges, visited tutorials and had long congenial conversations with Oxford and Cambridge dons. They came home convinced that a new college based on the "Oxbridge" model would be sufficiently different that it would not detract from the older college. Robert Burns, especially, was excited; such an innovative, academically oriented institution would bring splendid new prestige to his alma mater.

When he returned to the campus the President formulated the plan for "cluster colleges" in specific terms and then set out at once to convince the faculty and the Trustees of its promise. He reminded them of the critical role which had traditionally been played by America's independent colleges. They must continue to play that role, he argued. Because they could not compete with public, tax-supported institutions in finance, facilities or enrollment, they "must be something different and something unique."

> It is my belief that they must deal with small units within which there is a possibility of a common bond, or else they become cheap carbon copies of larger institutions. The smaller private colleges have less red tape, they have a chance to dream, a chance to imagine, and the possibility of pioneering in new ventures.[34]

This would be Pacific's answer to the mushrooming state institutions.

He told of his visit to Oxford and Cambridge, the most venerable, prestigious educational institutions in the English-speaking world. "While we would not want to copy them exactly...we studied Oxford and Cambridge to see what could be of value as demonstrated over the centuries." The President then outlined step-by-step proposals to implement his new dream for the College of the Pacific. He recommended first that the name be changed to University of the Pacific—a more accurate description of its status. The name "College of the Pacific" should be retained for the liberal arts college of the University. It would, like the schools of pharmacy, education, music, engineering and graduate study, be presided over by a dean. "This is the same as Harvard College's being the liberal arts college of Harvard University." The University would grant all degrees, and its governing body, the Board of Trustees, would be renamed the Board of Regents.[35]

Dr. Burns then went on to propose "that we establish a new college of the cluster type as developed at Oxford, as the first of the additional units of the University." To lead the new endeavor, a provost would be appointed "who would give this school identity over the years." The new college would offer undergraduate courses only, and "no specialties or vocationalism." It would be highly selective, its course of study highly demanding. Students would take fewer courses during the semester, perhaps having only three broad tutorials, "that would carry a value of approximately five units each." The criterion for graduation, however, would not be the total number of units accumulated, "but personal competence," which would be determined by rigorous examinations.[36]

This program, the President assured those who raised questions of finance, would not only be "educationally sound," but "financially expedient." The schools would share the same administration, the library, the laboratories, the gymnasium and the infirmary. Thus the only new investment required would be to buy the Stockton College campus and land across the river as it became available. In the meantime, Dr. Burns recommended that the College apply for a loan of $1,800,000 from the federal government to build a new dormitory on the Baxter Stadium site. It would be designed to accommodate the 250 men and women of the new college "with the necessary rooms, dining hall, social rooms, and lobbies. This quadrangle idea is a part of the genius of Oxford." To cover the higher instructional costs of the tutorial system, students would pay a higher tuition. He was convinced, though, that "the more colleges we have operating the more groups of people will focus their interest and support on them."[37] Generous donors would be found to endow the College and scholarships for worthy students.

Still, some critics continued to question the wisdom of establishing an institution which they feared would be competing with the century-old College of the Pacific. Dr. Burns countered their arguments with the statement that such competition would be healthy. "Oxford, Cambridge and the Claremont group have all said that this is part of the genius of their system—rather than this competition being destructive, it is one of the most constructive things that happens." When one school advances the others are on their mettle to improve. Thus, there would be a "gradual upgrading of academic standards throughout the University."[38]

Finally, he said, "it is a thrilling time to be associated with the College when something creative of this type is underway." Pacific could provide an alternative model, something unique in the world of higher education, where more and more massive institutions were being developed. Over and over again Dr. Burns emphasized the virtues of "growing larger by growing smaller." Pacific would

141

be reversing the process of unlimited growth "by emphasizing the selection of good students and by lodging them in small units where there is a common bond and where they feel they belong to something." Students in these small colleges could enjoy the rewards of personalized attention which had always been such an important part of the Pacific tradition. "In this way," he was convinced, "it is possible not only to develop brain power, but also to make the witnessing for Christian character and the good life possible for a selected group of people." [39]

Robert Burns' enthusiasm was infectious. On October 13, 1959, the faculty voted unanimously in favor of the plan. A week later, on October 20, 1959, the Faculty-Trustee Committee on the Future of the College met to discuss the project. They, too, recommended that the Trustees endorse the plan at their meeting on October 27, and urged President Burns to send each member of the Board a copy of the seven-page proposal for study prior to the meeting. So, after some time spent in discussion, the Trustees voted to apply for the loan to build the Baxter Stadium dormitory. Then this brief note concludes the minutes for the meeting:

> It was moved by Dr. Fisher and seconded by Bishop Tippett that necessary steps be taken to change the name of the College of the Pacific to the University of the Pacific; that we adopt the plan as outlined by President Burns and recommended by the Faculty-Trustee Committee and begin the new program by the establishment of a new college or colleges as soon as possible; that we authorize the Board of Trustees through its Executive Committee to begin negotiations for the purchase of the Stockton College campus... The question was called for and the motion carried unanimously. [40]

Thus in one fell swoop the hundred and eight year old institution was once again launched in a revolutionary new direction. Just two and a half years after President Burns had suggested the possibility, the Trustees voted to implement his ambitious proposal.

Then, only six months after the new development was announced, the plan was given a great boost by Mr. and Mrs. Raymond's bequest to the College of 3,500 acres of rich Sutter Basin farm land worth $1,500,000, the largest single gift in the

142

history of the College." It would "provide marvelous endowment for Raymond College which will be the first of the new cluster colleges."[41] The Raymonds had been benefactors of the College throughout the twelve years Jesse Rudkin had been Director of Development. He had met them while he was still a minister and subsequently convinced them, devout Methodists as they were, of the importance of the educational work done at Pacific. Never before, however, had they considered such a munificent gift. They proved the truth of President Burns' prophecy that the new venture would attract new generosity.

It would be some time, of course, before buildings would be habitable, the new provost and faculty hired, and students enrolled. Considerable discussion of details and more visits to Oxford and Cambridge would ensue before the College opened its doors. Nevertheless, it would be fair to say that Pacific had, indeed, lived up to Robert Burns' hopes. In the absence of the red-tape and the bureaucratic hurdles of larger institutions, the administration and staff at Pacific had been able to formulate and then implement this new pioneering venture within a remarkably short period of time.

During the decade of the 1960s Pacific's President was to test this readiness of the institution to explore new educational paths over and over again. Like the founders of the frontier College, Isaac Owen and Edward Bannister, like his predecessor Tully Knoles, Robert Burns demanded great flexibility and generosity of Pacific's trustees, its faculty and friends. Thanks to his own absolute dedication, his infectious enthusiasm, he, too, was usually able to win the assent he needed. Thus, as he had promised in his inaugural address, Pacific continued to move into new educational frontiers.

Chapter Six

THE LATE 1950s had been a period of expanding enrollments and expansive new vision for the College of the Pacific. On January 6, 1961, at the Founders Day Convocation, a symbolic seal of approval was affixed to these new directions for the institution: its name was officially changed to University of the Pacific. President Burns was elated. At last Pacific had lived up to the ambitious name its founders had given it. With its schools of education, pharmacy and engineering, its graduate school and conservatory, with its projected new cluster colleges and the traditional liberal arts core college (which retained the name College of the Pacific), the institution was at last truly a university. The Conservatory Auditorium was crowded with friends of Pacific who had come to witness this proud moment; the Convocation to celebrate the 110th anniversary of the founding of the University was a festive affair. Elizabeth Congdon, "untiring civic worker" and granddaughter of founding President Edward Bannister, was awarded an honorary Doctor of Public Services degree.

President Burns took advantage of the moment to announce his new plans for the University. "Pacific's Pattern for the Future" would consist, he promised, of the "sharpening of the mind within a small college atmosphere...We will provide something different by combining the best qualities of the old English system with newer American ideas." [1] His long range plans envisioned a university like Oxford, with cluster colleges (perhaps as many as fifteen) limited in enrollment to 250 students, grouped around the parent facilities. The first of these new institutions, Raymond College, would open in the fall of 1962.

At that same convocation Dr. Samuel Meyer announced the revolutionary proposal for the new Inter-American Studies Program. In his inaugural address Dr. Burns had voiced his concern that we develop closer relationships with those new nations bordering on the Pacific Ocean. His mentor Dr. Werner had lived and taught in South America for a number of years and had communicated to the young president his interest in that area. By

145

President Burns and Vice President Samuel Meyer in Lima, Peru, during their fact-finding trip to Latin America to explore the feasibility of Elbert Covell College.

the late 1950s a number of thoughtful observers (including John F. Kennedy) had joined him in being alarmed at the seeming lack of interest in those countries south of the Rio Grande. "As the years have gone by and the situation began to worsen rather than to improve," Dr. Meyer related, "it occurred to Dr. Burns...that this was an area in which the College might render conspicuous service."[2]

Located in California, which has historic ties with Mexico, the University of the Pacific was in an ideal location to foster better international understanding. Its library holdings in the California History Foundation would be a valuable resource. Furthermore, the new language laboratory, which had been funded primarily by Mrs. Winifred Olson, had brought the College's foreign language instruction the most advanced techniques and equipment. Another resource, surprising for a small college, lay in the number of faculty members who through professional interests were asso-

146

ciated with Latin America. Ample precedent could be found for such concern, Dr. Meyer indicated. "The Methodist Church to which this College is related has long been involved in extensive and significant missionary and educational projects in both Central and South America."[3]

To explore the possibilities of such a program, Dr. Burns and Dr. Meyer had spent six weeks the previous summer traveling through Panama, Colombia, Ecuador, Peru, Chile, Argentina, Uruguay, Paraguay, Brazil, and Venezuela. With Dr. Burns' friendliness and Dr. Meyer's perseverance, they managed to surmount the language barrier and talked with "literally hundreds of people." They questioned representatives of the Fulbright Commission and the Rockefeller Foundation, and educators, students and government officials—all with the goal of seeking information about how best Pacific might serve the educational needs of the area.

It was an exhausting schedule, but the President's sense of humor was never far from the surface. They had been traveling several weeks when Dr. Meyer, somewhat taut and anxious after having been delayed at the country's border for four hours, in the midst of struggling to communicate in Spanish to an unfriendly hotel clerk, discovered that his briefcase was gone. Packed with their passports, travelers checks, and notes, it was a critically important piece of luggage. Really alarmed, Dr. Meyer looked for Dr. Burns to tell him that his briefcase had been stolen. After enjoying the academician's dismay a few moments, the President confessed that he was the culprit. He had hidden the briefcase behind a flowering plant. Whether he was at home or abroad, Robert Burns was rarely ruffled and scarcely ever expressed irritation or anger. Instead, he found relief from the pressures and anxieties of traveling and of college presidency in levity.

The results, however, of this prolonged tour—these discussions with leading educators south of the border—were certainly not facetious. For, as the Academic Vice President announced at that Founders Day Convocation, Pacific was once again pioneering—moving into a new area of studies. Over and over again the Latin American leaders had spoken of the difficulty students from their countries experienced when they came to this country to study. Not only did they experience profound culture shock, but they also had the language barrier to surmount. The requirement

147

that students speak fluent English frequently limited enrollment of Latin American students in U.S. colleges and universities to the very wealthy, the only ones able to afford the special tutoring in conversational English necessary to augment their classroom study. On the other hand, graduates from the United States who were seeking professions in Latin American countries were frequently trained only in linguistics. They lacked the background in economics, geography, history and business which they needed if they were to find useful careers in Central and South America.

By the end of their travels, such unanimity had been expressed in these concerns, President Burns and Vice President Meyer sat down in their hotel room in Caracas, surrounded by the reams of notes they had taken, and outlined a twelve-point program of Latin American Studies. Subsequently refined and amended, this was the program Dr. Meyer presented at the Founders Day Convocation. First, the College would expand its own offerings in Latin American studies through utilization of its present faculty resources. Then "from time to time" additional faculty would be brought in. A program of exchange for professors, speakers, and students would also be developed. The library's resources would be expanded and, in recognition of "the economic potential, political significance and dynamic development" of Brazil, Portuguese would be added to the foreign language offerings.

Pacific also promised to cooperate with two well-established Methodist secondary schools in South America. Santiago College in Chile and Ward College in Buenos Aires were looking toward expansion to the junior college level. "Our contribution will be to provide advice and counsel in the development of courses and curricula, to make qualified members of our faculty available for teaching in the junior colleges...."[4] Ultimately, however, Pacific hoped to establish a cluster college in which all instruction would be in Spanish, "an academic innovation of major significance." "We believe," Dr. Meyer concluded, "that an investment in Christian, democratic education in Latin America is an investment in the future of Western civilization."[5]

Within a few weeks of the announcement, Dr. Arthur J. Cullen had been named to head Pacific's new Inter-American Studies program. Dr. Cullen had earned his doctorate from Middlebury College and had subsequently taught Spanish, Portuguese, Italian

Mr. and Mrs. Walter B. Raymond with President Burns. The college named in their honor was the first of the Cluster Colleges.

and French at a number of American Colleges. At the time of his appointment he was director of the Latin American Programs Center at the Inter-American University of Puerto Rico. He came to the College of the Pacific to be head of the modern languages department, director of the new Inter-American Studies major, and to initiate the preparation for the new Spanish language cluster college.

Later that spring the year-long search for the best person to direct the new Raymond College culminated in the appointment of Dr. Warren Bryan Martin, Chairman of the Department of Religion at Cornell College. Dr. Martin was known to be a serious scholar, contemptuous of anything less than the finest in academic achievement. He was excited about the possibilities inherent in the new college "where the program of academic excellence [will be] realized through the interplay of ideas and personalities working freely in the atmosphere of quiet dignity and culture." Raymond College, he hoped, would provide "a setting" within which the creative exchange of ideas between faculty and students would be encouraged, "without depreciating the personalities or commercializing the ideas."[6]

Dr. Martin spent a month on campus that summer. In October, accompanied by Dr. Burns, Dr. Meyer, Mr. E. M. Crigler (who had succeeded Art Farey the year before as Director of Public Relations) and Howard Bissell (one of the architects in charge of designing the new quad), he studied the Oxford-Cambridge system at first hand. Mr. W. J. Sartain, secretary general of the faculties at Cambridge, arranged the group's stay there. He set up meetings with professors and arranged for them to witness in person the tutorial method of education, to eat in the great halls and to visit the common rooms. At Oxford, too, the group "lived in" and discussed the proposed new cluster college with English educators experienced in that system of university organization.

By February of 1962, when Raymond's new Provost arrived on campus, he had a clearly delineated vision of the ways the new college could adapt the English system to the needs of American students. During that spring he and Dr. Meyer carried on an intensive dialogue—Dr. Meyer insisting on the conservative, prescribed curriculum every Raymond College student should take, and Dr. Martin insisting on the innovation of a 10-month three-year course of studies as opposed to the four years required traditionally for the B.A. degree. Both men agreed that Raymond College should demand the highest academic qualifications in its faculty and students. They set out at once to hire the professors who would open the new classes in the fall of 1962.

The innovation had attracted considerable attention. Articles appeared in a number of scholarly journals and the description of Raymond College's demanding program aroused unusual interest. For although new colleges were burgeoning across the country (this was a period of phenomenal expansion in American higher education), most of these new institutions promised relaxation of rules and standards. Raymond College was unique in its insistence on such academic rigor. As a result, although the College was to impose unusual demands on its faculty—a number of them were to live in the dormitories along with the students to provide a "total living and educational experience"—Dr. Martin had little difficulty in recruiting a topnotch faculty. On September 12, 1962, nine new faculty members welcomed Raymond's first class of sixty-seven freshman students.

Dr. Dean McHenry, Chancellor of the University of California campus at Santa Cruz (which was due to open its first cluster college in 1965) spoke at the formal opening. He complimented Pacific for its innovative courage. Raymond College, he said, "is the prototype of things to come in higher education...."[7] Mrs. Raymond was present; she accepted the thanks of the University's community for the gift which had made the new college possible. Evidently pleased with the aura of excellence they sensed in the College named in their honor, the Raymonds donated an additional 792 acres of farmland to the University a few weeks later.

One of the outstanding characteristics of the new school was its emphasis on a broad cultural experience for its students. A group of oil paintings on loan from the San Francisco Museum of Art was on exhibit in the Common Room at the time of the dedication, the first of a series of such exhibits to be held at the College. Religion was also an important facet of Raymond's cultural ambience. The Methodist Church contributed the altar and contemporary sculpture for the nightly religious services, which attracted the voluntary attendance of a number of faculty and students. There they sought "the meaning of spiritual values in an age of transition."

Attendance, in formal dress, was required for the weekly High Table. Copied from the Oxford-Cambridge model, this gracious custom brought all Raymond's faculty and students together for a formal dinner each Wednesday. The Provost, distinguished guests (President Burns, delighted with the graceful dignity of these gatherings, frequently attended), and the speaker of the evening sat at the High Table, on a raised platform at the head of the room. The liturgical, ceremonial quality of these evenings imbued Raymond's students and faculty with a sense of their distinctive identity.

An even more significant aspect of these weekly gatherings, however, lay in the intellectual stimulus of the scholarly address which followed the dinner. This portion of the evening took place in the elegantly furnished Raymond Common Room, and the entire

University community was invited to attend. Distinguished thinkers and artists brought new insights, new questions for the academic community to explore. At times these speakers were controversial, and at least on one occasion Mrs. Raymond objected. Provost Martin, President Burns, and Vice President Winterberg drove to Knights Landing to talk with her, though "there was never any question that the President would capitulate in this issue of academic freedom."[8] Together they were able to convince her of the necessity of confronting students with all sides of an issue.

In addition to these evening meetings faculty members who lived in the dorms were in demand at all hours. Occasionally, "time out" had to be called. When Provost Martin's wife, Elizabeth, walked through the Provost's Lodge with a sack over her head, students knew she wanted to escape for a while. There can be no doubt, however, that difficult though it may have been for faculty (and their spouses) at times, the informal colloquies held outside the classroom, at off hours in the dorms, contributed significantly to the totality of the educational experience at Raymond.

At the core of this intellectually stimulating program for learning lay the unusually demanding formal academic sequence. Every student was required to take at the end of his first year a series of three-hour written "pre-intermediate tests," examinations in each of the areas in the first year curriculum, i.e. language, mathematics, literature and history. Then during their third year students had to pass Senior Comprehensives, written examinations in each of the three major divisions of the curriculum: natural sciences, humanities, social sciences. These tests were followed by an oral examination during which Raymond faculty, as well as professors from other colleges, were invited to "probe the students' preparation in any of the three divisions." Combined with the inner discipline required by the independent study program, the imposed discipline of the examinations resulted in an intense and demanding academic experience. That it was beneficial to those students who could meet these demands is indicated by their astonishing success in the Graduate Record Examination. Ranked highest in the nation, as a group, their average scores were in the 98th percentile. In addition to numerous teaching assistantships and scholarships, two Rockefeller Foundation Fellowships and three Fulbright Fellowships were awarded to Raymond's first graduating class of 1965.

From the outset, Raymond College's Provost and its faculty sought ways to distinguish Raymond from the College of the Pacific. There were to be no sororities and fraternities, and only small intramural athletic contests. Those aspects of collegiate life which they felt dispersed Pacific's academic energies were never a part of Raymond's living and learning experience. The calendar also set the new College apart; interchange of students between the two schools was almost impossible because of the difference in schedules. Raymond's three semester academic year started earlier and ended later than the College of the Pacific's traditional two semesters.

Raymond's faculty, staff and student body deliberately sought "not unity but distinction."[9] When the older College's constituency complained about what they perceived to be Raymond's "superiority complex," neither the President nor the Academic Vice President was alarmed. President Burns wanted the new institution to be distinctive and he had foreseen from the beginning that such inter-collegiate academic competition could be a creative force. Dr. Meyer later remembered that his response was similar: "If Raymond College was a first class institution, that would make it much easier to see to it that the College of the Pacific was a first class institution, too."[10]

The second cluster college was even more distinguishable from the College of the Pacific, simply because of the fact that its instruction was in Spanish. Covell College (named for Pacific's generous benefactor, Elbert Covell) opened its doors in 1963—just a year after Raymond. Dr. Meyer took a special interest in this new school; he foresaw a great future for this unique educational venture (Covell was the only college in the country to offer its full curriculum in a foreign language). It would, he hoped, not only serve the cause of improving relationships between the two continents but also enrich the University's ethnic and cultural diversity through the infusion of Latin American students. The Academic Vice President was not able, however, to take as active a role as he had in Raymond's inception. The difficult task of finding professors who were not only bilingual but also specialists in their area of study was a demanding one. Frustrated by his lack of Spanish, Dr. Meyer had to rely wholly on the judgment of Covell's

Elbert Covell, Woodbridge vine-
yardist and generous benefactor of
the College.

linguistically-oriented provost, Dr. Cullen, for the recruitment of
the new faculty.

The office of admissions was also faced with new recruitment
challenges. Dr. Elliott Taylor, Dean of Admissions, visited ten
Central and South American countries in the spring of 1963 to
publicize the new program and to interview applicants. On
February 21, Voice of America broadcasts had announced the
forthcoming travels of Pacific's admissions officer. Subsequently
his visits were announced by the local press, by the Cultural Affairs
Officers of the U.S. Embassies and by Bi-National Centers. Dr.
Taylor discovered that Latin American students he interviewed
were primarily interested in practical subjects, engineering, science, and business administration. He also learned of the economic
difficulties students from many of these countries would face.
"The price of a North American education equals the price of a
very good house,"[11] he reported to the University's administration on his return. It would be necessary, therefore, to underwrite
a larger number of scholarships than had originally been intended.

Dr. Taylor was, nevertheless, even more enthusiastic about
Covell College when he returned from his travels. The interest
expressed by officials and educators in the new program, the
eagerness of the students to take advantage of the educational
opportunity, filled him with hope for its future. Many of the
students had made "substantial sacrifices to participate in the
interviews,"[12] traveling long hours by bus for the conference with
Dr. Taylor. Covell's first class was evidence of the success of his

efforts; thirty-nine students from thirteen Hispanic American countries—Bolivia, Peru, Chile, Paraguay, Argentina, Colombia, Nicaragua, Venezuela, Honduras, Guatemala, Mexico, El Salvador, and the Dominican Republic—joined twenty students from the United States to launch the revolutionary program.

All courses (except English as a Foreign Language, Materials and Methods for Teaching English as a Foreign Language, and U.S. Literature) were taught in Spanish. After students became proficient in English, they could also enroll in the regular courses of the College of the Pacific. As had been the case with Raymond College, however, the new cluster college's special identity was emphasized. To the Latin American student Covell College would offer the opportunity to take advantage of the United States' educational system. To the Anglo-American student Covell College would offer the unique opportunity of "total immersion" in the language and culture of Hispanic America. Both groups were to receive specialized training in "one of the critical needs of the Americas," training "which will help all nations to progress with actual benefit in their social, economic, and educational development." At the same time the graduates would learn something about the *manera de ser* of other cultures. Through living together, eating together, studying together in Covell's dormitories, dining hall and social hall, students would have a chance to become intimately acquainted with each other's traditions, manners, and values.

Occasionally problems arose because of this mixing of cultures. At first, most Anglo-Americans experienced some difficulty conversing with their Spanish-speaking roommates. They were forced for a while to communicate with sign language or *"con diccionario en la mano."* But more than mere words needed translation and understanding. The Latin American students' concept of time, for example, was radically different; promptness simply had not the value it had for North American students and teachers. And these students so far away from home needed places to stay during the holidays. More than once Elliott Taylor and his wife found themselves acting as surrogate parents. The University drew heavily on its reserves of generosity and "family" feeling in caring for these new Spanish speaking students in its midst.

The new cluster colleges attracted nationwide attention to the University. *Time* and *Newsweek* magazines featured Pacific in

155

their educational sections. *Time*'s article, entitled "Reform on the Coast," spoke of Pacific's former renown in intercollegiate football and praised the new academic direction, the program of tutorials for Raymond's 124 students, "its scholarly faculty and bold taste for guest speakers." The writer also described the important "cross-fertilization" which would occur at Covell College: "it will throw together 250 dissimilar students..." "Unless football creeps back," the article concluded, "Pacific may become one of the nation's most interesting campuses."[13]

As early as the fall of 1960 President Burns had concluded that a shifting of priorities would be necessary if the new academic programs were to be established. Pacific had fielded strong football teams in the late 1950s. Dick Bass led his teammates to a defeat of the powerful University of California team in 1958. But at the same time, costs had skyrocketed for travel, for the coaching staff, for athletic scholarships. And contrary to the hopes of 1950, when the stadium was built, home game revenues were never able to cover the losses of the intercollegiate athletic program. Year after year the President looked at diminishing gate receipts with increasing concern. The loss for the 1960 season (not including the 70 tuition scholarships) was projected to be $135,000. After consulting with the former football player and President of the Board, Ted Baun, and winning his support, the President called a special meeting of the Board of Trustees on December 2, 1960 to discuss the problem.

Acknowledging that a few years earlier, he had "stood on the rostrum at the Palace Hotel and defended the role of football in the modern college," the President reaffirmed his belief that "it has an important place in college life."[14] Whether it made sense, however, for Pacific to continue its present major emphasis on the sport, Dr. Burns seriously questioned. Television coverage of professional football games had decimated the crowds who once flocked to collegiate contests. Furthermore, in recent years, student attitudes toward academic achievement had changed. "In the wake of Sputnik a different academic emphasis is apparent among students, faculty, and public—an emphasis which demands more than is provided by a Saturday afternoon extravaganza."[15]

In keeping with this "new climate," Pacific had raised entrance requirements and was striving for academic excellence in its established schools. This phenomenon, together with "our dreams for educational ventures as great as California has ever known" ruled out, the President was convinced, the extravagant use of funds for intercollegiate sports. "The image we now envision," he told the Trustees, "is incompatible with a major program of cross-country proportions." Rather, he argued, it calls for "a community of scholars," with a "football-for-fun concept,"[16] and with an emphasis on all the sports, participated in by as many of the student body as possible.

Robert Burns believed that other schools would reach the same conclusion and that a new league would develop in the Bay Area "with schools of academic rather than athletic prestige . . . a medium powered, 'Ivy' type league."[17] In the meantime, Dr. Burns recommended that starting with the 1961 season, no more long cross-country trips be scheduled and that Pacific "try to get released from all our major far away commitments."[18] Football scholarships would also be phased out.

This "greatly deemphasized" intercollegiate athletic program that Dr. Burns proposed for Pacific was indeed revolutionary. From the time Amos Alonzo Stagg had come to the College in 1933, Pacific had been renowned for its football teams. Anticipating alumni objections to the new diminished program, Dr. Burns had invited a group of leading alums to study the problem. Bruce Orvis, a local rancher, Boyd Thompson and Jerry Kirsten came to the Board meeting to report their conclusions, "the work of many interested and devoted alumni." Although they hoped that intercollegiate athletics would continue to be "an integral part of the college program," they recognized after "studying the figures that a major adjustment is necessary to put it on a proper basis and give it back to the students."[19] The Board agreed, with surprisingly little discussion, to this radical departure from the school's tradition. Paul Stagg, Amos Alonzo's son, was hired to redirect Pacific's athletic program.

The faculty of the College of the Pacific applauded the deemphasis of football. And some of the new faculty members sought to extend even further the College's direction toward academic excellence. They prepared a paper outlining several concerns they wanted to be discussed at the faculty retreat early in 1961. Citing the criticisms of the Methodist Survey, they praised the strides which had already been made toward improvement of the academic milieu at Pacific. More improvement, though, was needed. In the area of governance they proposed that the Executive Committee be enlarged to include more than just department heads. They urged the improvement of the catalogue, the student newspaper, the book store, and the required weekly convocation programs.

Probably the most critical issue of this "Faculty Manifesto" (as it was subsequently called) lay in its "insistence" that the teaching load be reduced. "Given a high proportion of two unit courses, a teacher finds that the current fourteen unit load may result in as many as five or six different preparations." Beginning in the fall of 1961, they moved that the teaching load be reduced to twelve units per semester "as a first step toward a work load more consistent with the purposes Pacific has announced in its development of creditable work on a university level." [20]

The "Manifesto" criticized what its authors thought was "unsupported expansion" into new graduate programs, which led, they contended, to a "drag on faculty resources." In the fall of 1960 both the Chemistry and English Departments had initiated Ph.D. in Teaching programs, "to meet the increasing need for breadth as well as depth in the training of potential college teachers and administrators." [21] Candidates were required, therefore, not only to master their field of study, to pass foreign language exams, and to complete a research project and dissertation, they were also required to do "directed teaching." In comparison with the larger university graduate programs, Pacific's was acknowledged to be small. But as the pressure for academic achievement urged faculty members to do more research, the pressure to enlist the aid of competent graduate assistants was undeniable. Chemistry research had also been prodded by government grants in the amount of $300,000 during 1958 and 1959. The writers of the "Manifesto," nevertheless, questioned whether the College, committed as it was to the best in undergraduate education, should expand its graduate offerings. The departments of English and Chemistry argued, however, that their undergraduate programs would be enhanced by the presence of the advanced graduate students.

158

A number of older tenured faculty members joined the "Young Turks," as Sam Meyer subsequently dubbed them, in urging that the issues be discussed at the Retreat. And so they were. The authors of the "Manifesto" delegated themselves to every discussion group to assure that all the questions be dealt with. Jesse Rudkin saw in this move a conspiracy and communicated some of his alarm to Robert Burns. When he returned home that evening, therefore, the President called on his old college roommate, Dr. Harold Jacoby, one of the signers of the document. He was easily reassured. In a certain sense, though, Mr. Rudkin was correct—in the language of the Manifesto, in the actions of the young faculty members who wrote it, one can see the first step toward the adversary relationship which, to some extent, developed later.

The breaking up of the Pacific familial relationship was further accelerated by the formation of the deliberately isolated cluster colleges. Faculty members in the liberal arts core of the University, the College of the Pacific, resented what they perceived to be favoritism in the allotment of the resources to the new units. They were also angered by the condescension with which they were treated by the faculty and staffs of the new colleges. In the end, however, the tension was, as President Burns had predicted, creative. Throughout the decade of the 1960s the College of the Pacific continued the movement initiated by the Methodist Survey toward academic excellence.

It was apparent even before the clusters had opened, however, that the College of the Pacific needed its own advocate. The President and the Academic Vice President agreed that the best person to perform that function would be Dr. Harold Jacoby, who was at this time head of the Sociology Department. In January of 1962 they announced his appointment as Dean of the College. From that time until 1968, he directed the efforts of the College in its attempts to strengthen its faculty and curriculum. At Executive Policy Committee meetings he was indeed an able contender for the College in its competition with the cluster colleges and professional schools for the allocation of funds and personnel.

Not long after he was named Dean, some of the traditionally strong departments of the College announced new developments. From the inception in 1951 of the Tully Cleon Knoles Lectures in

Philosophy, Pacific's Philosophy Institute had published the Lectures, which attracted scholarly attention across the nation. The venture had, in fact, been so successful that Dr. Nietman embarked on an even more ambitious publishing project in September, 1962, *The Pacific Philosophy Forum*. The new quarterly, edited by Dr. Nietman, followed the design of the Knoles Lectures; a long essay to develop the thesis, followed by two shorter articles arguing the counter-thesis. Contributors, excited about the challenging format, were among the most prominent philosophers in the country. In October of 1962, it was adopted as a text for honors philosophy programs at Williams College in Massachusetts and the University of Oregon. Thus, the College of the Pacific's Philosophy Department continued to be remarkable for its nationwide standing and its dynamism. Philosophy classes attracted some of the best students in the College.

Under the leadership of De Marcus Brown, theater also continued to be a favorite with Pacific students. The summer sessions at Columbia's Fallon House had, in fact, become so popular the College was delighted to accept the State's offer to share the costs of refurbishing Eagle Cotage [sic] for a dormitory. The summertime productions were also popular with audiences—who frequently packed the small auditorium. Television, however, had eroded the size of audiences in Stockton. That fact, together with the continuing difficulty of sharing the Conservatory's Auditorium, led the theater director to look for a smaller, separate setting for his productions. He found it a few blocks from the campus in a 48 foot square building which had served previously as a bindery for the Atwood Printing Company.

Curt Ennen, Pacific Theater's technical director, designed the new theater's decor and was complimented highly by *The Sacramento Bee*'s theater critic. "The new theater itself is a small masterpiece of making something attractive and serviceable out of unpromising material...Ennen has provided imagination, taste and an unerring sense of color." This new theater-in-the-round required new techniques of acting and production, and De Marcus Brown and his enthusiastic troupe met the challenge. In May, 1962 capacity audiences enjoyed the opening productions.

Another division of the Speech Department, the forensic debate program, was also thriving. Dr. Paul Winters had succeeded Dean

160

Ed Betz as coach of debate in 1956. In subsequent years Pacific continued its traditionally strong showing in competition, annually winning tournaments throughout the country. That series of triumphs reached a peak in 1964 when College of the Pacific debaters Raoul Kennedy and Douglas Pipes won the most important contest in the country: the National Debate Championship, annually held at the U.S. Military Academy at West Point. It was a success of some moment. Never before had a Western college won the coveted trophy. The Pacific students then went on to defeat the University of Minnesota and win the National Television Debates broadcast each week on N.B.C. Intercollegiate debate at Pacific continued to be a fine testing ground, especially for future attorneys, but it also garnered a good deal of favorable publicity for the College.

The professional schools were also attracting considerable attention. In June of 1962, the Conservatory announced that the internationally famous American composer, Roy Harris, and his wife, the well-known concert pianist Johana, would be joining the faculty of the music school. Johana Harris, whose recordings and concerts were highly praised by the critics, played her first recital in Stockton in October, 1962, a benefit to raise money for scholarships. Throughout the year she embellished meetings of alumni and associates of the University with her gifted playing. Mr. Harris joined his wife on the Pacific campus in September of 1963 after finishing his Ninth Symphony, which had been commissioned by Eugene Ormandy for the opening of the Lincoln Center in New York. The presence of two such distinguished musicians and teachers added great new luster to the oldest school of music on the Pacific Coast. Dean Russell Bodley was understandably proud.

Pacific's newest professional school, the School of Pharmacy, was also in the limelight. In 1961 the first of its Doctor of Pharmacy degrees were awarded. And in the spring of 1962 a $44,000 grant from the Pfeiffer Research Foundation was awarded "in recognition of the excellent leadership of Dean Rowland and the progress of one of the youngest pharmacy schools in the nation." The grant was to be used to support research in the areas of pharmacy, pharmaceutical chemistry and physiology-pharmacognosy. Evidently impressed with the quality of the program offered by the Pharmacy School, the Pfeiffer Foundation subsequently awarded a $150,000 challenge grant to the institution, to be used in the development of new facilities across the Calaveras River from the main campus.

The School of Education was also in hopes of expanding its facilities. Constantly adapting to meet new requirements for credentials, adding new curricula in counseling and special education as they became necessary, the Education School continued to attract large numbers of students to the University. Starting in 1962, a unique new option was offered to Pacific's education students. Arrangements had been concluded with the Mexican government to allow a number of students to complete their practice teaching in Torreon and Durango, Mexico. The young future teachers were excited about the program, which enabled them to live with families in private homes. Thus, while completing their training as educators, they were able to gain broader understanding of the Mexican culture. They returned home better prepared to meet and teach California's large numbers of Mexican-American students.

Henderson McGee, one of the first graduates of Pacific's Department of Engineering, was named Dean of the School of Engineering in 1962. Like so many other alumni of this small department, he had had a distinguished career. A civil engineer, the new dean had to his credit varied professional accomplishments including the management of multi-million dollar construction projects for the U.S. Army Corps of Engineers, the design and planning of Veterans Administration hospitals and flood control projects. He brought to Pacific, in addition to his knowledge of engineering, administrative experience and "an intimate knowledge of and intense loyalty to Pacific." Under his leadership the annual Highway Conference reached new heights of popularity. Contractors, city and county public works officials and state highway engineers met for three days on campus to hear outstanding speakers. Requests for the published proceedings of the Conference were received from all over the country.

Without doubt the most significant event in the development of the University's professional schools during this period was the acquisition of the Dental School. The College of Physicians and Surgeons, which was amalgamated with the University in 1962,

162

had had a long and distinguished history. Founded in 1896 with departments of medicine, dentistry and pharmacy, the College Building, on Fourteenth between Valencia and Mission Streets in San Francisco, was completely destroyed in the 1906 earthquake and fire. But like the College of the Pacific, the institution and its staff were both resilient and persevering. Enough rebuilding had been completed by the fall of 1906 that classes were opened without interruption. Graduates of the College became outstanding medical and dental practitioners.

In 1918 the College of Physicians and Surgeons discontinued its medical and pharmaceutical departments. Costs had risen disastrously for the school and because of the expansion of Stanford and University of California medical schools there was no longer the demand for its services. The dental school continued, however, to train the professional dentists needed in Northern California. Then in 1923 another blow to the institution nearly caused its demise. Given the increasing costs and professional disapproval of proprietary schools (privately owned, profit-making ventures), the owners of the College announced that they were closing its doors. Five young alumni of the College refused to accept that verdict. Barely established in practices of their own, Dr. Henry C. Veatch, Dr. Arthur R. McDowell, Dr. Ernest C. Sloman, Dr. Bernard Kingsberry and Dr. Frederick T. West decided on a bold course of action.

Determined that their alma mater and their degrees would continue to be held in respect, they managed to raise $50,000 (a large sum of money in 1923) which they offered to the owners of the College. In return they received very little else than the promise of a future for the school—its charter, its name and the good will which had accrued over the years, the equipment and a lease on the building. They incorporated it then as a non-profit public trust of which they were the first Board of Directors. At their first meeting they recorded their objectives:

1. To make the College of Physicians and Surgeons academically and professionally the equal of the finest schools of dentistry in the nation.
2. To secure University affiliation.
3. To construct a new College building.[22]

It was to be many years before the last objectives were to be fulfilled, but the first was achieved with relative dispatch, thanks to the vigorous leadership of the Board.

The College's operation was dependent on tuition fees and the earnings from its public clinic—scarcely enough to support the expenses of providing a first class professional education. Undaunted, members of the Board persuaded other alumni to join them in volunteering a few hours of the week to augment the full time faculty. Year by year the standards were raised; the vigor of the program was such that it attracted distinguished practitioners from other schools. The growing strength of the institution also drew the attention of donors, who became aware of the great service to the community performed by the College. Not only did its efficiently managed dental clinic provide the best of care to people who could not otherwise afford the services of a dentist, P and S was also training significant numbers of dentists for the burgeoning population of Northern California. (Between 1897 and 1962, the graduating dentists of the College numbered 2,629.) As funds were raised, the full-time faculty was increased. By the time of its amalgamation with the University of the Pacific, the College had a full-time paid faculty of fourteen, a paid parttime faculty of forty-two, and a volunteer staff of 162!

For many years the dental school had had the best record in the western states in the Aptitude Test Scores, the Career Examination scores and the various State Board Dental Examinations. It had been the school's policy to require of their entering students, in general, four years of collegiate work, more than was required by the American Council for Dental Education. The Doctor of Dental Surgery Degree then required four additional years of study, the Master of Science in Dentistry seven years in the Dental School. The continuing education program for practicing dentists was another aspect of the school's training. On the whole the School of Dentistry fulfilled its founders' dreams; it was rated among the best in the country.

As the academic and professional quality of the school had improved over the years, so had the enthusiastic spirit and loyalty of its alumni. Shailer Peterson, secretary of the Council on Dental Education and dean of the University of Tennessee Dental School, characterized Physicians and Surgeons alumni as "the most dedi-

Completion of the new School of Dentistry building in 1967 was one of many construction projects carried out during the 1960s. President Burns is shown with Dental School Dean, John Tocchini.

cated in all dentistry." That the statement was no exaggeration is indicated by the fact that alumni had not only donated countless hours of volunteer assistance but also funds for the proposed new building. In 1954 Dean John Tocchini suggested the "Filling a Month Club," whose membership requirements involved working a little longer one day each month and donating the resulting fee to the Building Fund. Most of the 1,825 living graduates of the school had participated so generously that by 1961 the Building Fund amounted to $621,300. At their annual meeting that year the Alumni Association pledged themselves to raise another million dollars for the construction of the new facilities.

Proud as its alumni were of the College's position in the world of dental education, it had been clear since 1923 that it must became affiliated with a larger university. Accrediting groups strongly recommended the move; by 1960 the College of Physicians and Surgeons was the last independent dental school in the

United States. Originally it had been planned to form this association with Stanford University, which had at one time informally promised the board members that when the struggling school was firmly established, with at least two and a half million dollars in assets, such a merger might take place. But in 1960, when the necessary funds had been accumulated, Stanford moved its Medical School to Palo Alto. The board members, staff, faculty, and alumni of the dental school were loath to leave San Francisco, where their clinic was of such benefit to the city's poor and where so much good will had accrued over the years. Dr. Francis J. Herz, then President of the Board, discussed with Robert Burns, a fellow member of the Masonic Order, the possibility of amalgamation with Pacific, with the understanding that the school would remain in San Francisco. Before long both men agreed, as did their respective Boards, that it would be in the interest of both institutions to be amalgamated.

On January 3, 1962 it was publicly announced that the sixty-six year old school would become a part of Pacific. Its new unwieldy name proclaimed its tradition, "The College of Dentistry of the College of Physicians and Surgeons of the University of the Pacific." On July 2, 1962, the official transfer of the College's assets was signed and plans for the multi-million dollar building were unveiled. Two of the original five members of the Board, Dr. Kingsberry and Dr. West, witnessed the amalgamation and promised to continue their dedicated labors for the Dental School, as did other members of the Board.

The new building for the School of Dentistry was only one among many new construction projects the President included in his twelve year development plan in 1964, though several new buildings had been erected on campus between 1961 and 1964. The multi-million dollar quadrangle buildings with dormitories, common rooms and dining rooms for Raymond and Covell Colleges had been completed in 1962 and 1963. And on March 8, 1964 the gothic tower which Dr. Burns had so long dreamed of for Pacific was dedicated. He had always admired the towers he had seen on eastern college campuses, the campaniles at the University of California and Stanford. Not long after his inauguration as President he had spoken of the erection of such a structure at Pacific—symbolic to him of the vitality and upward thrust of its academic tradition. But he recognized that the hard pressed school had no money for mere decoration, be it symbolic or not, so although he had design sketches made, nothing was done about the project for years.

Throughout the late fifties and early sixties, far more difficult and practical problems had to be faced, among them the difficulty of pumping sufficient water to the new dormitories. Maintaining sufficient pressure with the College's old system was impossible; a new water tower had to be built. Faced with the challenge of placing the new structure on campus, Robert Winterberg laid out sketches of other proposed buildings on his desk. The designs for the gothic tower lay next to the water tower, and suddenly the projects merged in his mind. He called Dr. Burns at once, and the President was delighted with the idea. The new, *utilitarian* gothic tower's top section would enclose the 150,000 gallon water tank the campus needed, and the nine floors underneath would house the new FM radio transmitter, the President's office, a conference room and offices for the Vice President, development, alumni and public relations staff. Necessary new automatic telephone equipment and a vault for records were housed in the basement. Ted Baun recommended strongly to the Board that the new building be named for the University's dynamic president and they unanimously agreed. The Robert Burns Tower, the highest building in Stockton, rose like an exclamation point on the campus, a landmark punctuating the astonishing developments which Robert Burns had already brought to the campus during his seventeen and a half years as President.

The completion of the cluster colleges and the tower named in his honor did nothing, however, to allay or to slow the forward momentum of Dr. Burns' dynamic plans for the future of Pacific. At the Founders Day Convocation held after the dedication of the Tower, looking toward the 125th anniversary of the University's founding in 1976, he announced a twelve-year development plan to be launched in three four-year phases. Financing for the first phase from 1964-68 would require $28,299,714 in capital gifts. That sum would be spent in building the new pharmacy center, the new dental building, a science center to match Weber Hall on the south side of that quadrangle, additions to the Irving Martin Library, an academic classroom building, two new cluster colleges (one of which would be the proposed Episcopalian college, St. Michael's), new dormitories to take the place of South and West Halls which, he planned, would be refurbished for the School of Education's offices, classrooms, seminar rooms and educational laboratories. Funds were needed, too, to purchase additional land, to increase general endowment and scholarship funds, to improve faculty salaries, reduce teaching loads and to provide for sabbaticals, travel, and summer study grants for the faculty. He quoted government projections of the college student population in 1976 which indicated that there would be no difficulty in attracting students to the schools and colleges of the University. The challenge lay rather in being prepared for them. "There is a danger," President Burns warned, "that the needed facilities will be provided in a series of crash programs. Expediency rather than quality will be the byword. This the University of the Pacific intends to avoid." [23]

It was a heady time; the impetus toward expansion seemed inexorable. There appeared to be no limit to the things the University would accomplish. With unbounded optimism, the President's gaze was fixed on the future. But he also shared Samuel Meyer's pride in the accomplishments of the past few years. In 1956 the Methodist Survey had spoken firmly. "However skillfully its public relations may be conducted, however fortunate it may be in plant and surroundings or however widely known for its intercollegiate athletics, a college is measured by its educational excellence ....How best to obtain genuine excellence is the fundamental issue." [24] In a surprisingly brief period of time, Pacific had not only grappled with that fundamental issue, it had moved with giant steps forward in its "pursuit of academic excellence." By 1964 60% of the University's full-time faculty had earned doctorates. Entrance requirements had been raised and students' help along with faculty's had been enlisted to create a more challenging academic milieu on the campus.

Spurred on by the intensified interest in scholarship after Sputnik was launched, students were delighted that "academically, tremendous strides have been made at Pacific," [25] as one student writer commented. They recognized, though, more than they had before, that the quality of the education they received was in good measure their own responsibility. The student newspaper on May 18, 1962 contained a letter from a freshman woman:

In matters of curriculum, educational standards, and what the whole University stands for, it must be the students who care enough about something other than themselves to make their institution something that gives them more than a four year degree; something that awakens them to a higher standard than the mediocre and a life toward the goal of perfection.[26]

Altogether, therefore, thanks to higher standards and improved student awareness of their own responsibilities, things had changed at Pacific.

Another quality in students—a characteristic that had not been anticipated—accompanied this increased seriousness. Along with a more adult perception of their responsibilities came a growing impatience with parietal rules. Strict regulation of women's clothing was relaxed during this period; the University learned to be more flexible in its behavioral code. But it continued to be inflexible in its pursuit of higher academic standards. And the students responded sometimes with a wistful look at the past. As one student editor commented, "This place just isn't the country club it used to be."[27]

Recognition of the changed ethos was also received from outside the University. Representatives of the College of the Pacific were invited to participate in the Danforth Foundation's Campus Community Workshop in Colorado Springs in 1961. There, together with faculty members from Stanford, Tulane, Washington and Northwestern Universities, and from Bryn Mawr, Antioch, Kenyon, Mount Holyoke and Oberlin Colleges, they explored "ways and means of improving administration-faculty-student relationships." They carried out an intensive study of counseling and other student services, and they "sought ways to discover the relationship between religion and values and educational objectives."[28] It was a prodigious schedule, and the participants returned with new insights to share with their colleagues. The entire University community felt considerable pride in the invitation to participate. For, as Dr. Presley McCoy had pointed out in his letter of invitation, all of the institutions named were "highly respected for their academic achievements and continuing efforts to increase scholastic competence."[29]

The University also looked with pride to the commendation it received in the May 1962 issue of *Liberal Education*, the official bulletin of the Association of American Colleges. The editor, Dr. F. L. Wormold, himself a graduate of Oxford University, praised Pacific's scholastic strength and its innovative courage in the development of the cluster colleges. These accolades from their professional colleagues gave a powerful boost to faculty morale. But the improved standards also had tangible rewards—Pacific's new programs were attracting support from Foundations. In 1964 the President received a letter from the Stella and Charles Guttman Foundation announcing an unsolicited gift to the University of $20,000 for scholarship funds. "We believe," the letter said, that the College of the Pacific "as one of the twenty outstanding liberal arts colleges throughout the United States...is performing a vital service to the nation."[30]

Immediately after the Methodist Survey steps had been taken to strengthen Pacific's academic life; by the early 1960s the momentum of that transformation had become truly remarkable. In the time between 1961, when it officially became again a University, and 1964, when the President announced his Twelve Year Development plan, Pacific had established two new colleges and had acquired a fine dental school. The other professional schools—the Conservatory, the School of Education and the School of Pharmacy—had expanded and strengthened their programs. The College of the Pacific, in its competition with the new clusters, had "purged its curricula of excess and irrelevancies," had improved its teaching, and encouraged research. Within an astonishingly short period of time, Samuel Meyer reported to the alumni, the University of the Pacific had "gained new stature in the academic community...It is being transformed from a small, regional, liberal college into a medium-sized, multi-purposed university of national and international significance."[31]

Chapter Seven

THE OPTIMISM, the exhilarating innovative spirit, and the pursuit of excellence which marked Robert Burns' administration of the University of the Pacific during the early 1960s characterized many American schools and colleges during that time. After Sputnik was launched by Russia in the late 1950s, the federal government invested vast sums of money in the improvement and expansion of scientific education. And in 1961, John F. Kennedy's presidency brought with it urbanity, sophistication and a renewed concern for the arts and humanities. Like Dr. Burns, President Kennedy used the frontier metaphor. When he accepted his party's nomination, Kennedy spoke of "the New Frontier—the Frontier of the 1960s—a Frontier of Unknown opportunities and perils—a Frontier of unfulfilled hopes and threats." The key to many of these "new opportunities" lay in education, and the "unfulfilled hopes" were to be realized by the youth of the nation. There seemed to be no limits to the promise of the future on this Twentieth Century "Frontier."

But in November, 1963 President Kennedy was shot and killed in Dallas, Texas. Suddenly Americans were jolted into realization of the "threats" and "perils" of exploring "New Frontiers." Within a year, the world of higher education, on which he had based so much of his hope, was also touched with violence. Concerned educators, as well as citizens at large, were profoundly shocked when a group of students disrupted classes at one of the most prestigious public universities in the country, the University of California at Berkeley. Television screens revealed scenes of unprecedented riot on the campus—hundreds of students falling limp and being dragged to jail by uniformed policemen.

The student revolt of the 1960s had begun on September 14, 1964 when a group of students protested the University's ban on political activity on the sidewalk that bordered the campus. The events which followed were to become the paradigm for campus confrontations throughout the remainder of the decade. On October 1,

Jack Weinberg, one of the dissenting students (and author of the remark, "You can't trust anyone over 30") was arrested by campus police.[1] Students immediately surrounded the patrol car, however, and effectively immobilized it until the University's administration negotiated Weinberg's release. The crisis seemed to abate—until the Regents decided to press charges against four of the leaders of what was now called the Free Speech Movement. On December 2, a thousand student demonstrators took over Sproul Hall. Mario Savio, one of the leaders of the movement, accused the University of being an insensitive machine that used students for fuel: "We must put our bodies against the gears, against the wheels . . . and make the machine stop until we're free."[2] Eight hundred fourteen students were arrested. On December 3, a student strike closed nearly half of the University's classes. Finally, on December 8, the faculty voted to end the restrictions on political advocacy on campus. A semblance of peace was restored to the campus.

But the world of higher education had been tainted with disruptive violence. In 1965, student demonstrations of varying intensity and fury occurred at the University of Kansas, St. John's, Yale and Stanford. And during the following year the escalation of the war in Viet Nam was accompanied by a parallel escalation of the violence on college campuses. Academic pursuits were interrupted by major riots at San Jose, San Francisco and Long Beach State Colleges, and at the Universities of Wisconsin, Iowa and Cornell. In 1968 the National Student Association counted 221 demonstrations at 101 institutions which had involved an estimated 40,000 students! Even this disturbing record was eclipsed during the spring of 1970. Within a month of the Cambodian invasion, student protests disrupted classes at 415 colleges and universities.

The statistics alone, however, cannot communicate the profound malaise which afflicted the whole world of higher education during the late 1960s. (For the epidemic spread beyond the borders of the United States. Students in England, France, Germany, Japan, Hungary, and Czechoslovakia were also engaged in the riotous resistance of traditional authority.) Fear and distrust transformed cooperative relationships between administrators, faculties, and students into contentious rivalries. In the community at large there developed widespread suspicion of intellectuals and students. State legislatures enacted punishing cuts in university budgets.

Private donors hesitated to contribute to what they perceived to be anarchic institutions. Students, however, were undaunted. Berkeley had been their Bastille, and the disturbances there ushered in an unprecedented era of revolutionary upheaval on college and university campuses.

President Burns was determined to prevent such divisive clashes at Pacific. Soon after the disorders began, in the fall of 1964, the local chapter of the American Association of University Professors issued a statement praising his "open campus" policy. Students on the Pacific campus were free to urge varying political points of view. Early in 1965, the President formed a student-faculty-administration committee to hear complaints before they erupted in violence; for Robert Burns was convinced that one of the major causative factors of the student revolts lay in the impersonality, the lack of communication within the larger state university system.

In his book *The Uses of the University*, Clark Kerr had defined his role as President of the University of California as a kind of Captain of the Bureaucracy. Robert Burns disagreed. Although his office was now in the Tower, his door was always open and he was frequently seen walking about the campus, talking informally with students and faculty. He wanted to be directly in touch with all segments of the campus community and deliberately avoided the kind of bureaucratic structures which might have shielded him from the concerns of his constituency. Pacific could no longer be characterized as the small, close-knit family it had been when he became its President. Nevertheless, Robert Burns believed that continuing attention to the values of openness and friendliness could, even in the expanded University, forestall the breakdown of trust which led inevitably, during this troubled period, to disorder and turmoil.

The President emphasized these advantages of the comparatively small independent school when he spoke to denominational groups who were considering the establishment of cluster colleges. A group of Episcopalian laymen and ministers was especially interested in such an institution; in the spring of 1964 they had brought Wayne Gray to the campus to coordinate the fund raising effort. St. Michael's College was to be an autonomous college within the University. Its residence halls, dining facilities, classrooms, and chapel would be constructed across the river from the main campus. The anticipated 750 St. Michael's students would then be close enough to use the University's library, physical education and science facilities, its business office and admission services, "thus avoiding expensive duplication." Its brochure pointed out that "founding a new college currently costs approximately $20 to $25 million. By founding this new college within the University of the Pacific 'cluster' college concept, the cost will be approximately $3,150,000." [3]

Joseph Cotton agreed to be Honorary Chairman of the fund raising drive and made a short film to publicize the proposed new college. He explained that the name St. Michael's had been chosen because St. Michael, in the Old Testament Book of Daniel, was described as the angel holding the secret of the mighty word by which God created heaven and earth. Now, St. Michael's College was to be "a new creation" which would "guard the word, the truth." It would join the seven Anglican colleges in the East in "fostering the Anglican tradition in higher education." He asked, "Who of you haven't experienced the impact of the computer?" and emphasized the value of personalized education and close teacher-student relationships. St. Michael's would reject computerization of scholarship. Through individual attention to students, and the quality of its education, the new school would transmit "moral discipline" and the Christian tradition, "the wellspring of faith and learning." [4] Preliminary sketches of John Carl Warneke's design for the campus were displayed in the film, along with an aerial photo showing its potential location.

The concept was a valid one. Unfortunately, however, the leaders of the church later decided that the project was too costly, since during this period church revenues were contracting. Churchmen of many denominations had looked at the experiment with interest and hope, partly because it would have been another step toward ecumenical cooperation and partly because St. Michael's promised to be the model for other similar institutions.

President Burns also urged the state legislature to consider the advantages of the independent school. From the beginning of the decade, when the merger with the Dental School was first proposed, discussions had also been held with a group of San Francisco doctors who hoped that Pacific would reestablish a medical school on the site of the old Stanford University medical facility.

174

Robert Burns was more than a little interested in the new possibility for expansion. He was excited about the prestige such a school would bring to the University and was pleased to point out its historical relationship. The University of the Pacific had originated the first department of medical education on the West Coast in 1858.

Later, however, it had had to cede the medical school to an independent group of doctors because its own financial problems and the high cost of the program made it impractical to continue. This Cooper Medical College had subsequently become the Stanford University Medical School; under Stanford's aegis, it had carried on the tradition begun by Pacific early in California's history. In 1960, however, Stanford had moved its facility to new buildings in Palo Alto. Some of its physician faculty members had stayed on in San Francisco, and it was they who urged the University of the Pacific to reactivate the school it had originally founded.

On June 15, 1963, what it was hoped would be the first step in the process was completed when the Institute of Medical Sciences, a research center formerly a part of Stanford Medical School, became affiliated with the University. The Institute's staff consisted of distinguished scientists who were primarily interested in research. Within the Institute were four separate divisions: the Smith-Kettlewell Institute of Visual Sciences, the Institute of Neurological Sciences, the Heart Research Institute and the Research Data Facility. Grants from the Federal government were financing full time researchers who were working on varied projects: organ transplantation, disorders of the nervous system, and the development of a tactile vision substitution system for the blind.

Encouraged by this development, the former teaching faculty together with Dr. Burns continued to look for ways to develop a medical school at the site. But Dr. Winterberg and Dr. Meyer studied the proposal carefully and reached the conclusion that such a program would be too costly for the University to manage alone. Pacific's President was undaunted. He began investigating the possibility of a state subsidization for the project. California was a "debtor state," he pointed out, in the education of the doctors its burgeoning population needed. In 1964 its three private and three public medical schools had graduated only 467 physicians. (New York during that year had graduated 962.) [5] It was apparent, therefore, that new medical facilities had to be built, and objective estimates of cost indicated that the independent school would cost the taxpayers significantly less.

In the cost picture the best available estimates indicate the State of California appropriates $12,000 per student per year to cover operating costs for medical students enrolled at the University of California. But construction and equipment costs must be figured in as well. The cost of the new UCLA medical school appears to vary between $50 and $90 million. Using $70 million as an estimated cost figure for these facilities, together with estimated costs for facilities at the other two tax supported medical schools, it is reasonable to set the state subsidy for each medical student enrolled at Los Angeles, San Diego and Davis at $15,000 to $17,000 a year.[6]

The Pacific proposal would cost the State $8,000 per year per student, and the State would not be obligated for the capital outlay for new construction.

Senator "J." Eugene McAteer introduced legislation which would have authorized a State subvention to Pacific's projected 400 students in the amount of $8,000 per student per year. The school would consist of a new $16 million teaching facility that would be built next to the new 500-bed hospital that Presbyterian Medical Center intended to build. These would be built by funds from private sources. Ample precedent for such a subvention agreement had been set in the states of Pennsylvania and Florida. It made financial sense, and the legislature seemed to be looking with favor on the proposal after three months of discussion and hearings. Then, suddenly, a spokesman for the University of California Medical Center representing U.C. President Clark Kerr appeared before the Committee and registered the first objection to the plan. He argued that such a project would "dissipate tax funds and disrupt the California master plan for higher education."[7] Confronted with the opposition of the University system, which was at this time still immensely powerful in the state, the legislature retreated. Senator McAteer's bill died before reaching the Assembly floor.

Robert Burns' dreams of reactivating Pacific's medical education program had, therefore, to be postponed. (In reporting these legislative developments to the alumni President Burns wrote: "In terms of Pacific's point of view on California's medical education needs...we shall return.["8]) He continued to work with the Board of Directors of the Pacific Medical Center, and his expertise as a fund raiser was invaluable to that group when they were seeking funds to build the new hospital which was built near the site of the old Stanford-Lane Hospital. In 1968 the Graduate School of Medical Sciences was established through a cooperative agreement worked out among the University, the Institute of Medical Sciences and the Pacific Medical Center. Two divisions were created within the School, one for research and one for education. This latter sponsored programs of continuing education for practicing physicians, intern and resident programs, and graduate degree programs in Learning Disabilities and Visual Science. President Burns continued to hope that these would constitute the germinating impulse toward the development of a major medical school.

His vision of a professional medical school at least temporarily thwarted, Burns nevertheless pursued other areas of professional expansion with undiminished energy. As early as 1955 he had broached the possibility of establishing a law school with the Board of Trustees. After consulting with local attorneys, however, he had abandoned the project. Then in 1965 Judge Sherrill Halbert, a Trustee of McGeorge School of Law in Sacramento, spoke with him about the feasibility of a merger between that school and Pacific. Like the College of Physicians and Surgeons Dental School, McGeorge had been urged by accrediting bodies to become affiliated with a larger institution.

McGeorge had been founded in 1924 as the Sacramento School of Law by Verne McGeorge, "to serve the men and women of the Sacramento area who wished to secure professional training in law."[9] Its classes had been held at night in rented premises and were taught by part-time faculty members who were active attorneys in the capital city. Like the College of the Pacific, it had faced dire problems during the Depression and had been held together, as had Pacific, by the devotion and dedication of the faculty and staff. Yet the small school's achievement was remarkable. By 1966 twenty percent of the attorneys practicing law in the Sacramento-Stockton area were McGeorge graduates. Among the seventeen law schools in California it ranked fifth in the percentage of its

McGeorge School of Law in Sacramento amalgamated with Pacific in 1966. President Burns, left, is shown with Gordon Schaber, dean of the law school, and Judge Sherril Halbert, trustee of the School.

graduates passing the State Bar Examination on their first attempt. The 1966 class had moved that percentage even higher, with 89.6 percent passing in contrast to the statewide 52.5 percent.

In 1957, Gordon Schaber had succeeded John Harold Swan as Dean; under his forceful leadership the school had moved dramatically forward. In 1957, McGeorge moved into its first permanent quarters—a building which had formerly housed a well-baby clinic. And in 1963 McGeorge was accredited by the Committee of Bar Examiners of the State Bar of California. Now it was looking toward full accreditation by the American Bar Association. Amalgamation with a university and the establishment of day classes (in the fall of 1967) were two of the essential requirements for that accreditation.

McGeorge was offering a strong, widely respected program of legal education. In fact, a number of its loyal alumni and supporters urged it to continue as an independent college. When the decision was finally reached to seek an association with a larger school, a number of institutions were considered by the Board. Why did they choose Pacific? The answer lay partly in a shared "belief in the value and necessity of privately-supported education in our democratic society."[10] But another factor, according to Dean Schaber, lay in Pacific's "dynamic leadership, Robert Burns' known commitment to diversity and innovation."[11] As Superior Court Judge, Gordon Schaber had had first hand opportunity to observe lawyers in action. He had reached the conclusion that although young attorneys were well grounded in legal theory, they were frequently lacking the practical skills of trial preparation and courtroom advocacy. He wanted to inaugurate a "clinical" program which would inculcate these skills through practical experience in a model courtroom. And he became convinced that Pacific was the institution under whose aegis such an innovative program could be developed.

On October 26, 1966 the amalgamation agreement between the two schools was signed. For the remainder of the decade, the astute, energetic Dean of the Law School worked closely with Pacific's dynamic President. It was a fruitful relationship. Land and buildings were added to the School of Law's campus; programs were expanded and initiated; and McGeorge's pioneering training program in courtroom practice became the model for similar programs all over the country. In 1968 it won the coveted approval of the American Bar Association Section on Legal Education.

Pacific's Academic Vice President, Samuel Meyer, who had worked closely with President Burns in the discussions relating to the proposed medical school and in the initial conversations with McGeorge, resigned his post at the University in June of 1965. He had been named President of Ohio Northern University. President Burns and, in fact, the entire university community were sorry to see him go. Under his sometimes impatient, but always dedicated leadership the institution had made giant steps toward that goal of academic excellence which he had espoused on his arrival at Pacific. The curriculum had been strengthened. Standards had been raised. Scholarship had been nourished through the expanded sabbatical program for tenured faculty members and the Danforth Summer Study Grants. Dr. Meyer believed that church-relatedness in an institution of higher learning mandated the highest

possible academic standards. In an address entitled "Education...
Methodism's Splendid Obsession," he quoted Bishop Oxnam's
statement: "The Christian College is neither a rescue mission nor a
social settlement nor is it designed to be a psychiatric couch or the
healing service of a revival meeting... The Church expects its educational institution to be an educational institution in fact, to
maintain the highest of educational standards." [12] Dr. Meyer's insistence on this principle had brought Pacific to new heights in its
pursuit of academic excellence.

Dr. Wallace Graves succeeded Dr. Meyer as the academic
leader of the University. A political scientist, he had completed his
Ph.D. at the University of Texas and immediately prior to his
appointment at Pacific had served as Assistant to the President at
Texas Wesleyan College. He was to be at Pacific scarcely two
years, but those two years were significant ones in the life of the
institution; his influence was of more consequence than his brief
tenure in office would suggest. He not only participated in the
discussions which culminated in the McGeorge amalgamation, he
also guided the formation of the third cluster college.

Dr. Burns announced the establishment of Callison College at
the 115th Founders Day Commemoration March 6, 1966. "Few
announcements," he said, "in the twenty years I have served as
President of this University have equalled the importance of the
one I am now privileged to make." [13] Dr. and Mrs. Ferd Callison
had given property valued at $2.5 million to endow the new
college, which would fulfill the promise Dr. Burns had made in his
Inaugural Address—a curriculum in Asian studies. "Of the two and
one quarter billion people on the face of the globe, approximately
a billion and a quarter live in countries touched by the Pacific
Ocean." The College of the Pacific, he had promised, would do
everything in its power to promote understanding and a sense of
brotherhood among the peoples of the Pacific's Basin. "I pledge
you an expansion of our offerings in Oriental Studies." [14]

The College had already made important contributions to the
area through its programs of educational tours, its emphasis on
international relations, its alumni. One of these graduates, Tow
Sing Kow, Class of 1887, Dr. Burns reminded his listeners, had
been influential in bringing to an end the cruel practice of foot-
binding. "While on our campus he decided this practice, which he

Academic Vice President Wallace Graves.

had seen in his native land, was cruel and inhuman, and upon his return to China he persuaded the Empress to abolish the custom. It is conceivable," he concluded, "that if foot-binding could be abolished through the inspiration of a single student, mind-binding in many areas could be eliminated also." [15] Now, at last, concrete steps were being taken to eliminate the mind-binding lack of knowledge of Eastern civilizations. Callison College's curriculum would pay special attention to the Orient. It would "depart from outmoded but prevalent tradition by giving the student as thorough an understanding of the non-Western world and the problems of emerging nations as of his own Western heritage." [16]

The new college was to be housed in the newly constructed buildings of the quadrangle, adjoining the other two cluster colleges, Raymond and Covell. Each class in the four year, liberal arts college would consist of only about eighty students, because Callison was founded to expand the possibilities within Pacific for a personalized living-learning experience. Each Sophomore Class would spend a year abroad "as a means of personal confrontation with the problems of emerging nations." [17] Such an experience, President Burns believed, would give students "the capacity to

181

empathize with and understand non-Western cultures."[18] It was an exciting concept. Once again Pacific attracted national attention, receiving favorable note in an article in the *Saturday Review of Literature.*

Dr. Larry A. Jackson, who had been Dean of the Chapel from 1964-66, was appointed Provost of the new college. One of his first tasks was to find an appropriate site for the year abroad. On January 4, 1967, accompanied by President Burns and Ted Baun, he embarked on a seven-week tour through Japan, Malaysia, Thailand, India, Pakistan and Lebanon. While they were abroad, an event occurred on campus which the students found dull, but which the surrounding community found shocking. On January 26, 1967, Dr. Timothy Leary spoke at a chapel service.

The Methodist Survey Report of 1956 had expressed concern over the "weak chapel program" at Pacific and had recommended the hiring of a full-time chaplain for the College. Rev. Robert Stewart came to fill that post in 1957. In addition to teaching and student counseling, he had endeavored to develop a chapel program which would attract student attendance. He and the student chapel committee invited speakers and on one occasion sponsored a "jazz mass" which seemed revolutionary at the time and drew a good deal of favorable and some critical comment. Dr. Larry Jackson had succeeded Reverend Stewart in 1964 and for two years continued the effort to enliven the religious spirit on campus. In the spring of 1966 he invited Dr. Lawrence Meredith to come to Pacific to speak at the Interfaith Dinner.

Dr. Meredith infuriated a number of his listeners. Fully in tune with the disillusionment felt by many of the "youth culture," he questioned traditional authority—in the church, in the University, in the nation. Dr. Burns, though, saw in Dr. Meredith the kind of religious leader who might engender new life in the chapel program. "The church is not reaching the college-age students...," he told the Regents. Traditional chapel services were "poorly attended."

> The college chapel service [should be] different from the traditional Sunday morning church service. I believe it should be designed to stir up the student—to arouse him—to make him uncomfortable and dissatisfied with the world about him. If this is not done we perpetuate the status quo and thus there

is no progress. If we do not want empty pews on Tuesday mornings then we must try for provocative presentations that cause a student to think, to question, to accept, to reject, to understand, to mature, and thus in the higher sense—to worship... The problem is getting someone who speaks to this age.[19]

The President believed that Dr. Meredith was such a person and telephoned him in Michigan to persuade him to come to Pacific in the fall of 1966—when Dr. Jackson was to assume the position of Provost of Callison College. Dr. Meredith later remembered Dr. Burns' speaking of the "revolutionary situation" among students in California. He was concerned that at Pacific students have the opportunity to examine all sides of questions by exploring the arguments within the institution rather than by tearing it apart.

His arguments were, as they usually were, persuasive. Dr. Meredith agreed to come to Pacific. Immediately the chapel services began to attract excited attention among the students. By the time Timothy Leary came, to the accompaniment of rock music and psychedelic lights, there was standing-room-only at the weekly service. Soon after the barefooted "guru" had begun to speak, though, students began to leave. Barely audible, he seemed vague and disoriented. Students left speaking of his being "burnt out" by the drugs whose use he espoused. Instead of winning converts among the students, he had revealed himself as "a tired man, old before his time, a prophet with smelly feet, more to be pitied than followed."[20]

Dr. Ferd Callison.

Local newspapers, though, did not report student reactions in their stories of the incident. Several letters were sent to the President, criticizing the program. A few local churches sent resolutions of dismay and outrage to Bishop Tippett. Both men responded with strong affirmations of academic freedom. After explaining what the University was trying to accomplish with its chapel services, Robert Burns wrote: "Our policy will be to move ahead with our traditional stand on academic freedom *and* religious freedom. The price for anything else than this is too high—so high we cannot afford it. This policy of freedom—to think, to hear, to discuss and to speak, is our most precious heritage."[21] In his letter to the disgruntled Methodist congregations, Bishop Tippett chided them for basing their statements on the partial reporting found in the newspaper articles. If they had "talked to President Burns or Dr. Larry Meredith, Dean of the Chapel," they would have found that "Dr. Leary's presentation was one of a series" and that "the University had conducted a very scholarly and thorough symposium on drugs to explore the dangers and the real sinfulness of drug usage."[22] Once again the University's leadership had expressed its dedication to that freedom which is essential in the pursuit of knowledge and truth.

The actual experiencing of that principle was also brought to students later that spring in the All University Study Day. While students at numerous other institutions were disrupting classes, holding unauthorized "teach-ins" on the controversial Viet Nam war, students at Pacific were excused from classes on March 15, 1967—"so that all of the University's students could think and talk together about this nation's Far Eastern relations."[23] A panel of faculty members and students opened the discussions with pro and con presentations at 9 A.M. in the gym. Then small group discussions explored the issues—interrupted only by the distribution of box lunches—until 4 P.M., when Dr. Robert Scalopino of the State Department defended and Dr. Donald Grubbs of the History Department criticized U.S. policy. In subsequent years these All University Study days discussed the draft laws and other issues. They constituted another means by which the astute administration and faculty at Pacific fended off the threats of campus violence and disintegration through giving students the opportunity to discuss issues openly and critically *within* the institution, with the blessings of "the establishment."

As a result of this continuing sense of "peace at Pacific" the administration was able to pursue its development projects—unhampered by the time- and trust-consuming disruptions that were occurring on other campuses. In September, 1966, the new and badly needed Wood Memorial Hall addition to the library was opened. Although James Riddles, the University librarian, warned that "the south wing will be needed within a very few years to serve the expanding University population,"[24] this new north wing enlarged the library to nearly twice its original size. Now, for the first time, enough shelf space was available to house the University's entire collection of books and periodicals.

Another important new addition to the University's facilities was dedicated in San Francisco on May 7, 1967, the new $8.9 million dental school. Old friends of the College of Physicians and Surgeons and of Pacific joined Dean John Tocchini and President Burns for the proud moment. Streets were blocked off and after the ceremonies hundreds of visitors toured the new structure. A far cry from the now dilapidated old building which had, since 1906, housed the school, the new nine-story building contained over three million square feet—five times as much space as the older facility. The new dental school was the culmination of years of anticipation and planning, a monument to the loyalty and generosity of its alumni.

Even as this grand new addition was being dedicated, construction and planning for other new buildings were being completed: the academic facilities building (later named Wendell Phillips Center), the new student health center (a gift of the S. H. Cowell Foundation), additions to McGeorge School of Law and the new pharmacy school. In marked contrast to schools like Columbia University, where buildings were being wrecked and bombed and vandalized, Pacific continued its new building development throughout the late 1960s.

The fall of 1967 on campus witnessed the opening of Callison College. Eighty new students, excited by the innovative program, comprised the charter class. Dedication ceremonies were held on October 26, 1967, United Nations Day. Wendell Phillips, world traveler, explorer, and archaeologist, spoke, as did Dr. Burns, and Dr. John Bevan, who had come to the University from Florida in

185

Academic Vice President
John Bevan.

July, 1967 to succeed Dr. Graves as Academic Vice President. "It is
our plan," Dr. Bevan explained, "to confront our students with the
amenities and conflicts of culture, and to arouse within them feelings of anxiety which should intensify their search for meaningful
and applicable values..."[25] During their first year at Callison College, students studied science and economics, and in addition, the
Heritage of Man course, which was taught by a team of professors
representing the disciplines of history, political science, literature
and religion—"the amenities" of culture which, it was hoped,
would prepare them for the "conflicts" they would encounter
during their sophomore year abroad.

Sixty-six of the original class left for India in the fall of 1968, to
discover that no amount of "book learning" could prepare them
for the trauma of immersion in a totally alien society. Dr. Burns,
Dr. Jackson and Ted Baun had originally hoped that arrangements
could be worked out in Kuala Lampur for the Callison campus
abroad. Negotiations with the Malaysia government had aborted,
however, and subsequently arrangements were made with Indian
officials for the students to study at the University in Bangalore.
This city had once been a resort for British government officials.
Its climate was more favorable than that of many tropical Indian
cities, and housing was arranged for the students in the Shilton
Hotel. The group landed in Calcutta, though, before they went to
Bangalore. One of them, Judy Proulx, wrote home:

Our senses were assailed with the sight of hundreds of people sleeping on sidewalks and in gutters; with the smells of urine, cow dung, and musty hotel rooms. Our ears were filled with the cries of vendors and the wail of beggars. Our skin crept at the clutch of bony fingers at our arms and ankles. The hungry followed us for many blocks, and implored us with liquid eyes sunk in pock-marked faces. We stepped over pools of betel juice, mucus and blood; and slipped back sweating into our dusty rooms.[26]

After two days in the capital city, they went on to Bangalore, which was in comparison an affluent, industrial city.

It was, nevertheless, as the first faculty advisor reported, on his return, a difficult year—difficult not only for the American students, but also for the Indian educators, who "were chary of handling a group [of American students] with a reputation for iconoclastic individualism."[27] Much of this fear, though, was allayed after the students arrived. Except for their "enthusiasm and energy," they were not noticeable among the students at the University. "Despite a few trying moments," Professor Ramachandra B. Magal observed, "the overall effect of the first batch of Callison students was positive." They were no longer "feared as a bunch of yahoos descending on a traditional society for the purpose of wearing weird clothes and practicing strange rites..."[28]

Students' expectations were also radically revised in the actual encounter. Many of them had gone to India (in spite of faculty warnings) with a romantic notion of the "mysterious East." Ann Mayers wrote: "I somehow thought that the things I hated in America would be absent here: strict class and racial boundaries, religious dogmatism and materialism." She was "bitterly disappointed" and "disillusioned" to find in India the caste system, the conformity to superstitious religious sanctions, materialism. "I used to talk about the uptightness of American society—man I have really seen uptightness now..."[29]

Everything was strange: the food, the clothing, the ubiquitous poverty, even the educational system. University classes in India were still being taught by rote. Students were expected to memorize their lecture notes and then regurgitate them for exams. The Americans were tempted to abandon the repetitive, monotonous boredom of the classroom for the experience of real life outside. "Frustration, anger and plain confusion was often the lot of most of the students." [30] Nevertheless, in spite of all these barriers to understanding and the physical inconveniences, most of the students returned for their junior year at Callison, convinced that the experience had been one of growth and maturation. They returned aware of the fact that they had not "discovered India," because "the more I know about the country the less I know." [31] And that healthy intellectual humility was matched by a sense of the contingencies of life—how fortunate they had been to be born who they were rather than one of the "90% of the world that never eats enough, that dies with mucous crusts on their eyeballs and knots of worms in their bellies." [32] Ultimately the overseas program was transferred to a more westernized Asian nation, Japan. But for the first few years, students from Callison College did indeed experience these "feelings of anxiety" which accompanied severe culture shock, and those feelings did, as Dr. Bevan had promised at the Dedication, "aid them in evolving an understanding of themselves and their studies in relation to culture, creation and the Creator." [33]

Callison College seemed to be meeting the expressed needs of students for relevance, for experimental learning, for creative flexibility. Between 1967 and 1970 the enrollment of each class met the anticipated quota. Enrollment in the other two cluster colleges during that period, however, was declining. Both Raymond and Covell Colleges, with their more traditional curricula, were facing real problems in the recruitment of students. Under the leadership of Berndt Kolker, Raymond faculty began a reexamination of their program. At Covell College a program was developed which enabled American students to study in Costa Rica. In response to changing needs, the older schools of the University were also reappraising their curricula during the late 1960s.

Dr. Preston Stedman, who had become the Dean of the Conservatory of Music after Dean Bodley resigned in 1966, gradually expanded the music curriculum to include instruction in all the orchestral instruments. Dr. Dale Redig, in 1969 the new Dean of the Dental School, worked with that school's faculty to compress the course of studies into three years instead of the usual four. At the same time, Dr. Ivan Rowland was incorporating a similar

188

change in the Pharmacy School curriculum. In the summer of 1968, a group of College of the Pacific faculty members, together with their new Dean, Dr. William Binkley, traveled to Colorado Springs for another Danforth Foundation meeting; there they reevaluated the core College's traditional requirements in the liberal arts. They returned to campus with proposals for "a sweeping revision" of the college's curriculum, "to make it more relevant to today's better prepared and more socially conscious students." [34]

After prolonged and sometimes heated discussion, the faculty approved the changes, which were then implemented in the fall of 1970. The calendar was changed; instead of two semesters, breaking in February, the school year would consist of two semesters divided by a month-long "winter term" in January (during which the student was encouraged to immerse himself in intensive study of a single subject). During the fall and spring semesters, the course system was introduced. Instead of taking as many as six or seven two- or three-unit classes, each student would take four four-unit classes. Professors were pleased to be relieved of the multitude of small unit classes; instead they would teach five courses during the year.

Another innovation, however, met considerable resistance. Traditional undergraduate course requirements were to be dropped in favor of a group of thematically linked cross-disciplinary courses. This program of "Information and Imagination" (subsequently abbreviated to I and I) constituted the introductory program for freshmen and sophomores. Each student, with his advisor's help, chose three pairs of classes (24 units) from four groups of disciplines: historical-cultural studies, behavioral sciences, physical and natural sciences, and communicative creative arts. The program's designers hoped it would, "through exposing the students to a variety of disciplines and to many teaching styles and educational philosophies assist him in making the choice of a major field." [35] To work, however, the courses required a complete rethinking of a professor's area of professional competence. He would be required to abandon the old general survey courses which had traditionally introduced the students to collegiate study, and concentrate instead on some facet of his special field which could be shared with another discipline. Thus a professor of history and a professor of sociology might teach a pair of courses linked by the theme

189

"Revolution," and explore its manifestations from a historical and contemporary perspective.

Faculty critics argued that students needed the basic, groundwork courses of the traditional requirements and that although the linkages would sometimes be strong, natural ones, that more often they would be strained. Proponents countered that many introductory courses were repetitions of high school classes, that students would come to realize through the new method the necessary integration of all knowledge, and that disciplinary boundaries themselves were too often artificial and limiting. Everyone realized that this innovative approach to teaching and learning would require both creative flexibility and a great deal of continuing study to develop the new courses. Therefore, one faculty member commented, "The recommendation for an internal sabbatical, a semester off every four years, is in my opinion crucial to such an innovative program, for it would afford a faculty member time to rework and rethink course offerings, and time to do more concentrated research."[36] Months of debate between the two points of view finally convinced the majority of the faculty to embark on the creative new program. Raymond College Professor Clifford Hand was named Associate Dean in charge of the new curriculum. In general, faculties are known for their conservatism; indeed, their primary task is the conservation and transmission of the fund of knowledge mankind has accumulated over the centuries. The old College's faculty manifested remarkable openness and courage in their acceptance of "Information and Imagination."

The School of Engineering was also responding to new directions in that field. Together with the faculty, Dr. Robert Heyborne, who had been named to succeed Henderson McGee as Dean of the School, developed a cooperative education program. The new five-year degree program interspersed actual engineering training periods (of from three, four or five months) with classroom study. As soon as the student engineer finished the first two years of basic study on campus he would enter directly into his first semester of industrial employment. The program had many advantages. Students would have the opportunity to earn as much as $10,000 while attending college. Furthermore, the Dean promised, "This program has to produce a better engineer because the student will not only receive an engineering degree, but he will also have finished sixteen months in actual full-time engineering work." [37] Cooperative education would also enable the School to increase enrollment without increasing the size of classes, for groups of the three upper division classes would always be off campus working. Engineering educators looked with a good deal of interest and respect at Pacific's new program. The Engineering School was officially accredited by the Engineering Council for Professional Development in 1971.

During this period the School of Education was also responding to newly felt needs of the students and the community. In July, 1968, together with the Stockton Unified School District, the professional school initiated a pilot program to train elementary teachers for low income area schools. Designed especially to attract and train members of minority groups, the program was supported by the U.S. Office of Education. Recruited from among the vast numbers of junior college graduates, the new Pacific students spent half a day working in "disadvantaged area schools" and half a day attending University classes. One of the students told of her childhood: "Mom and Dad worked in this area as farm laborers and I can remember sleeping on blankets on dirt floors and my mother carrying me on her back as she worked in the fields." [38] Now she was becoming a teacher who would work with just such children as she had been, her teaching enhanced by a natural understanding of their problems and strengths.

This Teacher Corps Program was a pioneering one, partly because it was the first such undergraduate program in the country, but also because it enabled numbers of Mexican-American and black students to come to Pacific. The cost of a private school education had been beyond the reach of most students in those groups. As a result, the student body had been comprised almost totally of upper middle class whites. With the exception of Raymond and Callison Colleges, whose students tended to be more liberal, students at the University were characterized in the mid-1960s as "pleasant, socially and politically conservative." Most of them had chosen Pacific because it was "small, friendly and traditional."

In 1964, they had urged the President to reemphasize the traditional college game. After a cost analysis which indicated that it was as costly to conduct the de-emphasized football program as it was to conduct a moderately ambitious one, he assented. Students were pleased when he announced that the University would join the Pacific Athletic Conference, and play such teams as Fresno, Long Beach and San Diego State Colleges. And Pacific students cheered when the basketball team under the able coaching of Dick Edwards won its way to the NCAA finals.

Another mark of their traditional outlook in social affairs could be seen in Pacific's students' continuing interest in sororities and fraternities. While other institutions were phasing out the "Greeks," at Pacific they were being modified. The hazing, the Confederate flags, and that sort of customary activity were giving way to volunteer work in the community at the Children's Home, the Boys Club, the Family Service Agency. Nevertheless, they were a far cry from the literary societies to which President Burns had belonged when he was an undergraduate. He had had the unwelcome task of disbanding Rhizomia, his own fraternity, after a series of problems. And he continued to admonish all the groups to emphasize academic achievement. No serious thought, however, was given to eliminating the "Greeks" from the Pacific scene. For too many students they were an essential part of the College's appeal.

The volunteer work which served to expand the extracurricular experience of the fraternities and sororities was not confined to those groups. Volunteer activities arranged through the "Y" had been a tradition at Pacific. An extraordinarily large group of students looked forward to service professions, and the interest in working directly with people naturally followed. The curriculum, too, reflected and encouraged this community involvement: in the student teaching practicum, the music, speech, and learning clinics. The College won national notice in the mid-1960s with Professor William Byron's program of involving students in the work of the local California Youth Authority facilities. On the whole, however, student life at the University continued to be a relatively traditional, sheltered one. Students were encouraged to become conscious of, to minister to the needs of the local people, to move beyond their Gothic, ivy-covered campus into the troubled areas of the community outside. That community rarely, however, impinged on the life of the campus itself.

During the spring of 1969 a group of students decided that the generally conservative, Caucasian homogeneity of the student

192

body must be modified. On March 26, they "stormed" the Tower. A large group milled around the foot of the Tower, while about twenty-five crowded into the President's office to present their list of threatening "non-negotiable" demands:

> The present condition of this campus is oriented towards white middle-class students...this has resulted in a white racist campus lacking in perspective for both blacks and whites...this situation must be changed to educate more blacks and re-educate the whites. The following must be done by September of 1969. Two hundred fifty black students be admitted;...the basic requirements in admission be suspended;...the recruitment program must be headed by a black director and the program provide tutoring for students who desire it;...in addition to the 250 black students there be 250 Third World students allotted slots under the proposed minority Educational Opportunities Program![39]

They demanded an answer within two days, March 28. President Burns was alarmed—but not panicky. He called at once for an emergency meeting of the faculty governing board, the Academic Council. At their meeting, he presented the students' position and suggested that the University offer a compromise: to accept two hundred minority students. Faculty cooperation in the plan was essential because it would mean adding extra students to classes without extra revenue and extra recompense. Additional help would have to be given these new "culturally deprived" students. Some professors were concerned that even a compromised positive response to "non-negotiable demands" would invite more of the same. President Burns assured them that a tutorial program would be arranged and that he would make it clear to the students that their demands *were* negotiable, that they had, in fact, resulted in a compromise. After some discussion, the faculty assented.

President Burns called a student meeting for Thursday, March 27, one day before the "non-negotiable" deadline. Not unhappy about having gained the initiative, he read them a statement on the proposed policy.

> The University of the Pacific recognizes the plight of the culturally disadvantaged person in our society. It also recognizes that a primary avenue for the release of these persons

193

from their disadvantaged status is the opportunity for higher education. Consequently, the University has been gearing itself for a number of years to satisfy this need in extending itself to meet this problem... As a further expression of our commitment, we blaze new trails—students, faculty and administration in a bold adventure which incorporates three innovative parts: 1. That 200 culturally disadvantaged students be actively recruited from the Stockton community, 2. the students so recruited will be awarded tuition scholarships on the basis of their financial need, and 3. in order to help those recruited and enrolled to make significant progress towards meeting graduation requirements it proposes a tutorial program involving students and faculty; 130 faculty have already volunteered for this service. This program will be under the supervision of the Director of Community Involvement.[40]

Students cheered. The local minority community was grateful. It had been a magnanimous action on the part of the University, its administration and faculty. And in one fell swoop, a potentially destructive disturbance was averted.

Even before this incident, plans had been in the works for a "Summer Institute on Race, Deprivation and Human Dignity." Coinciding with the regular 1969 summer school, it offered a number of courses: Black American Heritage, the Nature of Prejudice, the Urban Environment and Its Problems, Methods of Social Change, and Music and the Negro American. Black lecturers who "tell it like it is" were invited to teach the series. They brought home to the students the cruel realities of racism, the dichotomy of the American dream of equal opportunity and American reality. In "searing, scholarly, penetrating" lectures they confronted students with the ramifications of prejudice and racial discrimination. This Institute, the Black Studies Department which was established in 1970, together with the presence of more minority students on campus helped to raise the consciousness of many of the previously unconcerned, affluent students to the problems of poverty and racial discrimination. The creative response of the University to crisis, together with its ongoing programs, was to contribute significantly to improved understanding and to the professional training of numbers of minority youth who could not otherwise have come to Pacific.

Once again, during the first fourteen days of May of 1970, demonstrations threatened to disrupt the educational process. On March 29, President Richard Nixon had announced the invasion of Cambodia. Many knowledgeable observers of the Viet Nam war disputed the military value of the move, and students were outraged. The President had promised gradual de-escalation of the war; now it seemed to be alarmingly expanded. No one really anticipated, however, the depth of the students' anger and frustration or the uncontrolled fury of those forces called to repress the demonstrations. By the end of the month, classes had been disrupted at 415 colleges and universities (286 of these were still paralyzed at the end of the semester and though 129 others had reopened many classrooms were empty). Three students were killed and nine others wounded in a tragic encounter between police and demonstrators in Jackson, Mississippi; thirteen students were shot (four of whom were killed) on the traditionally conservative Kent State campus. One Santa Barbara and one San Diego student were killed in California demonstrations. More than 100,000 students stormed Washington on the weekend after these dreadful events, calling for an end to the war.

The atmosphere was electric with tension even on the usually tranquil Pacific campus, in the usually quiet, out-of-the-way city of Stockton. On Sunday night, May 3, about 250 students and faculty members gathered at a rally to discuss ways of protesting the Cambodian invasion. Many student leaders believed the University should close. Once again Pacific's administration moved quickly. Academic Vice President John Bevan called a meeting of student representatives, administrative officers and faculty early Monday morning. After the meeting he announced that the University would stay open, but that Tuesday would be devoted to an All University Study Day to explore the invasion issue.

After they learned of the student deaths at Kent State, Jackson and the state colleges, students once again began to agitate for a closing of the College, but decided instead to hold a memorial service and cancel the traditional Mardi Gras activities. When they learned of Governor Reagan's decision to close state universities and colleges Pacific students sent him a telegram:

We students of the University of the Pacific received the closing of the California Universities and Colleges with deep regret. We remain open seeking a dialogue with the community that you have so effectively attempted to stifle. We have disavowed violence and mob action. The conclusion of our rational reflection is that we must work as hard as possible to erase the polarities ... [41]

And they were working—speaking before high school classes and local business organizations, explaining their belief that mobilized public opinion must bring an end to the Viet Nam war. Early in the week the administration considered canceling the Alumni-Parent Day which was planned for Saturday. Instead students and administrators worked together to modify the programming so that students, parents and alumni would have an opportunity to exchange views.

Still, during the second week of May some students and faculty members wanted the University to close from one to three days "to inform the students and the community on the war in Indo-China." A poll was taken Sunday night, May 10, in the midst of rumors that someone had placed a bomb in the Administration Building. Dr. Bevan asked the Strike Committee to meet with him for a planning session at 9 A.M. on Monday. At 3 P.M. he announced that it had been agreed that the University would stay open and that the faculty would be asked to authorize the release of students from classes so that they could set up information booths in the community and hold discussions with churches and civic groups. The name of Pacific Strike Committee, it was also agreed, should be changed to Peoples Alliance for Peace "to more accurately reflect its purpose." The students' concern about the issue, their work for a cessation of hostilities, continued throughout the semester. Sixty percent of the graduating seniors voted to contribute cap and gown rental fees for the campaign funds of legislators opposed to the war. Many of those who wore gowns wore white armbands with dove of peace emblems. It was a "multifaceted and colorful" commencement procession; but once again, with a creative, open response, Pacific's leadership had prevented an interruption of the education process.

The flexibility of the institution, its ability to move decisively and quickly, were important factors in averting the disruption of classes which had threatened on March 26, 1969, and again in May, 1970, as was the President's determination to settle the issue peacefully. But another factor, scarcely less important, lay in its Methodist tradition: the conscience of the administration and the Board of Regents could be appealed to. These governing bodies were sensitive to arguments of principle—the ethical responsibility of a Christian school to meet the needs of "disadvantaged" students and to foster peace. Bishop Tippett and the other churchmen on the Board were consistently vigorous spokesmen in favor of these responses of the University to the students' moral concerns as they were strong defenders of the principle of academic freedom. Their voice at Board meetings sometimes balanced the more pragmatic perspectives of its businessmen members. The result was decision-making based on ethical wisdom as well as practical exigency.

President Burns and, in fact, all the Board members were anxious that that voice continue to be heard although the University dissolved its formal relationship with the Church in 1969. The question had been originally raised at the January 30, 1968 Regents meeting. Dr. Burns reported that "There is a test case now in progress to determine whether any institution controlled by a church may have a problem of eligibility for government grants and subventions." [42] Already a number of Catholic schools had transferred control to boards composed of laymen. The election of Pacific's Board members by the two Methodist Conferences had actually involved no more than a *pro forma* affirmation of nominees the Board itself had recommended. Nevertheless, from a strictly legal point of view, the church controlled Board membership. Both Myron Wicke of the Methodist Board of Education, and Bishop Tippett agreed that a change in the Bylaws was probably necessary, though some Board members preferred to wait until the Supreme Court's action made it absolutely necessary.

Attorneys recommended, however, that the Board not wait until they were forced, that the University immediately seek the consent of the Conferences to the change. That consent obtained, on March 24, 1969, the Regents voted to amend the Bylaws. The accompanying resolution clearly affirmed the University's pride "in its 118 years of affiliation with the Methodist Church," and resolved that Pacific would "work diligently in future years in maintaining a meaningful relationship" with the Church. They were concerned, furthermore, that the change in legal status not be construed "as in any way diminishing the traditions of Christian life that the Methodist Church has cultivated and caused to flourish on the several campuses of the University."[43]

The University of the Pacific had changed substantially between 1964 and 1970. The new cluster college, Callison, had been created. Another professional school had joined the University and whole new facilities had been built for the Schools of Pharmacy and Dentistry. The demands of the students for relevance, together with the creative intellectual ferment among the faculties had led to extensive curricular changes. All of these were major positive achievements, even more remarkable when seen in the context of riot and destruction witnessed by so many institutions during the same period. For perhaps the most significant achievement of the University in the late 1960s was a negative one—it had avoided turbulence. In spite of the generally felt spirit of anger, frustration and rebellion, a spirit which had occasionally erupted at Pacific, the University had managed to deal with controversy and tension in a rational, peaceable way.

Late in 1969 the American Council on Education sent a team of educators to study all facets of campus life. They wanted to discover the ways Pacific had avoided violent disruption. President Burns was able to inform them that the absence of such chaos was no mere accident. It had resulted from thoughtful, determined effort, and policy. The decision to keep the size of each unit within bounds, the creation of the cluster colleges, mitigated the vast impersonality and the feeling that one was being manipulated by the system of larger institutions. The small size encouraged close friendly relationships between faculty and students. And the President's well-known "open door policy," his accessibility, meant that students and faculty would go directly to him with their frustrations. Pacific's tradition of academic freedom, the administration's willingness to explore controversial ideas and personalities within the milieu of the classroom and chapel programs eliminated the necessity students in other universities felt, to break down college walls. The University supported neither ROTC nor military research. On the contrary, its curriculum and extracurricular activities encouraged service, a sensitivity to the needs of the handicapped and the poor. Thanks to its Methodist tradition the governing bodies of the University were responsive to issues of conscience and principle.

Robert Burns did not include in his list of peace-preserving factors his own sense of humor, though he might have, for that too was undoubtedly important. When confronted, for example, with the outlandish costumes students wore at the 1970 commencement, instead of reacting with anger or disgust, he simply chuckled and murmured to Dean Schaber that "such things do happen from time to time but they always pass."[44] Nor did the list include his unflappable confidence in his own leadership and in the institution he loved. When unfavorable or mistaken comment appeared in the newspaper about various crises of the period, he would urge the staff not to worry. "Today's newspapers light tomorrow's fires,"[44] he would tell them. At the beginning of his twenty-fifth year as President, Robert Burns could look with justifiable pride at the University. Pacific had emerged from a tumultuous period, in considerable measure because of his own personality, his style of leadership, as one of the strongest institutions in the country. And it had lived up to its name.

Chapter Eight

PACIFIC EMERGED from the 1960s without experiencing the violence that too frequently erupted on hundreds of other campuses. Perhaps as remarkable was the fact that its administration had survived; the turnover in college and university presidencies during that unstable period was phenomenal. By the end of the decade, among all the academic administrators in California, Dr. Burns was the senior in tenure. Nevertheless, the tensions extracted their toll, even of Pacific's buoyant president. He was a patient at the Pacific Medical Center as he began the twenty-fourth year of his presidency, in October of 1969, undergoing treatment for the back pain which the doctors had diagnosed as cancer. They hoped that the treatments would be successful. Given a remission, Dr. Burns could expect to live a long and active life. With the optimism that was typical of his approach to all problems, Dr. Burns shared their hope. Other than his wife, Grace, and Dr. Winterberg, no one was told of the diagnosis. After several weeks in the hospital, he returned to Stockton, to the new Cowell Health Center on campus.

By January, the President was able to attend the Regent's Meeting, though he was confined to a wheel chair. Undaunted by the grueling series of tests and treatments, he presented a lengthy report to the Regents on the state of the University speaking of the discussions which were underway on a fourth cluster college in business administration, of the urgent need for a new science center and library wing, of the proposed purchase of the Pershing Town House Apartments for student residences. Because of his customary reliance on his assistants in administration, the University had operated efficiently during his absence. The President's office itself had been managed by his indispensable aide, Alice Saecker, Assistant to the President.

Gradually, as spring progressed, Dr. Burns assumed more and more of his presidential tasks and responsibilities. A bedroom wing was added to the President's House, so that he did not have to climb stairs. And once again he was to be seen on campus, in the little electric car the maintenance crew outfitted for him. By the end of March he had graduated from the wheel chair to crutches, and later he abandoned even these in favor of a cane. In April he traveled to Loyola University in Chicago, there to receive an honorary degree in recognition of his "distinguished contributions to American higher education."[1]

The academic leader on whom he depended during this period, Dr. John Bevan, capably handled the post-Cambodian crisis, and Dr. Burns regretted the Vice President's decision to move to Davidson College. Dr. Bevan had come to Pacific with a reputation for energetic, innovative leadership; under his administration of academic affairs all the curricular reforms of the late 1960s were effected. In the course of working out those changes, the Academic Vice President had become a controversial figure on campus; he told associates that he looked forward to a position with less pressure and tension in North Carolina. When the Dean of the Law School, Gordon Schaber, learned of Dr. Bevan's resignation, he asked the President if he was not distressed at the rapid turnover in this vital position (Dr. Graves had held the post only two years, Dr. Bevan, three). Robert Burns replied that as long as the financial management was handled under the extremely capable and continuous direction of Dr. Robert Winterberg that he was undisturbed by changing leadership in the academic area. New leaders could bring new ideas to the campus.[2] Nonetheless, he watched with interest the workings of the Search Committee and in July announced the appointment of Dr. Alistair McCrone to the position of Academic Vice President.

It was to be a more fateful decision than the Committee realized, for Dr. McCrone would become the Acting President of the University within a few months of his appointment. Dr. Burns did express his concern about Dr. McCrone's youth to the faculty. (Ironically, Alistair McCrone was the same age as Dr. Burns was when he became President.) He and some of the Board members were also concerned about the fact that Dr. McCrone was the first non-churchman to hold that guiding role. They abided with the Committee's decision, however, and Dr. Burns worked closely with the new Vice President. Not long after his arrival, Dr. Burns left on a trip to the Far East. And on the day after Christmas in 1970 he embarked on a round the world tour with his wife Grace and friends. Nine days after their return, on February 13, 1971, President Robert Burns died.

President Burns presented The Order of Pacific to Ellen L. Deering at the 1969 Commencement upon her retirement after serving forty years as Assistant Registrar and Registrar.

The news of his death came as a shocking blow to members of the University staff, and to friends and associates across the country. Only a few of those very closely associated with the University's administration knew of the gravity of the illness he had been trying to overcome, because he had not wanted pity, but rather to live as creatively and actively as was his normal life style. If that decision involved coping privately with pain, it was typical of the courageous way he had encountered problems throughout his lifetime. And as always his sense of humor was apparent—he was teasing visitors even during those last days.

The memorial service, held in the Conservatory auditorium, was crowded with University faculty and townspeople who genuinely mourned the death of the leader whose energy and wit had seemed indestructible. Bonnie Burns represented his family.

I have come to speak of a great man who was a loving father.
He didn't shed the joys of his work but shared that joy with us.

**Dr. Alistair W. McCrone,
Academic Vice President
and Acting President, 1971.**

He belonged to all of you and we shared him gladly, for there was always time for us—time to teach us to find our own ways, realizing that experience sometimes teaches better than words. He did not coddle us nor shield us but let us take our lumps with the rest of the world, and when we faltered or when we fell there was always time to talk of what we had learned. He taught us to laugh at ourselves and stand firm when others laughed at us. He did not choose who we should be, but set us on our way to finding out for ourselves, with kindness and understanding and encouragement. Because of him we shall never stop searching for our truest fulfillment of self, guided by his trust.[3]

Her description of his qualities as a father was echoed in the statements by University representatives.

Elliott Taylor spoke of his belief in freedom, his willingness to listen, his "sensitivity" to the voice of the students. Ted Baun reminded his listeners of the fact that during Robert Burns' presidency Pacific had developed from a two year upper division college to "a university of world wide influence." Dr. Burns, he said, "dreamed dreams for Pacific, chose well those with skills who developed those dreams . . . . His worry was that dreams and plans of today would be so small the future would be handicapped." The Pacific Student Association President, Greg Graves, spoke of his respect for Robert Burns, "because, unlike many, he allowed and insisted upon an honest disagreement that clarified rather than confused . . . ." And finally, the faculty representative Fay Goleman, spoke of his "informal friendliness," his openness and accessibility. All agreed with Elliott Taylor that "if you would see his monument, look about you."[4]

Robert Burns had never been the scholarly patriarchal figure that Tully Knoles had been—his style had always been more down-to-earth, warm and accessible; nevertheless, he, like his predecessor, had indeed given birth, fathered the University of the Pacific. During the nearly twenty-five years he was President, the institution not only grew, it changed in its very essence—from a small provincial upper division college to a major university with international dimensions. His capacity for leadership had developed under the tutelage of Dr. Knoles: first as his student, later during the fifteen years he had spent as recruiter, alumni director, fund raiser and registrar of the college. And there can be no doubt that he learned much of peril and promise of a college presidency working for the first two years with Dr. Knoles in their shared office. From Dr. Knoles, for example, he learned of the critical importance of academic freedom. Thanks to his own innate integrity and courage he was always an able defender of that principle—even when that defense conflicted with the other task which Dr. Knoles had known would be a primary one for Pacific's President during the next two decades, that of raising funds.

Robert Burns fulfilled Dr. Knoles' expectation of him; he was indeed "a remarkably talented beggar." He brought to that task a kind of persuasiveness that is the mark of a successful salesman; though he had not enjoyed selling shoes for the J.C. Penney Co., he spent a lifetime selling Pacific. The year's apprenticeship with Lyman Pierce was followed by thirty-nine more years of development work for the institution to which he was dedicated. He broached the subject wherever he went. In fact, a story is told about his invitation to become a member of San Francisco's elite Bohemian Club—where traditionally there has been an unwritten law against "money talk." Robert Burns warned the members that he would not keep that rule, because no matter where he went he talked about Pacific's needs. Some of the brashness his college teachers had noticed continued to be a characteristic throughout his life. But that brashness, that opportunism rarely offended, because it was rooted not in selfishness but in a genuine ambition for his University and concern for its vitally important task of educating young people. During his presidency nearly $46 million in gifts and grants enriched the coffers of the University.

He was among the first to point out that the assistance of able development officers had contributed significantly to that record. First Jesse Rudkin, and later Thomas Thompson and Carl Miller, helped him raise large sums of money for the institution's varied needs. Nor can there be any doubt, as he had observed to Gordon Schaber, of the critical importance of the Financial Vice President Robert Winterberg's assistance. Dr. Burns had an uncanny sense, an almost intuitive perspective of human nature which enabled him to match the person with the kind of position he was trying to fill. That sense of judgment was not enough, of course. He had also to persuade qualified persons to come to the little known, out-of-the-way college on the Calaveras. Here, too, his gifts as a salesman were called into play; over and over again he persuaded able administrators to come to Pacific.

After they arrived on campus, President Burns exploited to the fullest these members of the administrative staff he had hired—exploited them by giving them full responsibility in their given area. Samuel Meyer, now President of Ohio Northern University, remembered that quality of the Burns' presidency: "I learned from Robert Burns that you find the best person you can for the job and then don't interfere."[5] Occasionally, mistakes were made, but they were correctible. From most of the people he brought to Pacific Dr. Burns expected and received the best of responsible, intelligent leadership.

He was interested in their ideas. Stories abound of Dr. Burns' phone calls late at night to associates, "What do you think of this possibility?" At the meetings in Columbia he would suggest an idea and then sit back and listen to the other officers of the University argue about its strengths and weaknesses, sometimes goading them on with a provocative question. He was a gifted listener, a miner of ideas with genuine interest in what others had to say. As a result, he elicited creative responses from the deans and vice presidents with whom he worked.

This ability to work with people, to draw from them their best efforts and ideas in the interests of Pacific also affected the Board of Trustees/Regents. Observers frequently remarked on the extraordinarily close relationship between the President and the Board.

206

Especially fruitful was the friendship of Dr. Burns with Bishop Tippett and with the President of the Board during most of his tenure, Ted Baun. Ted and Alice Baun frequently traveled with the President and his wife—gathering ideas and support for the University. Like his predecessor, Tully Knoles, Robert Burns enjoyed the unquestioned backing of the Board in most of his decisions.

Board members spent long hours discussing, among other things, the new building projects which were completed between 1946-71. During that period the value of campus property increased from $1,600,000 to $31,900,000. Classroom space was multiplied many times and the library grew from a space adequate for 50,000 to 225,000 volumes. President Burns and the Board members were concerned that Pacific remain a residential college, believing that the values of a close community grew from the campus living situation. As a result, when enrollment increased, dormitory space was added. At the beginning of his presidency the three dormitories and sorority-fraternity houses provided board and room for 507 students. By the spring of 1971, 1973 students were housed in campus buildings. The fraternity and sorority houses had all been enlarged, West Hall, and the wings that connect it with South Hall; Grace Covell Hall, MacConchie Hall, the quadrangle residence halls, the Pershing apartments were all added during Dr. Burns' tenure.

TYPICAL EXAMPLES OF 20 YEARS OF GROWTH

	1946-47	1970-71
Student enrollment	701	5,534
Faculty	67	408
Instructional expense	$201,115	$7,621,000
Physical plant expense ...	72,826	1,571,000
Student aid	13,523	1,265,000
Faculty-staff benefits	8,826	889,000
Library expenditures	8,390	568,000
Student services	23,736	437,000
Endowment	682,987	4,908,094

The new buildings and land which he added to the campus in Stockton, in San Francisco and in Sacramento housed a greatly expanded student body and faculty and staff. The University's expenditures reflect that growth.

Between 1949-50 and 1959-60 the budget had doubled. By the end of the next decade it had quadrupled!

The statistics, though, merely hint at the changes which took place at Pacific from 1946 to 1971. Thanks in great measure to Dr. Burns' creative leadership, Pacific changed not only in buildings, budget and number of students but also in its very nature as an institution. When he became President the only academic programs which attracted attention beyond a very limited radius were drama, music, and education. Within the first few years of his administration, the Fallon House Theater and Dillon Beach Marine Station were added, the clinical and summer school programs greatly expanded. By 1971 Pacific was truly a university, with its core liberal arts college, three cluster colleges, professional schools in education, music, engineering, pharmacy, dentistry, law, and medical sciences. It had attracted international notice because of the innovative programs its pioneer-spirited president had developed.

That eagerness to move ahead, however, occasionally led him to mistaken judgments; for if there was a flaw in Robert Burns' administrative style it lay in his impetuousness. Frequently he boasted of the independent school's capacity for movement and change; sometimes he exercised that capacity without the kind of painstaking study which might have prevented subsequent problems. Had greater care, for example, been taken in the decision to affiliate with the Academy for Asian Studies, that institution's basic financial instability might have been discovered. Another example of precipitate judgment can be seen in the foundation of the cluster colleges: responding to the influx of students during the 1960s, Pacific's President was among the first to develop the cluster college concept. Raymond College was established in 1962; scarcely a year later Covell College was admitting students. Hindsight forces one to conclude that his eagerness to innovate led Robert Burns to establish these schools without the kind of financial base which would have assured their fiscal stability.

Sometimes it seemed to the older faculty members on campus that he was wearing a pair of blinders—blinders which kept him from looking at the needs of the already established programs and instead focused his vision wholly ahead, toward new possibilities for development. From the onset of his presidency the schools of education and music were presenting proposals for expanding their facilities. These schools, which had for decades sustained the institution, were badly in need of additional space and equipment. In addition, the core College's faculty felt that greater effort and attention should be spent on increasing the endowment of the institution, so that it would not be so much at the mercy of fluctuating enrollments. These groups felt some justifiable vexation, therefore, when the cluster colleges were built, when the newer professional schools of pharmacy, dentistry and law moved into new facilities. Dr. Burns answered their criticisms by pointing out that one must respond to the availability of funds in those areas. In fact, the cluster colleges did elicit some major gifts, and federal grants to health sciences buildings played a significant role in the development of the pharmacy and dental school centers. Nevertheless, the older faculties suspected that given the President's well known talent for fund raising, he might have found the money if he had been as excited about their established programs as he obviously was about founding new ones.

The decision to break the University's historic ties with the Methodist Church is probably another example of a premature move. The Supreme Court eventually decided that religious affiliated colleges and universities *were* eligible for most forms of government assistance. Those institutions which were more cautious in the face of the threatened negative decision continue to maintain their church relatedness today and are receiving federal loans and grants for buildings and other needs. Had more deliberate consideration of the change been given, the church's relationship with the University might have continued to benefit both.

In all fairness, however, it must be pointed out that the President's rashness, his eagerness to explore new frontiers, to consider new definitions for Pacific, led also to its becoming the strong university it became under his leadership. Because of his delight in pioneering, Pacific now includes the professional schools, which proved to be of such critical importance in the 1970s. When Dr. Rowland first saw the science facilities in Weber Hall, lighted by bare light bulbs hanging from the ceiling, he could not conceive how a pharmacy school might develop from such meager beginnings. It was Dr. Burns' imaginative vision which captivated the Dean of Idaho's established pharmacy school and persuaded him to leave the brand new facility there to come to Pacific. Dr. Burns' confidence proved to be well founded—in the dream he had of a pharmacy school at Pacific and in the man who was in great measure responsible for making that dream a reality.

Again, it was Dr. Burns who persuaded the Board of the wisdom of merging with the Dental School. Many of them were concerned about the problems attendant on administering a school at that distance from the main campus. Robert Burns' open-minded approach to new possibilities enabled him to leap the hurdle of the limiting concept of a self-contained campus to see the possibilities inherent in the expansion into San Francisco. He possessed an acutely practical intelligence, a mind that perceived opportunities for the institution in terms of pragmatic worth. But he also brought imagination to the task, a capacity to conceive wholly new directions, new images for his alma mater.

It was just this boldness, which led the McGeorge Law School administration to explore the possibilities of a merger with Pacific. It, too, was distant from the main campus, and its Board, like that of the dental school, wanted the legal facility to stay where it was in the capital city. Pacific had shown itself to be willing to work through the problems which such separation involved. Even more important, though, to the innovative leadership of the law school, was the fact that as a part of the University of Pacific McGeorge's faculty would be free to experiment with a new *modus operandi* in legal education.

In the balance, therefore, Robert Burns penchant for risk and innovation undoubtedly strengthened the institution to which he devoted 40 years of his life. That quality together with his other personal characteristics, his boundless energy, his optimism and self-confidence, his sense of humor and friendliness all left their mark on the history of Pacific. Without those qualities he could not have steered the University through the turbulent storms of the late 1960s. Even his "extra-curricular interests" affected the institution: his explorations of the Gold Rush country of California leading to the California History Foundation, Fallon House and Eagle Cottage; his delight in travel and the round-the-world tours to the international dimensions of Pacific's development. He was so absolutely dedicated to his alma mater that he related all new experiences to his interest in its becoming a "great University." Thus Pacific's shape as "a great university" was sculpted by the shape of Robert Burns' personality and enthusiasms.

That it would be a strong institution he had promised in his Inaugural Address. A mark of that strength lay in the orderly way the transition to new leadership was accomplished. Immediately after his death, Dr. McCrone was appointed Acting President, and a Search Committee composed of faculty, students, and alumni began the difficult task of sifting through the numbers of applications for what was now one of the major positions in American higher education. After months of meetings this Committee, under the extremely able leadership of Dr. Elliott Taylor, agreed with the Regents that three final candidates be invited to the campus for personal interviews. As a result of that process, Dr. Stanley McCaffrey was nominated to the Presidency.

Dr. McCaffrey, a graduate of the University of California, Berkeley, brought a varied background to his new position, having served for six years during World War II as a naval intelligence officer, for 12 years as Alumni Director and then Vice President of the University of California, and for a year as Executive Assistant to Vice President Richard Nixon. Between 1961 and 1971, he had served as President and Chief Executive Officer of the San Francisco Bay Area Council—the nine county regional organization — "dedicated to the civic, economic and environmental enhancement of the San Francisco Bay Area." The Search Committee believed that his experience working closely with civic and business groups, combined with his familiarity with academe, would prove invaluable as he confronted the complex problems of managing the University. Another important factor in his being chosen was his active membership in a Protestant church in Berkeley. Board members and old friends of the University were anxious that the guidance of Pacific continue to be in the hands of a committed churchman. They were pleased, also, to note his wife Beth's interest in church affairs, her membership on the Board of Trustees of Pacific School of Religion.

Stanley McCaffrey officially became President of the University of the Pacific on December 1, 1971, a little more than one hundred and twenty years after it was founded by those audacious Methodist ministers in the Gold Rush. Like all of his predecessors in that office, he was to face daunting obstacles in the path toward academic and financial development of the institution. And some of the vexing issues which Robert Burns had faced during his administration continued to be debated after his death: The question of how much emphasis to give to intercollegiate football, the controversial design of a system of governance which would be acceptable to administration, faculty and students. Fortunately, as President Burns had pointed out in his Inaugural Address, at Pacific "adjustment to new conditions has been a salient feature of our history." That historic flexibility, together with the pioneering perspective of Pacific's founders, their "frontier virtues of vision, faith, and courage," suggest models for overcoming present and future problems.

During his years as President, Robert Burns found strength and direction in that pioneering heritage. While remaining true to the traditional principles of academic life—the value of intellectual freedom, the continuing necessity of the pursuit of excellence in education—he yet explored wholly new thresholds, innovative ways of teaching and learning at the University of the Pacific. On that sunny June day in 1947 he had reminded his listeners that "A community of scholars is bound together by a dynamic idea. They either pioneer or perish. An institution becomes great by daring to dream and then bending every effort to make these dreams come true." During those twenty-four and a half years, Robert Burns fulfilled that promise. His pioneering leadership brought the University of the Pacific to new frontiers of greatness in the many and varied paths it offers to young people in their search for truth, within a concerned and friendly academic community.

Epilogue

As I UNDERTOOK my duties as the newly appointed President of the University of the Pacific in the late Fall of 1971, I was not only enthusiastic about the opportunity afforded me but was also favorably impressed by the University. While I had known of the University of the Pacific dating back many years to College of the Pacific days and had, in fact, played football against COP as a member of the California Golden Bear team, I had not known the University intimately. Thus, as I began intensive visits with officers of the University, members of the faculty and with the individual Schools and Colleges, I became increasingly impressed that the school which had been known earlier primarily for its Conservatory of Music and School of Education had indeed developed into a full-fledged University.

Ted Baun, long-time Chairman of the Board of Regents, tells the story of the time the COP football team played Cal in Memorial Stadium and beat the Bears. As some Old Blues gathered around in the stands of the Stadium after the game commiserating with each other over the defeat, one said to the other, "Imagine that, being beaten by those musicians from that little old Conservatory over there." Of course, those "musicians" were fellows like Dick Bass and other fine players of the Tiger team of that era. More importantly, however, this remark indicates what many people had thought of COP. They didn't realize that it had grown and developed into a University with many schools and colleges in a variety of disciplines and professions. In fact, coming from the San Francisco Bay area as I did, I was constantly surprised in the first months of my service by how little my friends in the Bay Area knew about Pacific. Oh, they had heard of Amos Alonzo Stagg and Eddie LeBaron, but they really didn't know of the University as it had developed in recent years.

The first quality which struck me as I visited the campus and as I began my service as President was the friendliness of everyone at the University—gardeners, maintenance men, receptionists, secre-

213

taries, students, faculty members; virtually every person one saw on the campus. While I had felt the University of California had a friendly atmosphere when I was there as an undergraduate in the years 1934-38, there really wasn't any comparison with the friendly spirit which prevailed on the Pacific campus at Stockton. Here, virtually everyone said hello to a passerby, and there was an easy informality and friendliness which was most impressive to me as a newcomer. I might add that, in the succeeding years in which I have served, I have found that this spirit of friendliness is the real thing and has continued to prevail and to pervade the atmosphere of the campus. It undoubtedly stems back to the very early years when Pacific was a small institution of under 1,000 students and almost everyone knew each other. The fact that this spirit has continued as the University has grown is a great tribute to all concerned, and certainly it represents one of the finest assets the University has. I have found that almost every visitor, after commenting on the beauty of the campus, speaks of the friendliness which he or she has experienced here.

A second quality which impressed me from the beginning, and which I have found to be an inherent quality of the University, is the *interest in the individual.* It is closely related to the spirit of friendliness I have just mentioned, but it carries over with great meaning into the classroom and to all relationships on the campus. Faculty members have a sincere personal interest in their students. Individuals on the campus have a respect for others, and it seems to me just about everyone has an interest in other individuals at the University. Again, this no doubt has developed from the small size and the personal character of the University in its earlier years. The fact that it has continued up to the present time certainly is a tribute to Bob Burns in his leadership of the institution and to all of those administrators and faculty members who have been such an integral part of Pacific for the past decades.

I might note that as we seek new students to maintain and strengthen our enrollment, these two qualities which I have noted— the spirit of friendliness and personal interest—are very important in attracting new students. These are qualities we have to offer, as a moderate-sized institution, which perhaps are not as readily apparent or available at larger institutions. They are precious qualities which fortunately have been preserved through the years and which stand as vitally important characteristics of the University of the Pacific.

Another quality which impressed me from the beginning was the devotion of members of the faculty and staff to the University. At most colleges and universities, one finds that faculty and staff members are quite devoted to their subject, to their particular responsibilities and, to an extent, to the institution, although this latter type of devotion varies from place to place. At Pacific, however, there was quite obviously an intrinsic devoted loyalty which members of the University felt toward this institution. While the description "family" was not looked upon with popular favor for a period, there was unquestionably a "family spirit" at Pacific, with the kind of devotion and loyalty to the institution which is found in a family group.

As I undertook the Presidency, the University of Pacific, along with other colleges and universities, was moving from the historic perception of the President as "pater familias," in which the President was the father figure and exercised strong control, to a more widespread participation in decision-making. Perhaps as long as President Burns was alive, the earlier tradition continued to an extent, but I believe there is evidence that the change had begun even in the later years of his Presidency. He had, for example, appointed a committee to study a system of governance for the University, and there were other indications of the faculty's assuming a larger role in University policy-decision making.

Even in this period of transition, there was a noticeable respect for the presidency at Pacific. From the beginning I was struck by the fact that on all occasions I was treated with friendly respect. Fortunately, this has continued to the present time, and it is something which a university president appreciates and which supports and strengthens him in his efforts. Unquestionably this spirit has grown, from the earliest years of the University under President Tully Knoles and subsequently with President Burns and represents a tribute to both of those leaders, as it does to the members of faculty, staff and succeeding student bodies. Even as I have held campus open meetings to discuss the University budget, a procedure which I initiated in my first year as President, I have found that as questions have been posed or even criticisms voiced, they have been presented in a respectful manner, appropriate, in my opinion, to the dignity of an institution of higher education.

215

Beyond these qualities and values which I have reviewed above, the element which most impressed me in my early months at the University, and in succeeding years, was the breadth of the University's academic development. From an institution which had offered relatively few courses in liberal arts, education and music at the time of the move to Stockton in 1924, the University had gradually expanded its offerings to those of a liberal arts college in succeeding years. Beginning in the late 1950s, and continuing into the 1960s under President Burns' leadership, the University made its "quantum leap" forward in the expansion of its academic curriculum, to become truly a full-fledged University. This period of growth and development has been well reviewed in earlier chapters of this history. It includes, of course, the initiation of the cluster colleges and their unique features. The clusters brought considerable national attention to the University and, in their earlier years, attracted a fair number of students who were interested in the innovative qualities they offered. However, I am fully convinced that the most important additions to the University's academic curriculum were those of the professional schools of pharmacy, dentistry and law.

These professional schools have not only grown and developed into programs of distinction, they have played a very important part in assuring the financial stability of the University. Thus, the decision of President Burns and the University Board of Regents to establish the School of Pharmacy and to bring the Schools of Law and Dentistry into the University must surely be, in the long history of Pacific, among the wisest decisions ever made by this University.

The story of the School of Pharmacy is a remarkable one. As President Burns initiated the School in 1955, upon the urging of Chemistry Chairman Emerson Cobb, in a classroom in Weber Hall with twenty students, it would have been difficult to envision the magnificent Pharmacy complex of today, with 750 students enrolled in the Pharmacy program. When one considers that the total enrollment on the Stockton campus is approximately 4,000, the fact that nearly one-fifth of that enrollment is in Pharmacy or Pharmacy-related programs is most impressive. Not only in enrollment has the School contributed to the University, but in providing financial support as well. The School of Pharmacy makes one of

216

the most important contributions to the fiscal stability of the institution of any of the Schools and Colleges of the University. Indeed, a strong case could be made that the decision to establish the School of Pharmacy was one of the most important and wisest decisions made by President Burns in his entire Presidency.

The addition of the School of Dentistry, by bringing old "P & S" (College of Physicians and Surgeons) into the University in 1962, was also a notable and significant decision. P & S was a respected professional school and brought good credentials to the University. With the financial support provided by Pacific, a splendid new dental facility was constructed in San Francisco at what was to become the Pacific Medical Center complex, and important new additions were made to the dentistry teaching staff. It would have been difficult to foresee the great interest in dentistry of prospective students that developed in subsequent years. For the past several years there have been over 3,500 applicants for the 135 places of admission in the Dental School, which has an overall enrollment of approximately 400. Thus, the Dental School, as well, has made a significant contribution to the University's enrollment stability and financial viability. It too has earned a national reputation for quality and is ranked among the leading dental schools in the nation.

The story of the addition of McGeorge School of Law, and its development since it became a part of the University, is an amazing one. McGeorge grew from an enrollment of about 400 part-time evening students in 1966, when it became affiliated with Pacific, to a present full-time enrollment of over 1,300. Its faculty has expanded from seventeen part-time to twenty-nine full-time and forty part-time. Its library volumes have increased from 14,600 to 115,000, and its plant value has grown from $246,640 to $4,717,364. McGeorge was regarded as an evening law school which did a good job of training practicing lawyers. In the years that it has been a part of the University, it has developed academically, in its physical plant, and in all other respects, and it now has national distinction. For the past five years McGeorge graduates have had the highest "passing rate" in the State Bar Examinations. Shortly after the School became part of the University, it was not only accredited by the American Bar Association, but also was accorded recognition by admission to the prestigious Association of

American Law Schools. Its Courtroom of the Future is hailed nationally as being a pioneer in innovating new procedures and methods in courtroom justice. Its program of trial advocacy received the highest national recognition last year when it won the Emil Gumpert Award of the United States Trial Lawyers.

Without the professional schools of Pharmacy, Dentistry and Law, Pacific would be a liberal arts college of quality. With these schools, plus the excellent professional schools of Music, Education and Engineering, it is a full-fledged University whose academic offerings are broad and distinguished. The addition of these schools must constitute one of the notable chapters in the history of the University and certainly of the Presidency of Robert Burns.

Another feature which impressed me as I became acquainted with the University was the fact that the Regents and succeeding administrations had been able to maintain a financial viability in spite of exceedingly difficult challenges. The history of the University, as I have studied it, represents a history of meeting challenges. As one reads the account of the past, from the very beginnings in 1851 through the early years, including the move to Stockton in 1924, every single year has been a year of challenges, if not crises. In most of those early years, the question was not of *economizing* but of *surviving!* Through the 1930s and the times of the depression, these fiscal concerns were accentuated, and minutes of the Board of Regents reflect, year after year, critical situations in which drastic actions were taken to enable the University to continue. At times it seemed the University would have to close its doors and that it was bankrupt. But somehow, through prayer and pleading, a last-minute loan or gift would pay the bills and keep the doors open. In the 1930s the Great Depression threatened the College's continued existence and, remarkably, the faculty and administration voted to take a forty percent salary cut to save the institution!

Thus, while the University's history is one of problems, almost all based on financial needs, it is most of all a record—a heroic record—of *meeting challenges.* No matter how difficult the problems were, they somehow seem to have been met. Always there were sacrifices by University personnel involved, and devoted effort by faculty, students, administrators, Regents, and all concerned. We have, indeed, a heritage of surmounting problems which seemed insurmountable and of emerging as an even stronger institution. It is a heritage which has given the University strength of character—a heritage of which we can be enormously proud.

Certainly great credit is due to Bob Burns for having developed support from among Regents and other benefactors not only to sustain the University but to enable it to grow. When one realizes that the capital value of the University's physical plant was approximately $1,600,000 in 1946, when he became President, and had developed to a value of $33,500,000 at the time of his death, one can appreciate not only the impressive growth of the institution but the enormous contribution which Bob Burns made to that growth.

The Regents of the University have shown the way in their generous and unfailing support. Long-time Board Chairman Ted Baun has supported all aspects of the University and has made special contributions to the School of Engineering, which is housed in a building that bears his name in recognition of that interest. Certainly Grace Covell made the most generous gift in the history of the University by her bequest amounting to nearly $5 million. Walter Raymond, Ferd Callison, Don Wood, Thomas and Joseph Long, Winifred Raney, John Crummey, the Paul Davies family and many others were generous in their support, enabling the institution to remain viable and to continue its progress. The element of careful financial management was an important factor through all these years and recognition must be given the Financial Vice Presidents (Controllers) of their respective eras, Ovid Ritter and Robert Winterberg. The fact that the University has been able to balance its budget has assured not only its continued operation but progressive development as well.

As I assumed the presidency in the fall of 1971, I was immediately impressed with the active interest in the University of the community of Stockton and San Joaquin County, indeed the Valley area. The record shows that the community has given strong support to the University from the time of its move to Stockton in 1924, when money and land were contributed by citizens to help the establishment of the new campus. "Town and gown" relationships are always important between a college campus and the community in which it is located. My observation is that these relationships at Pacific have been excellent all through the years—again, a tribute to Tully Knoles and Bob Burns. Both were active in meeting with and speaking before community groups, not only in Stockton but throughout the Valley and, as a result of their efforts, the University became very well known and highly regarded by citizens of this region.

I had not known Bob Burns although I had, of course, known of him. Interestingly, I had heard Tully Knoles speak on several occasions, before the Commonwealth Club of California and Rotary clubs, but I don't believe I had ever even heard Bob Burns speak. Now, having been at the University, having lived in the President's home—where Grace and Bob Burns lived for so many years—and having my office in the office which Bob Burns built in the Tower, I feel as if I have known him.

He must have been quite a remarkable man! His creativity and ingenuity are qualities which impress me as I look back over the developments for which he was responsible during his Presidency. I am sure there were many other fine qualities, certainly including splendid traits of character and human interest, which he possessed. From the standpoint of the University presidency, undoubtedly his innovativeness in meeting changing conditions and seizing upon what he saw as new opportunities were the qualities which most characterized him. His bringing the professional schools into the University, his establishing the cluster colleges, his personal contribution to the development of the Pacific Medical Center—all of these are evidence of his willingness to try new things, to branch out, and they reflect a lively imagination and willingness to dare. These characteristics are well reviewed in the preceding pages of this history and need not be recounted here. However, as his successor, facing many of the same problems which confronted him, I can appreciate from this special vantage point the importance which these qualities have had in the growth and development of the University of the Pacific as we know it today.

As this book is written, we are celebrating the 125th anniversary of the University of the Pacific. The first years of the University are marked by the faith which its founders had in it, faith which enabled the University to survive in spite of the most severe conditions of adversity. The fact that it continued was a tremendous tribute to the persistence and determination of the early leaders of the institution. Certainly the first period of significant growth and development of the University was under President Tully Knoles. He not only assured the growth of the institution by the courageous move to Stockton but, by his own strong personality and active speaking before hundreds of groups throughout California, he brought public recognition to Pacific, which enabled the institution to become established and to be known in its formative years. President Knoles presided over extremely difficult financial years of the institution, including those of the Great Depression, and the quality of institutional loyalty which he inspired in faculty and staff constitutes a great tribute to his leadership as he enabled Pacific to become firmly established as a fine institution of higher education.

Pacific became a University under the leadership of Robert Burns. The growth which has been documented in these pages, the expansion of the educational offerings, the addition of the professional schools, the innovative introduction of the cluster colleges— all of these represented development of a significant nature and truly qualified Pacific as a University.

What a legacy these two great Presidents have left! The University of the Pacific stands today as a living memorial to Tully Knoles and Bob Burns. Each made a magnificent contribution to the greatness of this institution. Their "mark for good" will remain indelibly inscribed upon Pacific for all time to come.

A university always faces challenges, and we at Pacific have had our share all through the years and will continue to have them. Life itself represents a series of challenges. But as I undertook the Presidency of the University of the Pacific in 1971, I found an institution built by great leaders, devoted to the ideal of service of their fellow human beings, with a faith and devotion that would surmount the greatest of difficulties to achieve the ideal of service. Thus, the University celebrates its 125th year with the highest recognition of its founders and of all those who have contributed to its progress through this century and a quarter. As we review this past quarter century in this historical account, we pay special tribute to the man who provided dedicated and inspired leadership to the University, Robert E. Burns. With his devoted and gracious helpmate, Grace, he strengthened the University and led it to new heights of excellence from which we, his successors, have the opportunity to continue to build in the never-ending search for new knowledge, and to educate succeeding generations of young men and women, all dedicated to the ideal of service to our fellow human beings. We continue this mission with the same sense of faith and devotion held by the University's founders and characterized by our leaders over the years. With the greatest of pride in past accomplishments, we look forward to the future with optimism and enthusiasm, confident that the University of the Pacific will be even greater in the years ahead.

Stanley E. McCaffrey,
President

Appendix I

University of the Pacific Board of Regents
July 1977

T. F. Baun	Fresno
Kenneth D. Beatie	Sacramento
R. L. Brandenburger	Portola Valley
Maurice Buerge	West Los Angeles
C. Robert Clarke	Honolulu, Hawaii
Mrs. James P. Darrah (Joan)	Stockton
Mrs. Paul Davies (Faith)	San Jose
Paul L. Davies, Jr.	San Francisco
Mrs. Frederick J. Early (Marguerite)	San Francisco
Robert M. Eberhardt	Stockton
President of the Board of Regents	
John R. Gamble, M.D.	San Francisco
Robert D. Haas	San Francisco
C. Vernon Hansen	Sacramento
Jaquelin H. Hume	San Francisco
Cecil W. Humphreys	Atherton
Richard G. Landis	San Francisco
Rev. Noel C. LeRoque	Sacramento
Thomas J. Long	Walnut Creek
Daren McGavren	Newport Beach
Eugene McGeorge	Mill Valley
Mrs. Percy Neitzel (Wilmere)	Suisun
Mrs. Gene Raney (Winifred)	Turlock
Justice Frank K. Richardson	San Francisco
Miss Lucy Ritter	Sacramento
Mason M. Roberts	Walnut Creek
Alex G. Spanos	Stockton
Bishop R. Marvin Stuart	San Francisco
Rev. Arthur V. Thurman	Redding
Mrs. Ben Wallace, Jr. (Bing)	Stockton

223

Frederick T. West, D.D.S.	San Francisco
Edward W. Westgate	Napa
George H. Wilson	Clarksburg
Thomas W. Witter	San Francisco
Carlos C. Wood	Napa
Herbert K. Yee, D.D.S.	Sacramento

Honorary Members

Henry R. Herold	San Marino
O. D. Jacoby	Oakland
Mrs. Percy Morris (Lillie)	Palo Alto
Bishop Donald H. Tippett	Berkeley
Don B. Wood	Lodi

Appendix II

Rev. Gerald Harvey	Los Angeles
Henry R. Herold	San Marino
Francis J. Herz, D.D.S.	San Francisco
J. Wesley Hole	Los Angeles
Dale G. Hollenbeck	Stockton
Mrs. Benjamin Holt (Anna)	Stockton
Simpson H. Hornage	Stockton
W. M. Hotle	Sebastopol
Mrs. C. M. Jackson (Harriet)	Stockton
O. D. Jacoby*	Oakland
Stanley James	San Jose
H. V. Jespersen	Placerville
Bishop Gerald Kennedy	Los Angeles
Rev. John R. Kenney	Bakersfield
Irving Kesterson	Atherton
C. N. Kirkbride	San Mateo
Francis N. Laird	La Habra
Harry W. Lange	Bakersfield
Thomas J. Long	Oakland
Rev. E. A. Lowther	Petaluma
Bert B. Malouf	Los Angeles
Fillmore Marks	Stockton
Rev. William H. Merwin	Los Angeles
Wally Moon	Encino
Mrs. Percy F. Morris (Lillie)	Berkeley
William E. Morris	Stockton
Marshall O. Nelson	San Fernando
Hubert E. Orton	Hollywood
William S. Orvis	Farmington
Rev. Alfred Painter	Costa Mesa
Rev. Theodore H. Palmquist	Palo Alto
Fred Parr	San Francisco
Rev. C. Russell Prewitt	Bakersfield
Chalmers G. Price	Placerville
Alstyne E. Pruner	Santa Barbara
Mrs. L. V. Richardson (Grace)	Stockton
L. Eugene Root	Sunnyvale
J. W. Rupley	Orinda
Newton Rutherford	Stockton
Charles Segerstrom	Sonora
Myron E. Smith	Los Angeles
Rev. C. B. Sylvester	Stockton

227

Appendix III

Construction on the Stockton campus was begun on April 14, 1924. By September some of the buildings were ready for use, though others were still under construction.

Facilities included in the original campus are:

Administration Building - Now known as Knoles Hall.

Anderson Dining and Social Hall - Named for Mr. and Mrs. W. C. Anderson, donors, in 1929.

Baxter Stadium - Named for Thomas Baxter, long-time president of the Board of Trustees.

The Conservatory of Music - Completed in February 1925.

The Gymnasium - Later destroyed by fire and rebuilt at its present location.

Heating Plant - Now Baun Hall and home of the School of Engineering.

Manor Hall - Originally Thalia Hall.

North and South Halls - Student residences.

President's Home.

Weber Memorial Hall - Given by citizens of Stockton in honor of Captain Charles M. Weber, founder of the city of Stockton.

Completed later were:

Fraternity and Sorority Houses:

Alpha Kappa Lambda (Omicron Chapter). The building was originally the Co-op House; Alpha Kappa Lambda moved into the home in 1954 and was established as Omicron Chapter.

Omega Phi Alpha. Organized in December 1921; moved into its present home in Fraternity Circle in June 1925; changed to Pacific Chapter of Delta Upsilon in 1959; changed back to Omega Phi Alpha in 1972.

Phi Kappa Tau (Gamma Upsilon Chapter). Organized in April 1854 as Archania Literary Society; adopted Greek name of Alpha Kappa Phi in 1926 when it moved into its present home in Fraternity Circle; established as Gamma Upsilon Chapter in 1961.

Sigma Alpha Epsilon (Rho Chapter). Founded November 1858 as Rhizomia Society (until 1957). Moved into its present home in Fraternity Circle in 1925. Revived as Phi Sigma Kappa from 1961 to 1966. Established as a service organization, Theta Tau, from 1966 to 1968. Changed to Phi Alpha from 1968 to 1970. Established as Rho Chapter of Sigma Alpha Epsilon in February 1970.

Alpha Chi Omega (Delta Sigma Chapter). Founded in 1935 as the Zetagathean Club; became Zeta Phi in 1945; moved into the old Tau Kappa Kappa House on Pacific Avenue in 1947; established as Delta Sigma Chapter in 1961.

Delta Delta Delta (Phi Rho Chapter). Founded as Athenaea Literary Society in 1917; changed to Tau Kappa Kappa before 1924; in 1927, purchased colonial home of Mrs. Adelaide Coburn on Pacific Avenue. In 1947, moved to present home in Sorority Circle. Nationalized in 1959 as Phi Rho Chapter.

Kappa Alpha Theta (Phi Chapter). Founded as Sopholechtia Literary Society in 1881; in 1912 assumed the name of Sigma Lambda Sigma; acquired the name of Alpha Theta Tau in 1923; nationalized in 1959 as Phi Chapter.

West Memorial Infirmary - Built in 1926 and made possible by a gift from Mrs. Charles M. Jackson in memory of her parents, George and Ellen West, and brother, Frank Allen West.

This was the campus as seen by Robert E. Burns when he first came to Pacific as a student. During the 1930s and 1940s, the following facilities were added:

Anderson Y - Completed in 1940 through a gift of Mrs. W. C. Anderson.

Knoles Field - The playing field was made possible through a gift from Mr. and Mrs. Amos Alonzo Stagg in the 1940s.

Morris Chapel - Dedicated in 1942 and made possible chiefly by the gift of Percy F. and Lillie B. Morris.

Swimming Pool - Completed in 1932 and financed through student donations and fees. Replaced in the 1970s by the Chris Kjeldsen Pool.

New Buildings During the Robert E. Burns Administration

Ballantyne (Jesse L. and John N.) Halls - Cluster College residence halls completed in 1964 and 1965, respectively, and named for Acampo orchardists.

Bannister Hall - A classroom and faculty office building acquired as war surplus after World War II; later a brick facade was added and the building named for Edward Bannister, the first president and founder of College of the Pacific.

Baun Hall - This building was named in 1958 for Ted F. Baun, graduate of the School of Engineering and long-time president of the Board of Regents. The building was the original heating plant for the campus, and served as the library prior to its becoming the home for the School of Engineering in 1955.

Robert E. Burns Tower - Dedicated on March 8, 1964, this structure combines Burns's wish for a campus landmark with the practical need for a new water tower. Various administrative offices are housed in the Tower.

Carter House - A student residence hall named for Mr. and Mrs. Robert Carter, Acampo farmer and supporter of Pacific. It was completed in 1965 as housing for Cluster College students.

Casa Jackson - A Cluster College residence hall completed in 1962 and named for Mr. and Mrs. Lester R. Jackson.

Casa Werner - A Cluster College residence completed in 1962 and named for Dr. Gustavus A. Werner, a history professor at Pacific for many years.

Grace A. Covell Hall - The largest residence hall on campus, this facility was completed in 1959 and named for Regent Grace A. Covell on January 20, 1960.

Cowell Student Health Center - Completed in 1969 as a result of a gift from the S. H. Cowell Foundation in San Francisco.

School of Dentistry (College of Physicians and Surgeons) - Founded in San Francisco in 1896 and merged with the University of the Pacific in 1962. Construction of the multi-million-dollar building at Sacramento and Webster Streets in San Francisco was completed in 1967.

Eiselen House - A Cluster College student residence named for D. Malcolm Eiselen, a member of the faculty for many years. Built in 1965.

Fallon House Theatre - Originally purchased by the University, this property was given to the State and then leased back by the University. It was used for the first time for a State Centennial Celebration in 1949, and as a summer theatre program in 1950; in 1961 Eagle Cotage was added.

Farley House - A Cluster College student residence named for D. Fred Farley, a long-time faculty member. Built in 1962.

Harris House - Originally conceived as an Alumni House in 1968, this building today serves as a center for various student religious organizations and the Anderson Y. It is named for the first dean of the School of Education, J. William Harris, who owned the property. Its name was changed from Alumni House to Harris House in 1976.

Irving Martin Library - Completed in 1955, this main wing of the library is named for Irving Martin, Sr., publisher of the *Stockton Record.*

McConchie Hall - Completed in 1960 and made possible by a gift from Fannie M. McClanahan in memory of her parents, John D. and Mariette McConchie. The building now houses Phi Delta Chi fraternity.

McGeorge School of Law - Founded in 1924 and amalgamated with the University in 1966. From a single building and an enrollment of 400 part-time students, it has grown to include a complex of buildings and an enrollment of 1,350 students.

Owen Hall - Today a music practice facility, this building originally was acquired as war surplus. Later it was faced with brick and named for Isaac Owen, one of the University's founders.

Pacific Marine Station - Although used as early as 1933, the property was given to the University in 1948 by the Lawson family. Subsequently, buildings were erected.

Pacific Memorial Stadium - Financed in part through contributions from the community, this stadium was dedicated October 21, 1950, in honor of deceased war veterans from the Central Valley and the Mother Lode.

Pharmacy Complex - Completed in 1969 as a center for the School of Pharmacy, various segments of this building are named for major contributors to the facility.

Price House - A Cluster College student residence completed in 1962 and named for Chalmers G. Price, a Placerville lumberman, and his wife.

Ritter House - A Cluster College residence completed in 1962 and named for Ovid H. Ritter, for many years comptroller and financial vice president of the University.

Sears Hall - A classroom addition to Morris Chapel dedicated June 16, 1950, this building was financed through a gift from Mr. and Mrs. Osro Sears in memory of Mr. and Mrs. Joseph Sears.

Student Union Building (End Zone and Bookstore) - Completed in 1949, this building was converted to the present Computer Center after completion of the University Center in the early 1970s.

University Townhouse Apartments - This apartment complex was acquired in 1971 for upper division and graduate student housing.

Wemyss House - A Cluster College residence completed in 1962 and named for Edwin Wemyss, Stockton businessman and donor to the University.

Wendell Phillips Center for International Studies - Originally designed as offices and classrooms for the Cluster Colleges, the building was completed in 1968 and named for businessman and world-traveler Wendell Phillips.

West Hall (and wings connecting with South Hall) - Student residences completed in 1947 and the mid-1950s respectively.

West Memorial Finance Center - Originally an infirmary, this building was converted to offices for financial services following completion of the Cowell Student Health Center in 1969. It originally was constructed in 1926 as a result of a gift from Mrs Charles M. Jackson, in memory of her parents, George and Ellen West, and her brother, Frank Allen West.

Donald B. Wood Bridge - Completed in 1969 to link the main campus and north campus over the Calaveras River. The bridge is named for Donald B. Wood, Regent of the University from Lodi.

Wood Memorial Hall - This addition to the Irving Martin Library is named in memory of John Thornton Wood, son of Mr. and Mrs. Donald B. Wood, donors.

In addition to these named facilities, eleven temporary quonset-type buildings were added to the campus soon after World War II and continued to be used throughout the years of the Burns administration.

Appendix IV

Enrollment During Burns' Years

Year	Full-time	Part-time	Total*
1947-48	740	201	941
1948-49	922	238	1160
1949-50	951	267	1218
1950-51	887	317	1204
1951-52	970	293	1263
1952-53	862	367	1229
1953-54	860	372	1232
1954-55	926	379	1305
1955-56	1086	648	1734
1956-57	1281	417	1698
1957-58	1347	676	2023
1958-59	1569	481	2050
1959-60	1646	468	2114
1960-61	1803	430	2233
1961-62	1774	376	2150
1962-63	2253	423	2676
1963-64	2362	396	2758
1964-65	2476	453	2929
1965-66	2674	502	3176
1966-67	2787	476	3263
1967-68	2955	815	3770
1968-69	3309	854	4163
1969-70	-	-	4636
1970-71	-	-	5064

*These totals do not reflect full-time-equivalents, but only the number of persons taking courses at Pacific.

Notes

Chapter One

1. "Minutes of the College of the Pacific Board of Trustees, October 22, 1946," p. 183, University of the Pacific, Stockton, Cal.

2. Tape recorded conversation with Leland Case, December 10, 1975.

3. "Board of Trustees Minutes," p. 185.

4. Ibid., pp. 185-86.

5. With the exception of Yeshiva and Brandeis, the Jewish community has not taken an active role in this development, preferring instead to rely on Hillel and similar associations within public or private secular colleges and universities. See C. Jencks and D. Reisman, *The Academic Revolution* (New York: Doubleday and Co., Inc. 1968), pp. 318-19.

6. Ibid., p. 1.

7. Ibid., p. 2.

8. Donald G. Tewksbury, *The Founding of American Colleges and Universities Before the Civil War* (New York: Bureau of Publication - Teacher College, Columbia University, 1932), p. 108.

9. J. O. Gross, "The Field of Education," *The History of American Methodism*, vol. 3 (Emory S. Bucks, general editor) (New York: Abingdon Press, 1964), p. 202.

10. Ibid., p. 217.

11. Jaroslav J. Pelikan, "Methodism's Contribution to America," *American Methodism*, vol. 3, p. 602.

12. Tewksbury, *Founding of American Colleges*.

13. Ibid., pp. 23-4.

14. William W. Guth, "What Methodism Has Done for Education in California," *California Christian Advocate*, February 22, 1912.

15. Rockwell D. Hunt, *History of the College of the Pacific* (Stockton, Cal.: College of the Pacific, 1951, p. 30.

16. Ibid., p. 33.

17. Ibid.

18. Robert E. Burns, "The First Half-Century of the College of the Pacific," (Master's thesis, College of the Pacific, 1946), p. 42.

19. Ibid.

20. Ibid., p. 43.

21. Ibid., p. 44.

22. *California Christian Advocate*, January 14, 1869, p. 19, quoted in Burns, Ibid., p. 47.

23. Hunt, *College of the Pacific*, p. 85.

24. Ibid., p. 69.

25. Ibid., p. 133.

26. Reginald and Grace D. Stuart, *Tully Knoles of Pacific: Teacher, Minister, College President, Traveler, and Public Speaker* (Stockton, Cal.: College of the Pacific, 1956), p. 14.

27. Ibid., p. 15.

28. Ibid., p. 29.

29. Ibid., p. 36.

30. Ibid., p. 66.

31. Hunt, *College of the Pacific*, p. 134.

32. Ibid.

33. Robert A. Altran, *The Upper Division College* (San Francisco, Cal.: Jossey-Bass, Inc., 1970), pp. 26-7.

34. Ibid., p. 27.

35. Ibid., p. 29.

36. Tully C. Knoles, "Report to the Trustees on the Occasion of the 25th Anniversary of His Becoming President of C.O.P., March 28, 1944," p. 3.

37. Hunt, *College of the Pacific*, p. 137.

38. Knoles, "Report to the Trustees, March 28, 1944," p. 4.

39. Tully C. Knoles, "Report of the President to the Board of Trustees, October, 1935," p. 1.

40. Hunt, *College of the Pacific*, p. 149.

41. Knoles, "Report of the President, October 27, 1936," p. 5.

42. U. S. Webb to Vierling Kersey, Superintendent of Public Instruction, correspondence, May 9, 1936.

43. Stuart, *Tully Knoles of Pacific*, p. 90.

44. Stockton Junior College, "Bulletin On Semi-Professional Courses," June 1, 1937, p. 1, University of the Pacific, Stockton, Cal.

45. In 1943-44, 399 V-12 trainees attended classes at the College of the Pacific. In the summer session of 1945, 134 sailors and marines participated in the closing session of the program.

46. Knoles, "Report to the Trustees, March 28, 1944," p. 6.

47. Tape recorded conversation with O. D. Jacoby, January 23, 1976.

48. E. R. Mirrielees, *Stanford, The Story of a University* (New York: G. P. Putnam's Sons, 1959), p. 125.

49. "Bulletin of the College of the Pacific, 1946," pp. 21-2, University of the Pacific, Stockton, Cal.

50. Tape recorded conversation with Marc Jantzen, February 9, 1974.

51. College of the Pacific, "Summer School Bulletin, 1946," p. 19, University of the Pacific, Stockton, Cal.

Chapter Two

1. Conversation with Alice Saecker, April 14, 1976.

2. Mary Burns to Grace Burns, correspondence, n.d.

3. Robert E. Burns, "Manuscript," (written shortly before his death), pp. 1-2.

4. Ibid., p. 2.

5. Ibid., p. 3.

6. Ibid.

7. Ibid.

8. Ibid.

9. Ibid.

10. Ibid., p. 4.

11. Ibid.

12. Ibid., p. 5.

36. Conversation with Grace Burns, March 9, 1976.

37. "Board of Trustees Minutes, October 27, 1942," p. 185.

38. "College of the Pacific Brochure," n.d.

39. "Board of Trustees Minutes, March 28, 1944," p. 311.

40. Burns, "First Half-Century," p. 43.

41. Ibid.

42. Ibid.

43. F. W. Reeves et al., *The Liberal Arts College: Based Upon Surveys of Thirty-Five Colleges Related to the Methodist Episcopal Church* (Chicago, Ill.: University of Chicago Press, 1932), p. 97.

44. "Board of Trustees Minutes, October 22, 1946," p. 185.

Chapter Three

1. Winston Churchill, quoted by Eric F. Goldman in *The Crucial Decade: America, 1945-1955* (New York: Alfred Knopf, 1956), pp. 37-8.

2. Robert E. Burns, "The Inaugural Address," (College of the Pacific, "Record of the events of the Inauguration of Robert Edward Burns as the nineteenth President, the induction of Tully Cleon Knoles as the first Chancellor, and the nineteenth Commencement of the College of the Pacific in Stockton, California on Monday, June the Sixteenth, Nineteen Hundred and Forty-Seven," 1947), p. 14.

3. Ibid., p. 13.

4. Ibid.

5. Ibid., p. 16.

6. Ibid.

7. Ibid., p. 17.

8. Ibid., p. 18.

9. Ibid., p. 19.

10. R. R. Hamilton, "Relations with the Veterans Administration: Report of Conference Group XVII," *Current Problems in Education* (Washington, D.C.: Education Association of the United States, Department of Higher Education, 1947), p. 182.

11. "Board of Trustees Minutes, April 23, 1947," p. 207.

15. Ibid.

16. W. B. Simpson, "Report on the American Academy of Asian Studies," n.d., p. 5.

17. Ibid., p. 6.

18. Tape recorded conversation with Jesse Rudkin, October 12, 1975.

19. Tape recorded conversation with Ivan Rowland, April 6, 1976.

20. R. N. Bender et al., "Survey Report to the President and the Board of Trustees of the College of the Pacific," (University Senate and Board of Education of The Methodist Church, January 1956), p. 29.

21. Ibid., p. 43.

22. Ibid.

23. Ibid., p. 209.

24. Ibid.

25. Ibid.

26. Ibid., p. 185.

Chapter Five

1. Arthur Farey, "President Burns Honored: 'To Lift Up Pacific,'" *Pacific Review*, February 1957, p. 4.

2. Ibid., p. 5.

3. Ibid., p. 4.

4. Ibid.

5. "Survey of (Faculty) Recommendations," p. 1, Office of the Academic Vice President (Lloyd Bertholf), University of the Pacific, Stockton, Cal.

6. Ibid., p. 2.

7. Ibid.

8. Ibid., p. 5.

9. Ibid., p. 8.

10. Ibid., p. 3.

11. Ibid., p. 2.

12. Ibid., p. 5.

13. "Board of Trustees Minutes, October 22, 1957," p. 54.

12. Ibid.

13. Robert E. Burns, "Report of the President to the Board of Trustees, October 28, 1947," p. 3.

14. Burns, "Report of the President, March 25, 1947," p. 2.

15. Ibid., p. 5.

16. Burns, "Report of the President, October 28, 1947," p. 5.

17. "Program for the Dedication of the Pacific Marine Station at Dillon Beach," August 24, 1948, University of the Pacific, Stockton, Cal.

18. Ibid.

19. Ibid.

20. Ibid.

21. "Board of Trustees Minutes, March 1943."

22. Burns, "Report of the President, October 28, 1947," p. 8.

23. Arthur W. Munk, "Sign of Creativity: a Unique Educational Experiment," *Journal of Teacher Education*, September 1964, (reprint).

24. Ibid.

25. *Pacific Review*, May 1947, p. 17.

26. John C. Crabbe, "KCVN-KAWO Radio Quonset," *Pacific Review*, October 1948, p. 9.

27. Ibid., p. 10.

28. *Pacific Review*, October 1947, p. 23.

29. De Marcus Brown, "The Little Theater at the College of the Pacific," (Master's thesis, College of the Pacific, 1935), p. vii.

30. Ibid., p. vi.

31. Franklin Wilbur, "Fallon House Theater: The First Twenty Years Occupancy by the Columbia Company of the University of the Pacific Plays and Players 1949-1968," (Master's thesis, Sacramento State College, Sacramento, Cal.), 1969, p. 59.

32. Wilhelmina K. Harbert, *Opening Doors Through Music: A Practical Guide For Teachers, Therapists, Students, Parents* (Rachel Keniston, editor) (Springfield, Ill.: Charles C. Thomas Publishers., 1974), p. vi.

33. Ibid.

34. Ibid., p. xv.

35. Ibid., p. xvii.

36. Ibid., p. xviii.

37. Ibid., p. xvii.

38. Arthur Farey, "The Story of the Christian Community Administration," *Pacific Review*, May 1947, p. 5.

39. Ibid., p. 36.

40. *Pacific Weekly*, October 18, 1946, p. 2.

41. *Pacific Weekly*, March 5, 1948, p. 1.

42. Burns, "Manuscript," p. 9.

43. *Pacific Review*, December 1950, p. 3.

44. *Stockton Record*, Clipping in Burns' scrapbook, n.d.

45. Robert E. Burns, "Looking into a Second Century," *Pacific Review*, May 1951, p. 4.

Chapter Four

1. *Pacific Review*, February 1950, p. 13.

2. *Pacific Review*, October 1951, p. 40.

3. "Board of Trustees Minutes, January 22, 1955," p. 501.

4. "Board of Trustees Minutes, October 15, 1950," p. 363.

5. "Board of Trustees Minutes, March 28, 1950," p. 329.

6. "Board of Trustees Minutes, October 20, 1950," p. 359.

7. Ibid.

8. "Board of Trustees Minutes, November 10, 1950," p. 371.

9. *Pacific Review*, May 1952, p. 16.

10. *Pacific Review*, May 1953, p. 6.

11. Ibid.

12. Robert E. Burns, "The Place of Football in the Modern College," *Pacific Review*, February 1954.

13. Ibid., p. 9.

14. American Academy of Asian Studies, "Bulletin," 1952, p. 1.

15. Ibid.

16. W. B. Simpson, "Report on the American Academy of Asian Studies," n.d., p. 5.

17. Ibid., p. 6.

18. Tape recorded conversation with Jesse Rudkin, October 12, 1975.

19. Tape recorded conversation with Ivan Rowland, April 6, 1976.

20. R. N. Bender et al., "Survey Report to the President and the Board of Trustees of the College of the Pacific," (University Senate and Board of Education of The Methodist Church, January 1956), p. 29.

21. Ibid., p. 43.

22. Ibid.

23. Ibid., p. 209.

24. Ibid.

25. Ibid.

26. Ibid., p. 185.

Chapter Five

1. Arthur Farey, "President Burns Honored: 'To Lift Up Pacific,'" *Pacific Review*, February 1957, p. 4.

2. Ibid., p. 5.

3. Ibid., p. 4.

4. Ibid.

5. "Survey of (Faculty) Recommendations," p. 1, Office of the Academic Vice President (Lloyd Bertholf), University of the Pacific, Stockton, Cal.

6. Ibid., p. 2.

7. Ibid.

8. Ibid., p. 5.

9. Ibid., p. 8.

10. Ibid., p. 3.

11. Ibid., p. 2.

12. Ibid., p. 5.

13. "Board of Trustees Minutes, October 22, 1957," p. 54.

14. "Board of Trustees Minutes, November 4, 1953," p. 555.

15. Bender et al., "Survey Report to the President and the Board of Trustees of the College of the Pacific," p. 26-7.

16. Tape recorded conversation with Samuel Meyer, April 26, 1976.

17. Ibid.

18. Ibid.

19. Ibid.

20. "Minutes of the Faculty Meeting, December 9, 1958," p. 2, University of the Pacific, Stockton, Cal.

21. Ibid.

22. "Faculty Meeting Minutes, October 14, 1958," p. 1.

23. Tape recorded conversation with Samuel Meyer, April 26, 1976.

24. "Board of Trustees Minutes, October 23-24, 1956," p. 36.

25. "Board of Trustees Minutes, May 25, 1957," p. 48.

26. "Board of Trustees Minutes, June 14, 1958," p. 72.

27. Mel Nickerson, "A New Framework for the Pacific Alumni Association," *Pacific Review*, May 1957, p. 6.

28. *Pacific Review*, October 1959, p. 4.

29. Ned Russell and Arthur Farey, "The Pacific Product - Part III," *Pacific Review*, October 1952, pp. 48-9; "The Pacific Product - Part IV," *Pacific Review*, October 1953, pp. 32-3.

30. "Board of Trustees Minutes, December 12, 1958," p. 91.

31. Ibid.

32. "Faculty Meeting Minutes, April 30, 1959," p. 1.

33. Ibid., p. 3.

34. Robert E. Burns, "Letter to the Board of Trustees, October 21, 1959," (included in the "Minutes"), p. 109.

35. Ibid., p. 110.

36. Ibid., p. 111.

37. Ibid., p. 112.

38. Ibid., p. 111.

39. Ibid., p. 112.

40. "Board of Trustees Minutes, October 27, 1959," p. 117.

41. "Board of Trustees Minutes, June 18, 1960," p. 132.

Chapter Six

1. *Pacific Review*, January 1961, p. 23.

2. Samuel Meyer, "A Statement For Tomorrow," *Pacific Review*, January 1961, p. 25.

3. Ibid.

4. Ibid., p. 27.

5. Ibid.

6. *Pacific Review*, May 1961, p. 7.

7. *Pacific Review*, November 1962, p. 11.

8. Conversation with W. B. Martin, June 14, 1976.

9. Tape recorded conversation with W. B. Martin, May 26, 1976.

10. Tape recorded conversation with Samuel Meyer, April 26, 1976.

11. Elliott J. Taylor, "Recruitment Spreads to Latin America," *Pacific Review*, April 22, 1963, p. 3.

12. Ibid.

13. *Time*, vol 82, #71, October 11, 1963, p. 71.

14. "Board of Trustees Minutes, December 2, 1960," p. 148.

15. Ibid., p. 149.

16. Ibid., p. 151.

17. Ibid., p. 150.

18. Ibid.

19. Ibid., p. 152.

20. "Proposal for Discussion Topics at the Faculty Retreat, February, 1961," n.d., University of the Pacific, Stockton, Cal.

21. Ibid.

22. *Pacific Review*, April 1962, p. 4.

23. *Pacific Review*, April 1964, p. 1.

24. Bender et al., "Survey Report to the President and the Board of Trustees of the College of the Pacific," pp. 30, 207.

25. Samuel Meyer, "Academic Progress: 1958-1964," *Pacific Review*, October 1964, p. 4.

26. Ibid.

27. Ibid., p. 3.

28. Ibid., p. 5.

29. Ibid.

30. Ibid., p. 6.

31. Ibid.

Chapter Seven

1. William L. O'Neill, *Coming Apart: An Informal History of America in the 1960s* (Chicago, Ill.: Quadrangle Books, 1971), p. 279.

2. Ibid., p. 280.

3. "St. Michael's College Brochure," University of the Pacific, Stockton, Cal.

4. "St. Michael's College," (fifteen minute sound-color film), University of the Pacific, Stockton, Cal.

5. *Pacific Review*, Summer 1965, p. 19.

6. Ibid.

7. Ibid.

8. Ibid.

9. *Pacific Review*, Winter 1967, p. 2.

10. Ibid., p. 3.

11. Tape recorded conversation with Gordon Schaber, September 30, 1976.

12. Samuel Meyer, "Education...Methodism's Splendid Obsession," *Pacific Review*, February 22, 1963, p. 6.

13. *Pacific Review*, Spring 1966, p. 12.

14. Burns, "Inaugural Address," p. 11.

15. Ibid., p. 12.

16. *Pacific Review*, Spring 1966, p. 3.

17. Ibid., p. 12.

18. Ibid.

19. "Minutes of the University of the Pacific Board of Regents, March 6, 1967," p. 8, University of the Pacific, Stockton, Cal.

20. Jack White, "Pacific Chapel: Commitment with Challenge," *Pacific Review*, Winter 1967, pp. 6-7.

21. *Pacific Review*, Winter 1967, p. 6.

22. Bishop Donald Harvey Tippett, correspondence, n.d.

23. Wallace B. Graves, "The All University Study Day," *Pacific Review*, Spring 1963, p. 11.

24. *Pacific Review*, Winter 1967, p. 8.

25. *Pacific Review*, Winter 1967-68, p. 3.

26. *Pacific Review*, Fall 1968, p. 2.

27. *Pacific Review*, Winter, 1970, p. 13.

28. Ibid.

29. Ibid., p. 14.

30. Ibid., p. 13.

31. Ibid., p. 14.

32. Judy Proulx, "A Letter to Friends," *Pacific Review*, Winter 1970, p. 3.

33. *Pacific Review*, Winter 1967-68, p. 3.

34. *Pacific Review*, Summer 1969, p. 2.

35. Ibid.

36. Donald J. MacIntyre, "Curriculum Revision: A Faculty Viewpoint," *Pacific Review*, Summer, 1969, p. 4.

37. *Pacific Review*, Spring 1970, p. 15.

38. *Pacific Review*, Winter 1969, p. 5.

39. "Statement of Demands of Concerned Students," addressed to "Dr. Burns, Dr. Bevan and Regents," March 26, 1969, University of the Pacific, Stockton, Cal.

40. Robert E. Burns, "Statement in Response to 'Concerned Students'," March 27, 1969.

41. Doyle Minden, "Two Weeks in May—1970," *Pacific Review*, Summer 1970, p. 15.

42. "Board of Regents Minutes, January 30, 1968," p. 2.

43. "Board of Regents Minutes, March 24, 1969," p. 5.

44. Tape recorded conversation with Gordon Schaber, September 30, 1976.

Chapter Eight

1. "Board of Regents Minutes, May 19, 1970," p. 1.

2. Tape recorded conversation with Gordon Schaber, September 30, 1976.

3. *Pacific Review*, Spring 1971, p. 14.

4. Ibid., pp. 4-5.

5. Tape recorded conversation with Samuel Meyer, April 26, 1976.

The Campus - 1946

The Campus - 1971

Bibliography

Altran, Robert A. *The Upper Division College.* San Francisco: Jossey-Bass, Inc., 1970.

Bender, R. N.; McConnell, T. R.; Mickle, J. J.; Gregg, H. C.; Wicke, M. F. "Survey Report to the President and the Board of Trustees of the College of the Pacific." University Senate and Board of Education of the Methodist Church, January 1956.

Bertholf, Lloyd. "Survey of (Faculty) Recommendations." Office of the Academic Vice President, College of the Pacific, Stockton, Cal., 1957.

Brown, De Marcus. "The Little Theater at the College of the Pacific." Master's thesis, College of the Pacific, 1935.

Burns, Mary. Correspondence with Grace Burns, n.d.

Burns, Robert E. "The First Half-Century of the College of the Pacific." Master's thesis, College of the Pacific, 1946.

—"The Inaugural Address." (College of the Pacific), University of the Pacific, Stockton, Cal., June 16, 1947.

—"Letter to the Board of Trustees, October 21, 1959." (Included in the bound book of "Minutes"), pp. 109-12.

—"Looking into a Second Century." *Pacific Review*, May 1951, p. 4.

—"Manuscript." Written shortly before the death of Robert E. Burns, University of the Pacific, Stockton, Cal., n.d.

—"The Place of Football in the Modern College." *Pacific Review*, February 1954, p. 9.

—"Report of the President to the Board of Trustees." March 25, 1947, pp. 2, 5; October 28, 1947, pp. 3, 5, 8.

—"Statement in Response to 'Concerned Students'," March 27, 1969.

California Christian Advocate. January 14, 1869, p. 19.

College of the Pacific Brochure: n.d.

—Brochure: "St. Michael's College," n.d.
—Bulletin: 1926-27, p. 23.
—Bulletin: 1946, pp. 21-2.

—Bulletin: "Summer School, 1946," p. 19.
—Film: "St. Michael's College," (fifteen minute sound-color).

__"Minutes of the Board of Trustees," 1930-1960. University of the Pacific, Stockton, Cal.

__"Minutes of the Faculty Meeting," 1946-1971. University of the Pacific, Stockton, Cal.

__Program: "Dedication of the Pacific Marine Station at Dillon Beach, August 1948."

__"Proposal for Discussion Topics at the Faculty Retreat, February 1961," n.d.

__"Student Handbook," 1929.

Considine, Bob. *The Unreconstructed Amateur: A Pictorial Biography of Amos Alonzo Stagg.* San Francisco: Amos Alonzo Stagg Foundation, Inc., 1962.

Crabbe, John C. "KCVN-KAWO Radio Quonset." *Pacific Review*, October 1948, p. 9.

De Vane, William C. *Higher Education In Twentieth-Century America.* Cambridge: Harvard University Press, 1965.

Farey, Arthur. "President Burns Honored: 'To Lift Up Pacific.'" *Pacific Review*, February 1957, pp. 4-5.

__"The Story of the Christian Community Administration." *Pacific Review*, May 1947, pp. 5, 36.

Goldman, Eric F. *The Crucial Decade: America, 1945-1955.* New York: Alfred A. Knopf, 1956.

Graves, Wallace B. "The All University Study Day." *Pacific Review*, Spring 1963, p. 11.

Gross, J. O. "The Field of Education." *The History of American Methodism*, vol. 3. Edited by Emory S. Bucks. New York: Abingdon Press, 1964.

Guth, William W. "What Methodism Has Done for Education in California." *California Christian Advocate*, February 22, 1912.

Hamilton, R. R. "Relations with the Veterans Administration: Report of Conference Group XVII." *Current Problems In Education.* Washington, D.C.: Education Association of the United States, Department of Higher Education, 1947.

Harbert, Wilhelmina K. *Opening Doors Through Music: A Practical Guide For Teachers, Therapists, Students, Parents.* Edited by Rachel Keniston. Springfield, Ill.: Charles C. Thomas Publishers, 1974.

Hunt, Rockwell D. *History of the College of the Pacific.* Stockton, Cal.: College of the Pacific, 1951.

252

Jacoby, Harold. Typescript of Eulogy for G. A. Werner. February 10, 1966.

Jencks, C. and Reisman, D. *The Academic Revolution.* New York: Doubleday and Co., Inc., 1968.

Knoles, Tully C. "Report of the President to the Board of Trustees," October 1935; October 27, 1936; October 25, 1938. University of the Pacific, Stockton, Cal.

—"Report to the Trustees on the Occasion of the 25th Anniversary of His Becoming President of C.O.P.," March 28, 1944.

Lucia, Ellis. *Mr. Football: Amos Alonzo Stagg.* New York: A. S. Barnes and Co., 1970.

MacIntyre, Donald J. "Curriculum Revision: A Faculty Viewpoint." *Pacific Review*, Summer 1969, p. 4.

Meyer, Samuel. "Academic Progress: 1958-1964." *Pacific Review*, October 1964, pp. 3-6.

—"Education...Methodism's Splendid Obsession." *Pacific Review*, February 22, 1963, p. 6.

—"A Statement For Tomorrow." *Pacific Review*, January 1961, pp. 25, 27.

Minden, Doyle. "Two Weeks in May—1970." *Pacific Review*, Summer 1970, p. 15.

Mirrielees, E. R. *Stanford, The Story of a University.* New York: G. P. Putnam's Sons, 1959.

Munk, Arthur W. "Sign of Creativity: A Unique Educational Experiment." *Journal of Teacher Education*, reprint. September 1964.

Nickerson, Mel. "A New Framework for the Pacific Alumni Association." *Pacific Review*, May 1957, p. 6.

O'Neill, William L. *Coming Apart: An Informal History of America in the 1960s.* Chicago, Ill.: Quadrangle Books, 1971.

Pacifican. September 1967, vol. 67 to December 1971, vol. 72.

Pacific Weekly. July 1945, vol. 40 to May 1967, vol. 66.

Pacific Review. September 1941, vol. 15 to December 1971, vol. 6.

Pelikan, Jaroslav J. "Methodism's Contribution to America." *The History of American Methodism*, vol. 3. Edited by Emory S. Bucks. New York: Abingdon Press, 1964.

Pierce, J. Lyman. Correspondence to the Board of Trustees, June 2, 1931.

Proulx, Judy. "A Letter to Friends." *Pacific Review*, Winter 1970, p. 3.

Reeves, F. W.; Russell, J. D.; Gregg, H. C.; Brumbaugh, A. J.; Blauch, L. E. *The Liberal Arts College: Based Upon Surveys of Thirty-Five Colleges Related to the Methodist Episcopal Church.* Chicago, Ill.: University of Chicago Press, 1932.

Russell, Ned and Farey, Arthur. "The Pacific Product - Part III." *Pacific Review*, October 1952, pp. 48-9.

—"The Pacific Product - Part IV." *Pacific Review*, October 1953, pp. 32-3.

Servin, Manuel P. and Wilson, Iris Higbie. *Southern California and Its University; a History of USC, 1880-1964*. Los Angeles, Cal.: Ward Ritchie, 1969.

Smith, G. Kerry, editor. *Twenty-five Years: 1945 to 1970*. San Francisco: Jossey-Bass, Inc., 1970.

Stockton Junior College Bulletin: "Semi-Professional Courses," June 1, 1937.

Stuart, Reginald and Grace D. *Tully Knoles of Pacific: Teacher, Minister, College President, Traveler, and Public Speaker*. Stockton, Cal.: College of the Pacific, 1956.

Taylor, Elliott J. "Recruitment Spreads to Latin America." *Pacific Review*, April 22, 1963, p. 3.

Tewksbury, Donald G. *The Founding of American Colleges and Universities Before the Civil War*. New York: Bureau of Publication - Teacher College, Columbia University, 1932.

Time magazine. Vol. 82, #71, October 11, 1963, p. 71.

University of the Pacific "Minutes of the Board of Regents," 1961-1971.

—"Statement of Demands of Concerned Students" addressed to "Dr. Burns, Dr. Bevan and Regents," March 26, 1969.

Webb, U. S. Correspondence to Vierling Kersey, Superintendent of Public Instruction, May 9, 1936.

White, Jack. "Pacific Chapel: Commitment with Challenge." *Pacific Review*, Winter 1967, pp. 6-7.

Wilbur, Franklin. "Fallon House Theater: The First Twenty Years Occupancy by the Columbia Company of the University of the Pacific Plays and Players 1949-1968." Master's thesis, Sacramento State College, 1969.

Interviews

Florence Armfield
Robert Bahnsen
Ted and Alice Baun
Charles Berolzheimer
Lloyd Bertholf
Ed Betz
Russell Bodley
Robert Breeden
Phillip Broughton
De Marcus Brown
Grace Burns
Lucy Carlson
Leland Case
Judith Chambers
Emerson Cobb
Catherine Davis
Ellen Deering
John Elliott
Arthur Farey

Marie Brenniman Farley
Fay Goleman
Wallace W. Hall
Monroe Hess
Harold Jacoby
O. D. Jacoby
Marc Jantzen
Harold Kambak
Peter Knoles
Berndt Kolker
Jeanette R. Mack
Warren Brian Martin
Virginia Short McLaughlin
Lawrence Meredith
Samuel Meyer
William Morris
William Nietman
Ralph Pederson
Martha Pierce

Dale F. Redig
Catherine Renwick
Ivan Rowland
Jesse Rudkin
Howard Runion
Alice Saecker
Gordon Schaber
Donald Smiley
Rev. Robert Stewart
Elliott Taylor
Bishop Donald H. Tippett
Alan and Cheri Waldo
Frederick West
Elois Grove Whitsell
George Wilson
Robert Winterberg
Carlos Wood

Index

Irving Martin Library, 66,89,113, 185

Jackson, Larry A., 182,183,186
Jacoby, Harold, 75,159
Jacoby, Olin D., 2,3,27,28,123
Jantzen, Marc, 30-31,70,75
J. C. Smith Co., Stockton, 17
Jonte, Herbert, 127
Jordan, David Starr, 16,28,43,101
Junior college, within COP, *see* General College. *See also* Stockton Junior College

Keither, Willard, 74
Kennedy, John F., 146,171
Kennedy, Raoul, 161
Kerr, Clark, 173,176
Kersey, Vierling, 21
Kingsberry, Dr. Bernard, 163,166
Kirsten, Jerry, 105,157
Knight, Goodwin, 119
Knoles, Emily, 12,13
Knoles, Tully Cleon, early life, 11; as student, 11-13; as teacher, 13, 14,45,59; as President, 1-3,14-24 *passim*, 27-30 *passim*, 32,51,55 60,143; as Chancellor, 60-61,68, 91,96,98,102,119,128,205; death, 128-129
Knowland, Joseph, 74
Knox, John L., 74
Kolker, Berndt, 188
Kress, Samuel H., 57

Landau, Rom, 107
Lange, Alexis F., 16,101
Latin American studies, *see* Inter-American Studies. *See also* Covell College
Lawson family, of Dillon Beach, 72-73
Leary, Timothy, 182-183,184
LeBaron, Eddie, 88
Lee, Jason, 7
Leonard, Paul, 37
Lester, Robert, 20

Library, *see* Irving Martin Library
Lindhorst, Frank A., 83
Literary societies, *see* Social clubs

MacLaren, John, 22
McAteer, Senator "J." Eugene, 176
McCaffrey, Beth, 211
McCaffrey, Stanley, 211,212
McCall, Roy C., 79,80
McCown, William E., 112
McCoy, Presley, 169
McCrone, Alistair, 202,211
McDowell, Dr. Arthur R., 163
McGee, Henderson, 162,190
McGeorge, Verne, 177
McGeorge School of Law, 177-179,210
McHenry, Dean, 151
Maillard, J. W., Jr., 74
Marine biology, *see* Pacific Marine Station
Martin, Elizabeth, 152
Martin, Irving, Sr., 89
Martin, Warren Bryan, 149-150, 151,152
Mayers, Ann, 187
Medical school (a proposed addition to UOP), 174-177
Meredith, Lawrence, 182-183, 184
Methodist Board of Higher Education, 1,6,17,69,83,125
Methodist church, affiliation with UOP, 3-4,7,27,69,83,113-114,120,125,151,197-198,209
Methodist church schools, in U.S., 4,5-6,7,11; in South America, 146,148
Methodist Survey Committee *Report*, of 1956, ment., 114,115, 116,117,120,122-123,124,131, 158,159,168,170,182; ex., 114, 115-116,124

Tippett, Bishop Donald H., 127, 142,184,197,207
Tocchini, John, 165,185
Topping, Norman, 37
Tow, Sing Kow, 180-181
Truman, Harry S., 96
Trustees, *see* Board of Regents
Tsanoff, Radislov, 74
Tuthill, Professor D., 9

University of California, Berkeley, 15,16,40,63,171-172,176
University of California, Los Angeles, 16
University of Southern California, 10,11,73
University of the Pacific, founding, 3-4,7,8; move to Stockton, 16-17; from college to university, 1959, 140,142

V-12 program, 23,29
Van Fleet, Jo, 77
Veatch, Dr. Henry C., 163
Veterans program, 65-66
Von Kleinsmid, Rufus B., 91

Wallace, B. C., 54
Wallace, Felix, 71
Warneke, John Carl, 174
Warren, Earl, 89,91
Watts, Alan, 107
Webb, Attorney General U.S., 21
Wedemeyer, General Albert, 89
Weinberg, Jack, 172
Werner, Gustavus Adolphus, 46-47,145
West, Dr. Frederick T., 163,166
Wheeler, Lois, 77
Wicke, Myron, 197
Wilbur, Ray Lyman, 12,16
Wilson, George, 76
Winterberg, Robert, 129-130,131, 152,167,175,201,202,206
Winters, Paul, 160
Winton, Martin, 111-112
Wood, Carlos, 71,74
Wood Memorial Hall, 185
Wormold, F. L., 170

YMCA, 37-38,39-40,43,54